D0746684

Ethical Futures in Qualitative Research

For
Katherine E. Ryan
and
Elizabeth S. Pittelkow

*International Congress of
Qualitative Inquiry*

Ethical Futures in Qualitative Research

Decolonizing the Politics of Knowledge

Norman K. Denzin
Michael D. Giardina
Editors

Left Coast
Press inc.

Walnut Creek, California

LEFT COAST PRESS, INC.
1630 North Main Street, #400
Walnut Creek, CA 94596
http://www.LCoastPress.com

Left Coast Press inc.

Copyright © 2007 by Left Coast Press, Inc.

ISBN 978-1-59874-140-7 hardcover
ISBN 978-1-59874-141-4 paperback

Library of Congress Cataloguing-in-Publication information available

Printed in the United States of America

∞™   The paper used in this publication meets the minimum requirements

of American National Standard for Information Sciences—Permanence of Paper for Printed Library Materials, ANSI/NISO Z39.48–1992.

07 08 09 10 11   5 4 3 2 1

CONTENTS

Acknowledgments

We thank Mitch Allen at Left Coast Press for his enthusiastic support of this project. We also thank Carole Bernard for her editorial expertise and patience with us throughout the production process and Hannah Jennings for her production design of the volume.

Many of the chapters contained in this volume were presented as plenary or keynote addresses at the Second International Congress of Qualitative Inquiry, held at the University of Illinois, Urbana-Champaign, in May 2006. We thank the Department of Advertising, the Institute of Communications Research, the College of Communications, and the Center for Qualitative Inquiry for institutional support of the Congress, as well as those campus units that contributed time, funds, and/or volunteers to the effort.

The conference, and by extension this book, would not have materialized without the tireless efforts of Himika Bhattacharya (diplomatic liaison), Li Xiong (communications guru), Yiye Liu (webmistress), Maria Silva (ADIS), Kevin Dolan (program designer), Grant Kien (organizational sage), and James Salvo (the glue who holds the whole thing together). We also recognize the nearly one thousand participants who attended the conference and helped to inaugurate the International Association for Qualitative Inquiry (IAQI). For information on this association, please visit http://www.iaqi.org

Norman K. Denzin and Michael D. Giardina
Champaign, Illinois
December 2006

Introduction

Ethical Futures in Qualitative Research

Norman K. Denzin and
Michael D. Giardina
University of Illinois, Urbana-Champaign[1]

It's a benefit to science, probably. But I'm not convinced it's a benefit to the tribes.
—Dr. Mic LaRoque, discussing the
Genographic Project, 2006 (Harmon, 2006)

A lot of it, story-wise, I just made up.
—*Apocalypto* writer/director Mel Gibson, 2006
(Hoberman, 2006)

We are not myths of the past, ruins in the jungle or zoos. We are people and we want to be respected, not to be victims of intolerance and racism.
—Rigoberta Menchú, 1992 (Riis-Hansen, 1992)

Proem

Three separate but interrelated glimpses of daily life in 2006 set the stage for what follows throughout—the Genographic Project, Mel Gibson's Mayan-themed film *Apocalypto*, and the broad-reaching, politically motivated disregard for science espoused by the current Bush administration.

To wit:

In the December 10, 2006, edition of the *New York Times*, an article titled "DNA Gatherers Hit Snag: Tribes Don't Trust Them," discussed the National Geographic Society's multi-million dollar Genographic Project to collect DNA samples from indigenous groups around the world "in the hopes of reconstructing humanity's ancient migrations has come to a standstill on its home turf in North America" (Harmon, 2006, p. 1). Proponents of the project claim that results may shed light on such questions as "How did descendants of the hunter-gatherers who first left humanity's birthplace in east Africa some 65,000 years ago come to inhabit every corner of the Earth?" "What routes did they take?" "Who got where, and when?" (Harmon, 2006, p. 1). Opponents counter with a litany of well-reasoned points, arguing instead that the findings could, among other things, "undermine [groups'] moral basis for sovereignty and chip away at their collective legal claims," as well as "clash with long-held beliefs" that threaten a sense of cultural history" (Harmon, 2006, p. 1).

At roughly the same time, we witnessed Mel Gibson's (2006) latest exercise in rendering "masculine suffering unto glory"—the controversial film, *Apocalypto*—(mis)representing a faux universalized "Mayan" civilization as a "blatantly sadistic spectacle" complete with savage scenes of women being raped, children butchered, and men disemboweled (Fuchs, 2006; Hoberman, 2006). But critics concerned with moral, ethical, and respectful portrayals of indigenous culture and life be damned, apparently. As Gibson relayed in an interview with *Time* magazine when discussing the film and its representations, particularly those of human sacrifice: "After what I experienced with *The Passion* [*of the Christ*], I frankly don't give a flying fuck about much of what those critics think" (quoted in Padgett, 2006, p. 1).[2]

And, more generally, we've experienced a pathological aversion to the politics of truth and evidence running throughout much of the Bush administration's approaches to "scientific" inquiry. As former U.S. vice president Al Gore has noted,

> If you look carefully ... [the Bush administration's] practice has been in almost every case to appoint people whose immediate prior careers have been aimed at the destruction of the laws they are now being asked to enforce. It really is institutionalized corruption. It is deeply unethical and its effect is to place the private, narrow interests of wealthy and powerful industrial groups above the interests of the American people. [quoted in Levenson, 2004, n.p.][3]

This politicized practice is far-reaching, manifesting itself in public policy initiatives ranging in scope from foreign policy endeavors (read: Iraq) to such things as the religiously inflected arguments concerning the age of the Grand Canyon. That is to say, although virtually every geologist has dated the Grand Canyon's formation back some two *billion* years, a (creationist) movement is afoot to declare the Canyon only 4,500 to 10,000 years old and caused by "the great global flood described in [the Book of] Genesis as God's punishment for humanity's sin" (Vail, quoted in Wilgoren, 2005, p. 1). This "Young Earth creationist" perspective is unsettling in itself; however, the fact that Tom Vail's (2003) controversial book, *Grand Canyon: A Different View*, is sold in the state-sanctioned bookstore of the Grand Canyon raises serious questions concerning the extent to which facts that are troublesome to the radical right have become seemingly irrelevant. Because of pressure from Bush administration officials, the Grand Canyon National Park service (as of January 1, 2007) "is not permitted to give an official estimate of the geologic age of its principle feature ... [in effect] suspend[ing] its belief in geology" (PEER press release, 2006).[4] (But should we expect anything less from the administration of a president who has claimed that "the jury is still out" on something as elementary as evolution?[5])

Thus, whether "having your genealogy and identity (cell-lines) stolen, patented, or copied" (Smith, 1999, p. 100), having your cultural heritage misrepresented in popular media portrayals, or struggling against the fundamentalist politicization of science, the above examples illustrate the degree to which ethical issues concerning the politics of truth, evidence, and knowledge have moved to the fore of popular discourse. At the same time, and complicating matters, government agencies are attempting to regulate scientific inquiry by defining what counts as "good" science.[6] Conservative regimes are enforcing evidence- or scientifically based biomedical models of research (see Denzin, Lincoln, & Giardina, 2006). Yet, as with such ill-conceived legislation as the No Child Left Behind Act of 2002, this experimental quantitative model is ill suited to:

> examin[e] the complex and dynamic contexts of public education in its many forms, sites, and variations, especially considering the

... subtle social difference produced by gender, race, ethnicity, linguistic status or class. Indeed, multiple kinds of knowledge, produced by multiple epistemologies and methodologies, are not only worth having but also demanded if policy, legislation and practice are to be sensitive to social needs. [Lincoln & Canella, 2004, p. 7]

Born out of a "methodological fundamentalism" that returns to a much-discredited model of empirical inquiry in which "only randomized experiments produce truth" (House, 2006, pp. 100–101), such activities raise fundamental, philosophical epistemological, political, and pedagogical issues for scholarship and freedom of speech in the academy. *Qualitative researchers have a moral, ethical, and professional obligation to insert themselves into this space and be heard.*

In response to the challenges that lie ahead, a methodology of the heart, a performative, indigenous, feminist, communitarian ethic that embraces an ethics of truth grounded in love, care, hope, and forgiveness is needed. Love, here, to borrow from Antonia Darder and Luis F. Mirón (2006):

means to comprehend that the moral and the material are inextricably linked. And, as such, [we] must recognize love as an essential ingredient of a just society. Eagleton (2003) defines this concept of love as a political principle through which we struggle to create mutually life-enhancing opportunities for all people. It is grounded in the mutuality and interdependence of our human existence—that which we share, as much as that which we do not. This is a love nurtured by the act of relationship itself. It cultivates relationships with the freedom to be at one's best without undue fear. Such an emancipatory love allows us to realize our nature in a way that allows others to do so as well. Inherent in such a love is the understanding that we are not at liberty to be violent, authoritarian, or self-seeking. [p. 150]

Indigenous scholars are leading the way on this front. During the "Decade of the World's Indigenous Peoples" (1994–2004), a full-scale attack was launched on Western epistemologies and methodologies. Indigenous scholars asked that the academy decolonize its scientific practices (Battiste, 2006; Grande, 2004; Smith, 2006). At the same time, these scholars sought to disrupt traditional ways of knowing, while developing "methodologies and approaches to research that privilege indigenous knowledges, voices, and experiences" (Smith, 2005, p. 87). An alliance with the critical strands of qualitative inquiry and its practitioners seemed inevitable.

Today, progressive-minded scholars are building these connections, learning how to dismantle, deconstruct, and decolonize traditional ways of doing science, learning that research is always already both moral and political, learning how to let go. Ironically, as this letting go occurs, a backlash against critical qualitative research gains momentum. New "gold standards" for reliability and validity, as well as design, are being advanced (St. Pierre, 2004). So-called evidence-based research—including the Campbell and Cochrane models and protocols—has become fashionable once more (Pring, 2004; Thomas, 2005), even while its proponents fail to recognize that the very act of labeling some research as "evidence-based" implies that some research fails to mount evidence—a strongly political and decidedly nonobjective stance. Institutional review boards (IRBs) are routinely ignorant of or unsympathetic to new developments in interpretive approaches. The criticisms, it seems, are coming in from all sides.

In what follows, we discuss indigenous and critical methodological responses to the prevailing biomedical model of ethics currently at play in the United States and elsewhere; present an overview of a performative, indigenous, feminist, communitarian ethic; and briefly summarize the chapters contained in this volume. We end with a call to action for qualitative researchers who seek to be present to the scene and change the future of our/their field(s).

Cultural Politics and an Indigenous Research Ethic

We have much to learn from indigenous scholars about how radical democratic practices can be made to work. Maori scholars Linda Tuhiwai Smith (1999) and Russell Bishop (1998) are committed to a set of moral and pedagogical imperatives and, as Smith expresses it, "to acts of reclaiming, reformulating, and reconstituting indigenous cultures and languages ... to the struggle to become self-determining" (1999, p. 142). Such acts lead to a research program that is committed to the pursuit of social justice and radical progressive democracy. In turn, a specific approach to inquiry is required. In his discussion of a Maori approach to creating knowledge, Bishop (1998) observes that researchers in Kaupapa Maori contexts are

> [r]epositioned in such a way as to no longer need to seek to *give voice to others*, to *empower* others, to *emancipate* others, to refer to others as *subjugated* voices, but rather to listen and participate ... in a process that facilitates the development in people as a sense of themselves as agentic and of having an authoritative voice. ... An indigenous Kaupapa Maori approach to research ... challenges colonial and neo-colonial discourses that inscribe "otherness." [pp. 207–208]

This participatory mode of knowing privileges subjectivity, personal knowledge, and the specialized knowledges of oppressed peoples and groups. It uses concrete experience as a criterion of meaning and truth. It encourages a participatory mode of consciousness that locates the researcher within the Maori-defined spaces in the group. The researcher is led by the members of the community and does not presume to be a leader, or to have any power that he or she can relinquish (Bishop, 1998, p. 205).

As a way of honoring the group's sacred spaces, the researchers give the group a gift. In laying down this gift, the researcher rejects the ideology of empowerment. There is no assumption that the researcher is giving the group power. Rather, the laying down of the gift is an offering, a pure giving. And in this act, the researcher refuses any claim to anything the group might give him or her in return. If the group picks up the gift, then a shared reciprocal relationship can be created (Bishop, 1998, p. 207). The relationship that follows is built on understandings involving shared Maori beliefs and cultural practices. In turn, the research is evaluated according to Maori-based criteria, not criteria imported from international literature, including Western positivist and postpositivist epistemologies as well as certain versions of critical pedagogy that think in terms of grand narratives and "binaries" or "dialectical linear progressions" (Bishop, 1998, pp. 209–211).

Like Paulo Freire's revolutionary pedagogy (1999), Cornel West's prophetic pragmatism, and Patricia Hill Collins's feminist moral ethic, the Maori moral position values dialogue as a method for assessing knowledge claims. The Maori culture also privileges storytelling, listening, voice, and personal performance narratives (Collins, 1990, pp. 208–211). This moral pedagogy rests on an ethic of love, care, and personal accountability that honors individual uniqueness and emotionality in dialogue (Collins, 1990, pp. 215–217). This is a performative, pedagogical ethics grounded in the ritual, sacred spaces of family, community, and everyday moral life (Bishop, 1998, p. 203). It is not imposed by some external, bureaucratic agency.

Within the Kaupapa Maori community, this ethic sets out specific guidelines for respecting and protecting the rights, interests, and sensitivities of the people being studied (Smith, 1999, p, 119). These guidelines ask that Maori researchers make themselves present, that they meet face to face with the members of the community they are studying. In these encounters, Maori scholars listen, show respect, and share knowledge while behaving in a cautious, gentle, and humble manner, thus displaying many of the personal qualities that the Maori value (Smith, 1999, p. 120). These ethical codes are the same protocols that govern the relations the Maori have with one another and their environment. Through such shows of respect, "the place of everyone and everything in the universe is kept in balance and harmony" (Smith, 1999, p. 120). Among the Maori, respect is a principle that is felt as it is performed, experienced, and "expressed through all aspects of social conduct" (Smith, 1999, p. 120).

In the Maori context, the concept of "person" applies to a being who has a series of rights and responsibilities that are basic to the group. These obligations include a commitment to warm, respectful interpersonal interactions as well as respect for actions that create and preserve group solidarity. There is also a commitment to a shared responsibility for one another, which extends to corporate responsibility for the protection of the group property, including the knowledge, language, and customs of the group (Bishop, 1998, p. 204). In this context, as Bishop (1998, p. 204) notes, group achievement often takes the form of group—not individual—performance.

This view of performance parallels the commitment within certain forms of "red pedagogy" to the performative as a way of being, a way of knowing, a way of expressing moral ties to the community (Grande, this volume; Graveline, 2000, p. 361). Frye Jean Graveline (2000) a Metis woman, speaks:

> As a Metis woman, scholar, activist, teacher, healer
> I enact First Voice as a pedagogy and methodology
> Observing my own lived experience as an Educator
> Sharing meanings with Others ...
> My Voice is Heard
> In concert with Students and Community Participants ...
> I asked: What pedagogical practices
> Enacted through my Model-in-Use
>   contribute to what kinds of transformational learnings?
> For whom?

The Performative as a Site of (Indigenous) Resistance

Because it expresses and embodies moral ties to the community, the performative view of meaning serves to legitimate indigenous worldviews. Meaning and resistance are embodied in the act of performance itself. The performative is political, the site of resistance. At this critical level, the performative provides the context for resistance to neoliberal and neoconservative attacks on the legitimacy of the worldview in question. Indigenous discourses, such as those of the Maori, are constantly under assault. Neoliberals and neoconservatives deny indigenous cultures any legitimacy and blame the members of these cultures for the problems that they experience. Liberals encourage assimilation and melting-pot views of race and ethnic relations. As Bishop (1998) notes, radical, emancipatory theorists "claim that they have the formula for emancipation of Maori as oppressed and marginalized people" (p. 212).

Bishop, Collins, and Smith all remind us that these positions presume that persons inside an indigenous culture are incapable of solving their own problems. Neoconservatives and postpositivists want to control the criteria that outsiders use to evaluate indigenous experience, and these criteria usually involve statistics and outcome measures that record the appalling conditions in the culture (Bishop, 1998, p. 212). Liberals rewrite school curricula, and "radical emancipationists argue that Maori cultural practices do not conform to their perspectives of how emancipatory projects should develop" (Bishop, 1998, p. 212). Under the guise of objectivity and neutrality, neoconservatives deny indigenous cultures' rights to self-determination. Multicultural curriculum revisionists rewrite the cultures' narratives to fit a hegemonic liberal discourse. And some radical theorists think that only they and their theories can lead such cultures into freedom, as if members of these cultures suffer from an indigenous version of false consciousness (Bishop, 1998, p. 213).

Each of these political positions undermines the integrity of indigenous cultures and these cultures' commitments to the performance as a way of being, a way of knowing, and a way of being political. The performative is where the soul of the culture resides. The performative haunts the liminal spaces of the culture. In their sacred and secular performances, the members of indigenous cultures honor one another and their cultures.[7] Smith (1999) states the issue clearly: "The struggle for the validity of indigenous knowledge may no longer be over the *recognition* that indigenous people have ways of knowing the world which are unique, but over proving the authenticity of, and control over, our own forms of knowledge" (p. 104; emphasis in the original).[8]

Resisting Colonialism

In response to the continuing pressure of colonialism and colonization, Smith (1999, pp. 142–162) outlines some twenty-five different indigenous projects, including those that create, name, restore, democratize, reclaim, protect, remember, and celebrate lost histories and cultural practices.[9] These indigenous projects embody a pedagogy of hope and freedom. They turn pedagogies of oppression and colonization into pedagogies of liberation, hope, and healing. They are not purely utopian, for they map concrete performances that can lead to positive social transformations. They embody ways of resisting the process of colonization.

Smith's moral agenda privileges four interpretive research processes. The first, *decolonization*, reclaims indigenous cultural practices and reworks these practices at the political, social, spiritual, and psychological levels. *Healing*, the second process, also involves physical, spiritual, psychological, social, and restorative elements. The third process, *transformation*, focuses on changes that move back and forth among psychological, social, political, economic, and collective levels. *Mobilization*, at the local, national, regional, and global levels, is the fourth basic process. It speaks to collective efforts to change Maori society.

These four complex, interdependent processes address issues of cultural survival and collective self-determination. In each instance, they work to decolonize Western methods and forms of inquiry and to empower indigenous peoples. These are the states of "being through which indigenous communities are moving" (Smith, 1999, p. 116). These states involve spiritual and social practices. They are pedagogies of healing, pedagogies of recovery—practices that materially and spiritually benefit indigenous peoples.

A Moral Code

In turn, these processes require a set of moral and ethical research protocols. Fitted to the indigenous (and nonindigenous) perspective, these are moral matters. They are shaped by the feminist, communitarian principles of sharing, reciprocity, relationality, community, and neighborliness (Lincoln, 1995, p. 287). They embody a dialogic ethic of love and faith grounded in compassion (Bracci & Christians, 2002, p. 13; West, 1993). Accordingly, the purpose of research is not the production of new knowledge per se. Rather, the purposes are pedagogical, political, moral, and ethical, involving the enhancement of moral agency, the production of moral discernment, a commitment to praxis, justice, an ethic of resistance, and a performative pedagogy that resists oppression (Christians, 2002, p. 409).

A code embodying these principles interrupts the practice of research, resists the idea of research being something that white men do to indigenous peoples. Further, unlike the Belmont Principles, which are not content driven, this code is anchored in a culture and its way of life. Unlike the Belmont Principles, it connects the moral model to a set of political and ethical actions that will increase well-being in the indigenous culture. The code refused to turn indigenous peoples into subjects who are the natural objects of white inquiry (Smith, 1999, p. 118). These principles argue that Western legal definitions of ethical codes privilege the utilitarian model of the individual as someone who has rights distinct from the rights of the larger group, "for example, the right of an individual to give his or her own knowledge, or the right to give informed consent ... community and indigenous rights or views in this area are generally not ... respected" (Smith, 1999, p. 118). Bishop's (1998) and Smith's (1999, pp. 116–119) ethical and moral models call into question the more generic, utilitarian, biomedical Western model of ethical inquiry (see Christians, 2000).

The Biomedical Model of Ethics and the Belmont Principles

The rules governing human subject research are rooted in scandal: the Tuskegee Syphilis Study (AAUP, 1981), the Willowbrook Hepatitis Experiment, Project Camelot in the 1960s, and a series of events in the 1970s, including Milgram's deceptions of experimental subjects, Laud Humphreys's covert research on homosexuals, and the complicity of social scientists with military initiatives in Vietnam (Christians, 2000, p. 141; Gunsalus, 2002). As Christians (2000) notes, concern for research ethics during the 1980s and 1990s, support for foundations, the development of professional codes of ethics, and extensions of IRB apparatus "are credited by their advocates with curbing outrageous abuses" (p. 141). However, these efforts have been framed, from the 1960s onward, in terms of biomedical models of research (see also Denzin & Giardina, 2006a; Denzin, Lincoln, & Giardina, 2006). As implemented, this model involves IRBs, informed consent forms,

Models of Critical, Interpretive Inquiry

The IRB framework assumes that one model of research fits all forms of inquiry, but this is not the case. This model requires that researchers fill out forms concerning subjects' informed consent, the risks and benefits of the research for subjects, confidentiality, and voluntary participation. The model also presumes a static, monolithic view of the human subject. Performance autoethnography, for example, falls outside this model, as do numerous interpretive paradigms such as reflexive ethnography, many forms of participatory action research, and qualitative research involving *testimonios*, life stories, life-history inquiry, personal narrative inquiry, performance autobiography, ethnopoetics, conversation analysis, and ethnodrama. In all of these cases, subjects and researchers develop collaborative, public, pedagogical relationships. The walls between subjects and observers are deliberately broken down. Confidentiality disappears, for there is nothing to hide or protect. Participation is entirely voluntary, hence there is no need for subjects to sign forms indicating that their consent is "informed." The activities that make up the research are participatory; that is, they are performative, collaborative, and action and praxis based. Hence, participants are not asked to submit to specific procedures or treatment conditions. Instead, acting together, researchers and subjects work to produce change in the world.

The IRB model presumes a complex ethical framework (see below) that is inherently problematic. This leads to a peculiar conception of harm, for why would collaborative researchers bring harm to those they study? In short, the Belmont Principles (see below) need to be recast in light of contemporary understandings of interpretive inquiry.

The Professional Associations and Societies

In 1998, numerous professional associations, including the AHA, the Oral History Association, the Organization of American Historians, and the AAA, started communicating with one another and with more than 700 IRBs to encourage the IRBs to take account of the standards of practice relevant to the research in their specific disciplines (AAUP, 2001, p. 56). Concerns among the members of the professional societies involved the biomedical definitions of research applied by IRBs and the corresponding definitions of harm, beneficence, respect, justice, and informed consent. The problems start with how research is defined in Title 45, Part 46, of the U.S. Code of Federal Regulations. According to the regulations, research is

> any activity designed to test an hypothesis, permit conclusions to be drawn, and thereby to develop or contribute to generalizeable knowledge expressed in theories, principles, and statements of relationships. Research is described in a formal protocol that sets forth an objective and a set of procedures designed to reach that objective.

This definition turns human beings into research subjects who may be exposed to harm because of the protocols that implement the research design.

The model works outward from the Belmont Report (the 1978 report of the U.S. National Commission for the Protection of Human Subjects in Biomedical and Behavioral Research) and its ethical principles (see AAUP, 2001, 2002; Christians, 2000; Lincoln & Cannella, 2002; Lincoln & Tierney, 2002; Pritchard, 2002). The current version of these rules—the 1991 regulations and their revisions—are also known as the "Common Rule" (AAUP, 2001, p. 55, 2002). The Common Rule describes the procedures of review that are used by more than seventeen different federal agencies in the United States. It is often presumed that this single regulatory framework will fit all styles and forms of "research," but, as Pritchard (2002, p. 8) notes, this is not always the case. In principle, the Common Rule is implemented through informed consent.

The Belmont Report sets forth basic ethical principles: respect for persons, beneficence, and justice. Respect involves treating persons as autonomous agents and protecting them from harm, as well as protecting persons who exhibit diminished autonomy. Respect implies the subject's voluntary participation in the research project. The principle of beneficence asks that the research maximize benefits to the subject, and the collectivity, while minimizing harm. Typically, harm has been determined through application of the Common Rule, which requires that harm or risk to the subject not exceed what is "ordinarily encountered in daily life" (AAUP, 2001, p. 56). This rule asks that members of society accept the fact that long-term benefits may result from research that harms certain subjects or places them at risk. Justice, the third ethical principle, requires that researchers treat persons equally; particular groups should not be disadvantaged in terms of being selected as subjects or in terms of being able to benefit from the research.

The three principles of *respect*, *beneficence*, and *justice* are implemented through disciplinary codes of ethics and through a set of procedures administered by IRBs that follow the Common Rule. The principle of respect is implemented through the obtainment of subjects' *informed consent* (passive versus active). Informed consent involves at least three issues: ensuring that subjects are adequately informed about the research, although deception may be allowed; ensuring that the information is presented in an easily understood fashion, which may also include seeking third-party permission; and ensuring that consent is voluntarily given.[12]

The principle of beneficence is applied through a complex set of procedures designed to assess the *risks and benefits* to the subjects of participation in the research. The term *risks* refers to potential harm to subjects, and *benefits* refers to potential positive value to the subjects' health or welfare. If an IRB determines that subjects in a given research project are at risk, it then asks whether the risks are minimal or can be minimized and whether the risks are warranted (Pritchard, 2002, p. 8). Under the risk-benefit model, risk is measured in terms of the probability of benefits, and benefits are contrasted with harms, rather than risks. There are multiple forms of harm—psychological, physical, legal, social, economic, cultural—and corresponding benefits. Risks and benefits must be assessed at the individual, familial, and societal levels. Risks must be exceeded by benefits, although risks at the individual level may be justified if the benefits serve a larger cause. Although not specified in the Belmont Report, the codes of ethics developed by many scholarly professional associations also insist on "safeguards to protect people's identities and those of the research locations" (Christians, 2000, p. 139).

The principle of justice is expressed in the assurances that the procedures used in the selection of the research subjects are fair. Special populations should not be unduly burdened by being required to participate in research projects. In addition, the benefits of the research should not be unfairly distributed throughout a subject population or made available only to those who can afford them.[13]

Internal Criticisms of the Model

The above-described model, with the apparatus of the IRB and the Common Rule, has been subjected to considerable criticism. The arguments of most critics center on the four key terms and their definitions: *human subject*, *human subject research*, *harm*, and *ethical conduct*.

First, we should address the issue of science and ethics. As Christians (2000) notes, the Common Rule principles "reiterate the basic themes of value-neutral experimentalism—individual autonomy, maximum benefits and minimal risks, and ethical ends exterior to scientific means" (p. 140). These principles "dominate the codes of ethics: informed consent, protection of privacy, and non-deception" (Christians, 2000, p. 140). However, these rules do not conceptualize research in participatory or collaborative formats. They do not prevent other ethical violations, such as plagiarism, falsification or fabrication of data, and violations of confidentiality. Rather, as Christians points out, IRBs are structured so as to protect *institutions*, not individuals.

There is room for ethical conflict as well (see Pritchard, 2002, pp. 8–9). The three principles contained in the Common Rule rest on three different ethical traditions: respect, from Immanuel Kant; beneficence, from John Stuart Mill and the utilitarians; and justice, as a distributive idea, from Aristotle. These ethical traditions are not compatible; they rest on different moral, ontological, and political assumptions and different understandings of what is right and respectful (e.g., the Kantian principle of respect may contradict the utilitarian principle of beneficence).

Respect, *beneficence*, and *justice* are all problematic terms. Surely there is more to respect than informed consent, more than simply getting people to agree to participate in a study. Respect involves caring for another, honoring that person, and treating him or her with dignity. Obtaining a person's signature on an informed consent form is not the same as demonstrating true respect.

Beneficence, including risks and benefits, cannot be quantified, nor can we attach a clear meaning to *acceptable risk* or clearly define what benefits may serve the large cause. Smith (1999) and Bishop (1998), for instance, argue that the collectivity must determine the costs and benefits of the group's participating in research. Further, individuals may not have the right, as individuals, to allow particular forms of research to be done if the research results are likely to affect the greater social whole. A cost-benefit model of society and inquiry does *injustice* to the empowering, participatory model of research (see below) that many Fourth World peoples are now advocating.

Justice extends beyond fair selection procedures or the fair distribution of the benefits of research across a population. Justice involves principles of care, love, kindness, fairness, and commitment to shared responsibility, to honest, truth, balance, and harmony. Taken out of their Western utilitarian framework, respect, beneficence, and justice must be seen as principles that are felt as they are performed—that is, they can serve as performative guidelines to a moral way of being in the world with others. As currently applied by IRBs, however, they serve as cold, calculated devices that may turn persons against one another.

And now to address research. Pritchard (2002) contends that the model's concept of research does not deal adequately with procedural changes in research projects, with unforeseen contingencies that lead to changes in the purposes and intents of studies. Often researchers cannot maintain their participants' anonymity, nor is this always even desirable; for example, participatory action inquiry presumes full community participation in a research project.

The staffing of IRBs presents another level of difficulty. IRBs are often understaffed, and many include members who either reject or are uninformed about the newer, critical qualitative research tradition. Many IRBs have not instituted suitable appeal procedures or methods for expediting the identification of research that should be exempted from IRB review.[14]

Recent summaries by the American Association of University sity Professors (AAUP, 2001, 2002) raise additional reservations about IRBs that center on the following issues:

Research and Human Subjects

- Failure on the part of IRBs to be aware of new interpretive and qualitative developments in the social sciences, including participant observation, ethnography, authoethnography, and oral history research.
- Application by IRBs of a concept of research and science that privileges the biomedical model and not the model of trust, negotiation, and respect that must be established in ethnographic or historical inquiry, where research is not *on* but rather *with* other human beings.
- IRBs' event-based rather than process-based conception of research and the consent process.

Ethics

- Failure on the part of IRBs to see human beings as free, moral, social agents located in complex historical, political, and cultural spaces.
- Infringements on academic freedom by IRBs in not allowing certain types of inquiry to go forward.
- IRBs' inappropriate applications of the Common Rule in assessing potential harm to subjects.
- IRBs' overly restrictive applications of the informed consent rule.

IRBs as Institutional Structures

- IRBs' failure to have adequate appeals system in place.
- IRBs' failure to recognize the need to include members who understand the newer interpretive paradigms.

Academic Freedom

- IRBs' infringements on researchers' First Amendment rights and academic freedom.
- IRBs' policing of inquiry in the humanities, including oral history research.
- IRBs' policing and obstruction of research seminars and dissertation projects.
- IRBs' constraints on critical inquiry, including historical or journalistic work that contributes to the public knowledge of the past while incriminating or passing negative judgment on persons and institutions.
- IRBs' failure to consider or incorporate existing forms of regulation into the Common Rule, including laws concerning libel, copyright, and intellectual property rights.
- IRBs' general extension of their powers across disciplines, creating negative effects on researchers' choices concerning what they will or will not study.
- IRBs' vastly different applications of the Common Rule across campus communities.

The AAUP has also noted the following items as important areas that are not addressed by IRB reviews:

- The conduct of research with indigenous peoples (see below).
- The regulation of researchers' unorthodox or problematic conduct in the field (e.g., sexual relations with subjects).
- Relations between IRBs and ethical codes involving universal human rights.
- Disciplinary codes of ethics and new codes of ethics and moral perspectives coming from feminist, queer, and racialized standpoint epistemologies.
- Appeal mechanisms for human subjects who need to grieve and who seek some form of restorative justice as a result of harm they have experienced as research participants.
- Fourth World discourses and alternative views of research, science, and human beings.

Disciplining and Constraining Ethical Conduct

The consequences of these restrictions, as Lincoln and Tierney (2002) and Lincoln and Cannella (2002) observe, is a disciplining of qualitative inquiry that extends from granting agencies to the policing of qualitative research seminars and even the conduct of qualitative dissertations. In some cases, lines of critical inquiry have not been funded and have not gone forward because of criticisms of local IRBs. Pressures from the political Right discredit critical interpretive inquiry. From the federal level to the local level, a trend is emerging. In too many instances, there seems to be a move in IRBs' purposes away from *protecting* human subjects and toward *increased monitoring* and *censuring* of projects that are critical of right-wing ideologies.

Lincoln and Tierney (2002) observe that these policing activities have at least five important implications for critical social justice inquiry. First, the widespread rejection of alternative forms of research means that qualitative inquiry will be heard less and less in federal and state policy forums. Second, it appears that qualitative researchers are being deliberately excluded from the national dialogue. Third, consequently, young researchers trained in the critical tradition are not being listened to in important policy matters. Fourth, the definition of research has not changed to fit newer models of inquiry. And fifth, in rejecting qualitative inquiry, "traditional" researchers are endorsing a more distanced form of research that is compatible with existing stereotypes concerning persons of color, sexual orientations, etc.

Christians (2000) summarizes the abject poverty of this model. It rests on a cognitive model that privileges rational solutions to ethical dilemmas (the rationalist fallacy), and it presumes the scientist is a single subject (the distributive fallacy). It presents the scientist as an objective, neutral observer. Private citizens are coerced into participating in scientific projects in the name of some distant public good (e.g., the Genographic Project, discussed above). The rights-, justice-, and acts-based system ignores the dialogic nature of human interaction. The model creates conditions for deception, for the invasion of private spaces, for the duping of subject, and for challenges to the subjects' moral worth and dignity. Christians calls for its replacement with an ethics based on the values of a feminist communitarianism, an ethic of empowerment, a care- and healing-based, dialogic ethic of love, hope, and solidarity.

This is an evolving, emerging ethical framework that serves as a powerful antidote to the deception-based, utilitarian IRB system. It presumes a "community that is ontologically and axiologically prior to persons" (Christians, 2005, p. 150). This community has common moral values, and research is rooted in a concept of care, of shared governance, of neighborliness, of love, kindness, and the moral good. Accounts of social life should display these values and should be based on interpretive sufficiency. They should have sufficient depth to allow the reader to form a critical understanding about the world studied. These texts should exhibit an absence of racial, class, and gender stereotyping. They should generate and lead to resistance, empowerment, and social action, and to positive change in the social world.

A Performative, Indigenous, Feminist, Communitarian Ethic

Against this background, indigenous peoples debate codes of ethics and issues of intellectual and cultural property rights. In this politicized space, as Smith (1999) observes, "indigenous codes of ethics are being promulgated ... as a sheer act of survival" (p. 119). Thus, the charters of various indigenous peoples include statements that refer to collective—not individual—human rights. These rights include control and ownership of the community's cultural property, its health and knowledge systems, its rituals and customs, the culture's basic gene pool, rights and rules for self-determination, and an insistence on who the first beneficiaries of indigenous knowledge will be.

These charters call on governments and states to develop policies that will ensure these social goods, including the rights of indigenous peoples to protect their cultures' new knowledge and its dissemination. These charters embed codes of ethics within this larger perspective. They spell out specifically how researchers are to protect and respect the rights and interests of indigenous peoples, using the same protocols that regulate daily moral life in their cultures. In these ways, Smith's arguments open the space for a parallel discourse concerning a feminist, communitarian moral ethic.

In the feminist, communitarian model, participants have a coequal say in how research should be conducted, what should be studied, which methods should be used, which findings are "valid" and acceptable, how the findings are to be implemented, and how the consequences of such actions are to be assessed. Spaces for disagreement are recognized at the same time that discourse aims for mutual understanding and for the honoring of moral commitments.

A sacred, existential epistemology places humans in a noncompetitive, nonhierarchical relationship to the earth, to nature, and to the larger world. This sacred epistemology stresses the values of empowerment, shared governance, care, solidarity, love, community, covenant, morally involved observers, and civic transformation. This ethical epistemology recovers the moral values that were excluded by the rational, Enlightenment science project. This sacred epistemology is based on a philosophical anthropology that declares that "all humans are worth of dignity and sacred status with exception for class or ethnicity" (Christians, 1995, p. 129). A universal human ethic that stressed that the sacredness of life, human dignity, truth telling, and nonviolence derives from this position (Christians, 1995, pp. 12–15). This ethic is based on locally experienced, culturally prescribed proto-norms (Christians, 1995, p. 129). These primal norms provide a defensible "conception of good rooted in universal human solidarity" (Christians, 1995, p. 129; see also Christians, 1997, 1998). This sacred epistemology recognizes and interrogates the ways in which race, class, gender, and sexuality operate as important systems of oppression in the world today.

Looking ahead in the Third Millennium, interpretive, indigenous methods, democratic politics, and feminist, communitarian ethics offer progressives a series of tools for countering reactionary political discourse. At stake is an "insurgent cultural politics" (Giroux, 2000, p. 217) that challenges neofascist state apparatuses. This cultural politics encourages a critical race consciousness that flourishes within the free and open spaces of a "vibrant democratic public culture and society" (Giroux, 2000, p. 217). Within the spaces of this new performative cultural politics, a radical democratic imagination redefines the concept of civic participation and public citizenship. This imagination turns the personal into the political. Struggle, resistance, and dialogue are key features of its pedagogy. The rights of democratic citizenship are extended to all segments of public and private life, from the political to the economic, from the cultural to the personal. This pedagogy seeks to regulate market and economic relations (including scientific) in the name of social justice and environmental causes (see, e.g., Gore, 2006).

The Chapters

Ethical Futures in Qualitative Research is comprised of three sections that outline a vision for a qualitative research paradigm that takes seriously the challenges ahead in our neoliberal era. Section I (Ethical Challenges in Qualitative Research) offers compelling critical perspectives on ethics and ethical forms of qualitative research in the new millennium. Section II (Indigenous Moral Ethics) turns its attention to issues of decolonizing/Red pedagogies operative within a global context of human rights and ethical practices. And Section III (Performing Ethics) looks ahead, presenting a vision of the future of critical, interpretive research that is organized around the spirit of a performative, indigenous, feminist, communitarian ethic. The sections are linked by an understanding that "the cultural is always performative and pedagogical, and hence always political, and too frequently racist and sexist" (Denzin, 2003, p. 230; see also Giroux, 2000).

Clifford G. Christians ("Neutral Science and the Ethics of Resistance") starts us on our journey with a philosophical reflection that argues that the social sciences must reinvent themselves in qualitative terms after the humanities if they are to realize an ethics and politics of resistance. After first introducing notions of John Stuart Mill's philosophy of social science, value neutrality in the work of Max Weber, and the politics of IRBs, Christians counters this positivistic frame and works forward to speak to the need for interpretive sufficiency in reinventing power and transforming IRBs with the goal of "enabling the humane transformation of the multiple spheres of community life." This social ethics of resistance, he argues, ultimately works to reintegrate human life with the moral order.

Yvonna S. Lincoln and Gaile S. Cannella's chapter ("Ethics and the Broader Rethinking/Reconceptualization of Research as Construct") is a bold, hard-hitting piece that pushes the boundaries of qualitative research in several directions and continues on the theme of progressive ethical transformation within qualitative research. Lincoln and Cannella begin by giving an overview of ethics in the realm of human subject research, particularly as related to its advent following the revelations of the Nuremberg Trials and subsequent horrors such as the Tuskegee and Miltown experiments. They similarly discuss academic illusions related to "objectivity," "freedom from values," and the ethical treatment of "subjects." From there, they argue that we must move beyond such close-minded, modernist perspectives to rethink and reconceptualize our research practices along the lines of a radical ethical perspective, one in that sees social science itself being "radically revisioned in ways that are egalitarian, anti-colonial, and embedded within a non-violent revolutionary ethical consciousness."

Thomas Schwandt's chapter ("The Pressing Need for Ethical Education") presents a multi-layered commentary on the current state of IRBs in relation to the ethics of scientific investigations. Schwandt speaks specifically to three distinct episodes—a university-sponsored conference on human subject protection regulations/research outside the biomedical sphere; an industry-oriented biotechnology conference that deals with such fields as genomics, stem-cell research, and proteomics; and a dissertation research project he is codirecting on the ways in which young children without disabilities understand, construct, and make sense of their peers who have disabilities—and the ways in which each episode illuminate different aspects of controversy vis-à-vis IRBs.

Closing the section is Julianne Cheek's chapter ("Qualitative Inquiry, Ethics, and the Politics of Evidence"), a probing examination of the unfolding metric-based terrain of qualitative research in Australia and the United Kingdom. Locating her discussion within the boundaries of neoliberal and neopositivism, she details various efforts on the part of various regulatory bodies to establish certainty with respect to the prevailing buzzwords of the day: the measures and assurances of "quality" and "excellence." She then engages with a series of questions (such as "How do *we* want excellence in qualitative research to be defined?" and "How do we keep the critical/risky edge on our research with a fundamentally conservative context?") that are aimed at encouraging qualitative researchers to take seriously the regulatory efforts afoot to stifle such research. She closes with a call for new forms of activism that focuses on forces operating *within* the field as much as those operating against it from the outside.

Marie Battiste ("Research Ethics for Protecting Indigenous Knowledge and Heritage") opens Section II by addressing the importance of indigenous knowledge for all peoples and its vitality and dynamic capacity to help solve contemporary problems and addresses Eurocentric biases, the cultural misappropriations that are endangering indigenous peoples, and the benefits they may receive. In the process, she presents an overview of the current regimes of ethics that impinge on indigenous knowledge as well as efforts being done to counteract such regimes. She concludes by offering a process for Aboriginal communities to address protection of their knowledge, culture, and heritage through a double door process, calling to mind the protective actions taken internationally and regionally among indigenous communities to stop the erosion of indigenous knowledge and heritage.

Sandy Grande's chapter on Red pedagogy continues this section's focus on indigenous methodologies. Tying together narratives concerning such varied topics as Hurricane Katrina, documentary filmmaking, and research on Native New Yorkers, Grande further develops her notion of Red pedagogy; that is, an indigenous pedagogy that operates at the crossroads of Western theory, specifically critical pedagogy, and indigenous knowledge. In so doing, she challenges us to examine our own communities, policies, and practices, taking seriously the notion that "to know ourselves as revolutionary agents is more than an act of understanding who we are." She concludes by outlining seven precepts of Red pedagogy in the hopes that a transformative "*decolonial imaginary*" where indigenous and non-indigenous peoples build transcultural and transnational coalitions to construct a nation free of imperialist, colonialist, and capitalist exploitation can rise from the ashes.

In a similar vein, Eve Tuck and Michelle Fine ("Inner Angles") turn to a range of ethical responses to/with indigenous and decolonizing theories. Rooted in the deep particularities of history, colonized spaces, and minds—yet also seeking to recognize a solidarity of structural violence in the United States and globally by the United States that cuts deep across time, place, and community—the chapter focuses on four specific areas of analysis germane to critical, indigenous methodologies: (1) the hegemonic voice-over of colonization; (2) that which is obscured by colonizers' guilt; (3) how indigenous and decolonizing theories might/already inform an epistemological shift; and (4) participatory action research praxes as praxes of self-determination. Tuck and Fine close with an invitation for us all "to consider how participatory action research that takes sovereignty as a prerequisite to democracy seriously might open up new possibilities for our theoretical work and for our sovereign approaches to education, subsistence, wellness, and knowledge in our communities."

Corrine Glesne ("Research as Solidarity") concludes Section II and offers an insightful view into practices of ethical, indigenous resistance forged in/through interpretive inquiry as set against Western ideologies of science and research. Turning away from such historically rigid notions as research purpose, data collection through participant observation and individual prestructured interviews, and data interpretation through pre-set lenses, Glesne argues instead for an ethic of community and an ethic of hospitality that honors in solidarity our research participants rather than exploits them for personal/professional gain.

In Section III, attention is turned to the performance of ethics within critical, interpretive inquiry. Ronald J. Pelias's chapter ("Performative Writing") inquires into the ethics of performance, first outlining its definitional complexities before proceeding to identify a number of ethical issues in regard to performative writing as a representational form. In so doing, he focuses his gaze most specifically on the embodied, the evocative, the partial, and the material forms. He closes with a resounding performative writing oath for ethical performative writing that embraces the risks associated with such writing in the name of a transformative vision of activism and social justice.

Arthur P. Bochner ("Notes toward an Ethics of Memory in Autoethnographic Inquiry") follows with a striking essay that posits the idea of memory as the performance of personal history. His pragmatic theory of the mind contests the nineteenth-century psychological view of memory—one of a presumed blank slate of the mind. In so doing, he opens a space for an ethics of personal narrative that includes memory as the site for reconstructing the past, which is always done in the present and through which each iteration (as Husserl reminds us) it is experienced as a new event against the horizon of all previous constructions. In the end, Bochner establishes a new ethics of *narrative* that moves us to reconsider our location to and understanding of memory-work.

Carolyn Ellis ("I Just Want to Tell *My* Story") continues this discussion of the performative by delving into an examination of relational ethics in writing about intimate others. Presenting a series of "remembered experiences" with her students, Ellis addresses pressing questions such as: "What can I assume is appropriate for me to tell about my relationship with the participant in my study and/or the person in my story?" "How will this person feel about what I have said?" "Must I get this person's consent to write my story?" "What if this person doesn't like or agree with the way I portray what happened?" "Given our relationship, what are my responsibilities to my participants?" "How will what I write affect our relationship?" Moreover, Ellis comes to terms with pedagogical questions associated with teaching such writing practices, presenting us with both roadmap and cautionary tale for others who seeking to engage with such a project.

The volume closes with a performative text by Carolyn Ellis, Arthur P. Bochner, Norman K. Denzin, Yvonna S. Lincoln, Janice M. Morse, Ronald J. Pelias, and Laurel Richardson. Moderated and stitched together by Carolyn Ellis, the text is drawn from a closing roundtable discussion held at the Second International Congress of Qualitative Research and focuses on the current and future state of qualitative research.

By Way of a Conclusion

The collected authors outline a radical path for an ethical future in qualitative research. In so doing, they transcend the Belmont Principles, which focus almost exclusively on the problems associated with betrayal, deception, and harm. They call for a collaborative, performative social science research model that makes the researcher responsible not to a removed discipline (or institution), but to those he or she studies. This model stresses personal accountability, caring, the value of individual expressiveness, the capacity for empathy, and the sharing of emotionality (Collins, 1990, p. 216). This model implements collaborative, participatory, performative inquiry. And it forcefully aligns the ethics of research with a politics of the oppressed, with a politics of resistance, hope, and freedom.

Most importantly, this model directs scholars to take up moral projects that decolonize, honor, and reclaim indigenous cultural practices. Such work produces spiritual, social, and psychological healing. Healing, in turn, leads to multiple forms of transformation at the personal and social levels. These transformations shape processes of mobilization and collective action. And these actions help persons realize a radical politics of possibility, of hope, of love, care, and equality for all humanity.

Our challenge is clear: to transform and change the spaces in which we exist in the academy; to take hold of the terms that define our existence in relationship to the other disciplines and the journals and the apparatuses and the departments, and tenure, and recruitment, and teaching, and instruction, and funding, and publishing, and journals; to take hold of our own existence, our own history, and make it into a dream that was there from the beginning when we were called into this space of qualitative research.

In the end, as Bochner reminds us, we have a responsibility—*an ethical and moral responsibility*—to do whatever we can, individually and collectively, to shape the future: "Meet your colleagues in other departments who are doing similar work. Talk to each other. Have conversations. Form institutes. Form work groups and reading groups. Get involved with each other. Don't isolate yourselves" (quoted in Ellis et al., this volume, p. 262).

We have a job to do; let's get to it!

Notes

1. This chapter draws on and reworks arguments in Denzin (2003) and Denzin and Giardina (2006a, 2006b).

2. The Internet Movie Database (www.imdb.com) also notes two glaring historical anachronisms in the film: (1), the buildings in the city co-mingle architectural styles from three separate Mayan civilizations: Tikal Classic Maya (800 CE), Puuc (c.1050 CE), and El Mirador, a pre-Classic metropolis that existed around the year 0 CE; and (2) the murals in the tunnel scene are nearly exact replicas of ones dating from 100 BCE, or more than a thousand years *before* the movie is supposedly set. *The only difference is that the real murals don't show people brandishing bleeding, severed heads.* Moreover, and aside from the architectural inaccuracies and artistic license taken, we see little of the thriving, culturally advanced civilization that was at the forefront of mathematics, astronomy, and artistic accomplishment known to have existed in the pre-Columbian epoch.

3. With respect to the War on Terror™, Matthew Yglesias (2006, July 18) points out roughly the same trend, which is to say: "the current campaign to defend and spread liberal principles against 'Islamist extremism' is being spearheaded by people who neither understand those principles nor have any real affection for them."

4. A press release from the Public Employees for Environmental Responsibility (PEER), a national alliance of local, state, and federal resource professionals, further states:

Park officials have defended the decision to approve the sale of *Grand Canyon: A Different View,* claiming that park bookstores are like libraries, where the broadest range of views are displayed. In fact, however, both law and park policies make it clear that park bookstores are more like schoolrooms rather than libraries. As such, materials are only to reflect the highest quality science and are supposed to closely support approved themes. Moreover, unlike a library, the approval process is very selective. Records released to PEER show that during 2003, Grand Canyon officials rejected 22 books and other products for bookstore placement while approving only one new sale item—the creationist book.

For more from PEER, see http://www.yubanet.com/artman/publish/article 48306.shtml.

For a scathing review of Vail's book, see Elders (2003), in which Elders states unequivocally that:

Grand Canyon: A Different View is not a geological treatise. It is "Exhibit A" of a new, slick strategy to proselytize by biblical literalists using a beautifully illustrated, multi-authored book about a spectacular and world-famous geological feature ... [whose] continued sale ... within the National Park will undermine the work of the NPS [National Park Service] interpreters who work so hard to educate the public.

The official statement by Grand Canyon administrators as to the canyon's geological age is "no comment."

5. This blatant dismissal and disregard of (scientific) evidence follows a long line of right-wing prevarication on the general subject, such as former Speaker of the House Tom DeLay (R-TX) dismissing evolution and the need for the Environmental Protection Agency because "God charges us to be good stewards of the Earth" (quoted in Thompson, 2003); former President Ronald Reagan refusing to endorse evolution in 1980 because, "Well, [evolution] is a theory—it is a scientific theory only, and it has in recent years been challenged in the world of science and is not yet believed in the scientific community to be as infallible as it was once believed" (Thompson, 2003); and the present Bush administration appointing right-wing religious-conservative ideologues to high-profile science/technology positions (such as the appointment of Dr. W. David Hager, an avowed anti-choice advocate, to a post on the Food and Drug Administration's Reproductive Health Drugs Advisory Committee in 2002). As the eminent evolutionary biologist, Richard Dawkins (2006) writes in his magisterial polemic, *The God Delusion*, such adherences to religious fundamentalism within the political arena necessarily "subverts science and saps the intellect" (p. 284).

6. For the case in Australia, see Cheek (2006); for the case in the United Kingdom, see Torrance (2006); on "Bush Science," see Lather (2004).

7. Smith (1999, p. 99) presents ten performative ways to be colonized, ten ways in which science, technology, and Western institutions place indigenous peoples—indeed, any group of any human beings—their languages, cultures, and environments, at risk. These ways include the Human Genome Diversity Project as well as scientific efforts to reconstruct previously extinct indigenous peoples and projects that deny global citizenship to peoples while commodifying, patenting, and selling indigenous cultural traditions and rituals.

8. The *testimonio* has a central place in Smith's list of projects. She begins her discussion of the *testimonio* with these lines from Menchú (1984): "My name is Rigoberta Menchú, I am twenty-three years old, and this is my testimony" (p. 1). The *testimonio* presents oral evidence to an audience, often in the form of a monologue. As Smith (1999) describes it, the indigenous *testimonio* is "a way of talking about an extremely painful event or series of events" (p. 144). The *testimonio* can be constructed as "a monologue and as a public performance" (Smith 1999, p. 144).

9. Other projects involve a focus on testimonies, new forms of storytelling, and returning to—as well as reframing and regendering—key cultural debates.

10. Federal protection of human subjects has been in effect in the United States since 1974, now codified in Title 45, Part 46, of the U.S. Code of Federal Regulations. Part 46 was last revised November 13, 2001, effective December 13, 2001. IRBs review all federally funded research involving human subjects to ensure the ethical protection of those subjects.

11. As early as 1969, Vine Deloria, Jr. proposed that an anthropologist wanting to study a Native American culture should be required to apply to a tribal council for permission to do the research, and that the council should give permission only if the researcher "raised as a contribution to the tribal budget an amount of money equal to the amount he proposed to spend in his study" (p. 95).

12. The Family Education Rights and Privacy Act, the Protection of Pupil Rights Amendment, and the Parental Freedom of Information Amendment extend additional privacy rights to children (see Shavelson & Towne, 2002, pp. 152–153).

13. Researchers are exempted from the Common Rule if they can show that their research involves (1) normal educational practice; (2) the use of educational tests, interviews, survey procedures, or the observation of public behavior *unless* confidentiality cannot be maintained or disclosure of participation would place subjects at risk of criminal or civil liability (Puglisi, 2001, p. 34); and (3) collecting or studying existing data, documents, or records if they are publicly available, and they can maintain confidentiality (that is, private information must not be linked to individual subjects). An IRB review may be expedited if the research involves (1) materials previously collected for nonresearch purposes; (2) collection of data from voice, video, digital, or image recordings for research purposes; or (3) research on language, communication, cultural beliefs, or cultural practices that presents no more than minimal risk to subjects. An IRB may waive the requirement of informed consent when four conditions are met: (1) the research presents no more than minimal risk to subjects; (2) the waiver does not adversely affect

the rights and welfare of the subjects; (3) the research cannot be carried out without the waiver, and (4) where appropriate, the subjects are provided with additional pertinent information after participation (Puglisi, 2001, p. 34).

14. The College of Communications at the University of Illinois, Urbana-Champaign, is one exception to the rule. For a complete overview of the policies and procedures currently in place, visit http://www.comm.uiuc.edu/icr/faculty/research/ICR_IRB.html.

References

American Association of University Professors (AAUP). (1981). Regulations governing research on human subjects: Academic freedom and the insititutional review board. *Academe, 67*(4), 358–370.

American Association of University Professors (AAUP). (2001). Protecting human beings: Institutional review boards and social science research. *Academe, 87*(3), 55–67.

American Association of University Professors (AAUP). (2002). Should all disciplines be subject to the common rule? Human subjects of social science research. *Academe, 88*(1), 1–15.

Battiste, M. (2006). The global challenge: Research ethics for protecting indigenous knowledge and heritage. Keynote address, 2nd International Congress of Qualitative Inquiry. Urbana, IL, May 4, 2006.

Bishop, R. (1998). Freeing ourselves from neo-colonial domination in research: A Maori approach to creating knowledge. *International Journal of Qualitative Studies in Education, 11*(2), 199–219.

Cheek, J. (2006). The challenge of tailor-made research quality: The RQF in Australia. In N. K. Denzin & M. D. Giardina (Eds.), *Qualitative inquiry and the conservative challenge: Confronting methodological fundamentalism* (pp. 109–126). Walnut Creek, CA: Left Coast Press.

Christians, C. G. (1995). The naturalistic fallacy in contemporary interaction-ist-interpretive research. *Studies in Symbolic Interaction, 19*(1), 125–130.

Christians, C. G. (1997). The ethics of being in a communications context. In C. G. Christians and M. Traber (Eds.), *Communication ethics and universal values* (pp. 3–23). Thousand Oaks, CA: Sage.

Christians, C. G. (1998). The sacredness of life. *Media Development, 2*(1), 3–7.

Christians, C. G. (2000). Ethics and politics in qualitative research. In N. K. Denzin & Y. S. Lincoln (Eds.), *Handbook of qualitative research*, 2nd ed. (pp. 133–155). Thousand Oaks, CA: Sage.

Christians, C. G. (2002). Introduction. In "Ethical Issues and Qualitative Research" [Special Issue]. *Qualitative Inquiry, 8*(4), 407–410. *Handbook of Qualitative Research*, 3rd ed. (pp. 139–165). Thousand Oaks, CA: Sage.

Christians, C. G. (2005). Ethics and politics in qualitative research. In N. K. Denzin & Y. S. Lincoln (Eds.), *Handbook of qualitative research*, 3rd ed. (pp. 139–164). Thousand Oaks, CA: Sage.

Collins, P. H. (1990). *Black feminist thought*. New York: Routledge.

Darder, A., & Mirón, L. F. (2006) Critical pedagogy in a time of uncertainty: A call to action. In N. K. Denzin & M. D. Giardina (Eds.), *Contesting empire/globalizing dissent: Cultural studies after 9/11* (pp. 136–151). Boulder, CO: Paradigm.

Dawkins, R. (2006). *The God delusion*. Boston: Houghton Mifflin.

Deloria, Jr., V. (1969). *Custer died for your sins: An Indian manifesto*. New York: Macmillan.

Denzin, N. K. (2003) *Performance ethnography: Critical pedagogy and the politics of Culture*. Thousand Oaks, CA: Sage.

Denzin, N. K., & Giardina, M. D. (Eds.) (2006a). *Contesting empire/globalizing dissent: Cultural studies after 9/11*. Boulder, CO: Paradigm.

Denzin, N. K., & Giardina, M. D. (Eds.) (2006b). *Qualitative research and the conservative challenge: Contesting methodological fundamentalism*. Walnut Creek, CA: Left Coast Press.

Denzin, N. K., Lincoln, Y. S., & Giardina, M. D. (2006). Disciplining qualitative research. *International Journal of Qualitative Studies in Education, 19*(6), 769–782.

Eagleton, T. (2003). *After theory*. New York: Basic Books.

Elders, W. (2003). Bibliolatory revisted: A review of *Grand Canyon: A different view*. Available online at http://home.austarnet.com/au/bibliolatory_revis-ited/elders.htm. Accessed January 3, 2007.

Freire, P. (1999). *Pedagogy of hope* (Robert R. Barr, Trans.). New York: Continuum (Original work published 1992).

Fuchs, C. (2006). Bring the pain: *Apocalypto* film review. PopMatters.com. Available online at http://www.popmatters.com/pm/film/reviews/8581/apocalypto-2006. Accessed January 5, 2007.

Giroux, H. A. (2000). *Impure acts: The practical politics of cultural studies.* New York: Routledge.

Gore, A. (2006). *An inconvenient truth: The planetary emergency of global warming and what we can do about it.* Emmaus, PA: Rodale Books.

Grande, S. (2004). *Red pedagogy: Native American social and political thought.* Lanham, MD: Rowman & Littlefield.

Graveline, F. J. (2000). Circle as methodology: Enacting an aboriginal paradigm. *International Journal of Qualitative Studies in Education, 13*(2), 361–370.

Gunsalus, C. K. (2002). Point of view: Rethinking protections for human subjects. *Chronicle of Higher Education, 49*(12), B24.

Harmon, A. (2006). DNA gatherers hit snag: Tribes don't trust them. *New York Times.* Available online at http://ww.nytimes.com/2006/12/10/us/10dna.html. Accessed December 27, 2006.

Hoberman, J. (2006). Mel Gibson is responsible for all the wars in the world: OK, slight exaggeration, but he's at least to blame for this one he made up. *The Village Voice.* Available online at http://www.villagevoice.com/film/0649,hoberman,75217,20.html. Accessed January 5, 2007.

House, E. R. (2006). Methodological fundamentalism and the quest for control(s). In N. K. Denzin & M. D. Giardina (Eds.), *Qualitative inquiry and the conservative challenge: Confronting methodological fundamentalism* (pp. 93–108). Walnut Creek, CA: Left Coast Press.

Lather, P. (2004). This *IS* your father's paradigm: Government intrusion and the case of qualitative research in education. *Qualitative Inquiry, 10*(1), 15–34.

Levenson, M. (2004). Gore calls Bush worst-ever president for the environment. *The Boston Globe.* Available online at http://www.boston.com/news/nation/articles/2004/10/07/gore_calls_bush_worst_president_for_environment. Accessed December 23, 2006.

Lincoln, Y. S. (1995). Emerging criteria for quality in qualitative and interpretive inquiry. *Qualitative Inquiry, 1*(3), 275–289.

Lincoln, Y. S., & Cannella, G. S. (2002). Qualitative research and the radical right: Cats and dogs and other natural enemies. Paper presented at the 66th annual meeting of the American Educational Research Association, New Orleans, April 1–5.

Lincoln, Y. S., & Tierney, W. G. (2002). "What we have here is a failure to communicate...": Qualitative research and institutional review boards (IRBs). Paper presented at the 66th annual meeting of the American Educational Research Association, New Orleans, April 1–5.

Menchú, R. (1984). *I, Rigoberta Menchú: An Indian woman in Guatemala.* New York: Verso.

Padgett, T. (2006). Apocalypto now. *Time.* Available online at http://www.time.com/time/magazine/article/0,9171,1174684,00.html. Accessed January 5, 2007.

Pring, R. (2004). Conclusion: Evidence-based policy and practice. In G. Thomas & R. Pring (Eds.), *Evidence-based practice in education* (pp. 210–223). Buckingham, UK: Open University Press.

Pritchard, I. A. (2002). Travelers and trolls: Practitioner research and institutional review boards. *Educational Researcher, 31*(1), 3–13.

Public Employees for Environmental Responsibility (PEER). (2006). How old is the Grand Canyon? Park service won't say. Available online at http://www.peer.org/nwes/news_id/php?row_id=801. Accessed January 2, 2007.

Puglisi, T. (2001). IRB review: It helps to know the regulatory framework. *APS Observer, 1*(1), 34–35.

Riis-Hansen, A. (1992). Interview with Rigoberta Menchú Tum: Five hundred years of sacrifice before the aliens go. Available online at: http://race.eserver.org/rigoberta-menchu-tum.html. Retrieved January 23, 2007.

Shavelson, R. J., & Towne, L. (Eds.) (2002). *Scientific research in education: Committee on scientific principles for education research.* Washington, DC: National Academy Press.

Smith, L. T. (1999). *Decolonizing methodologies: Research and indigenous peoples.* Dunedin, New Zealand: University of Otago Press.

Smith, L. T. (2005). On tricky ground: researching the native in the age of uncertainty. In N. K. Denzin & Y. S. Lincoln (Eds.), *Handbook of qualitative research*, 3rd ed. (pp. 85–108). Thousand Oaks, CA: Sage.

Smith, L. T. (2006). Choosing the margins: The role of research in indigenous struggles for social justice. In N. K. Denzin & M. D. Giardina (Eds.), *Qualitative inquiry and the conservative challenge: Confronting methodological fundamentalism* (pp. 151–175). Walnut Creek, CA: Left Coast Press.

St. Pierre, E. A. (2004). Refusing alternatives: A science of contestation. *Qualitative Inquiry, 10*(1), 130–139.

Thomas, G. (2005). Introduction: Evidence and practice. In G. Thomas & R. Pring (Eds.), *Evidence-based practice in education* (pp. 1–20). Buckingham, UK: Open University Press.

Thompson, N. (2003). Science friction: The growing—and dangerous—divide between scientists and the GOP. *Washington Monthly*. Available online at http://www.washingtonmonthly.com/features/2003/0307.thompson.html. Accessed March 12, 2006.

Torrance, H. (2006). Research quality and research governance in the United Kingdom: From methodology to management. In N. K. Denzin & M. D. Giardina (Eds.), *Qualitative inquiry and the conservative challenge: Confronting methodological fundamentalism* (pp. 127–148). Walnut Creek, CA: Left Coast Press.

Vail, T. (2003). *Grand Canyon: A different view*. Green Forest, AZ: New Leaf Publishing Group.

West, C. (1993). *Keeping the faith: Philosophy and race in America*. New York: Routledge.

Wilgoren, J. (2005). Seeing creation and evolution in the Grand Canyon. *New York Times*. Available online at http://www.nytimes.com/2005/10/06/science/sciencespecial2/06canyon.html. Accessed December 23, 2006.

Yglesias, M. (2006). Leo Strauss, Unrehabilitated. *The American Prospect* (Online Edition). Available online at http://www.prospect.org/weblog/2006/07/post_862.html. Accessed December 23, 2006.

Part I
Ethical Challenges in Qualitative Research

Chapter 1 | Neutral Science and the Ethics of Resistance

Clifford G. Christians
University of Illinois, Urbana-Champaign

The subject-object dichotomy dominated the Enlightenment mind.[1] Isaac Newton's *Principia Mathematica* (1687) described the world as a lifeless machine built on uniform natural causes in a closed system, and Newton inspired the eighteenth century as much as anyone. Descartes (1596–1690) presumed clear and distinct ideas, objective and neutral, apart from anything subjective. The physical universe became the only legitimate domain of knowledge. On the positive side, it unlocked an excitement to explore and rule the natural world that formerly had controlled them. In fact, Descartes limited his interests to precise mechanistic knowledge because he wished that "we should make ourselves masters and possessors of nature" ([1637] 1916, pt. VI). Natural science played a key role in setting people free. Achievements in mathematics, physics, and astronomy provided unmistakable evidence that by applying reason to nature and to human beings in fairly obvious ways, people could live progressively happier lives. Crime and insanity, for example, no longer needed repressive theological explanations, but instead were deemed capable of mundane empirical solutions. Science gained a stranglehold on truth, with its ideology of hard data versus subjective values.

It is a hallmark of modernity that the character of the social sciences revolves around the theory and methodology of the natural sciences. As the social sciences and the liberal state emerged and overlapped historically, Enlightenment thinkers in eighteenth-century Europe advocated the techniques of experimental reasoning to support the state and citizenry. The basic institutions

of society were designed to ensure "neutrality between different conceptions of the good" (Root, 1993, p. 12; cf. pp. 14–15).[2]
Objects and events situated in space-time were considered to contain all the facts there are. Value-free experimentalism in Enlightenment terms has defined the theory and practice of mainstream
social science until today. Only a reintegration of research practice and the moral order provides an alternative paradigm. For an
ethics and politics of resistance, the social sciences must reinvent
themselves in qualitative terms after the humanities.

Value-Neutral Experimentalism

Mill's Philosophy of Social Science

For John Stuart Mill, neutrality is necessary to promote autonomy. Planning our lives according to our own ideas and purposes
is sine qua non for autonomous beings in his *On Liberty* ([1859]
1978): "The free development of individuality is one of the principal ingredients of human happiness, and quite the chief ingredient of individual and social progress" (p. 50; see also Copleston,
1966, p. 303, n. 32). This neutrality, based on the supremacy of
individual autonomy, is the foundational principle in his *Utilitarianism* (Mill, [1861] 1957), and in *A System of Logic* (Mill, [1843]
1893) as well. In addition to bringing classical utilitarianism to
its maximum development and establishing with Locke the liberal state, Mill delineated the foundations of inductive inquiry as
social scientific method. In terms of the principles of empiricism,
he perfected the inductive techniques of Francis Bacon as a problem-solving methodology to replace Aristotelian deductive logic.

According to Mill, syllogisms contribute nothing new to
human knowledge. If we conclude that because "all men are mortal" the Duke of Wellington is mortal by virtue of his manhood,
then the conclusion does not advance the premise (see Mill, [1843]
1893, II, 3, 2, p. 140). The crucial issue is not reordering the conceptual world but discriminating genuine knowledge from superstition. In the pursuit of truth, generalizing and synthesizing are
necessary to advance inductively from the known to the unknown.
Mill seeks to establish this function of logic as inference from the

known, rather than certifying the rules for formal consistency in reasoning (Mill, [1843] 1893, bk. 3). Scientific certitude can be approximated when induction is followed rigorously, with propositions empirically derived and the material of all our knowledge provided by experience.[3] For the physical sciences, he establishes four modes of experimental inquiry: agreement, disagreement, residues, and the principle of concomitant variations (Mill, [1843] 1893, III, 8, pp. 278–288). He considers them the only possible methods of proof for experimentation, as long as one presumes the realist position that nature is structured by uniformities.[4]

In Book 6 of *A System of Logic*, "On the Logic of the Moral Sciences," Mill ([1843] 1893) develops an inductive experimentalism as the scientific method for studying "the various phenomena which constitute social life" (VI, 6, 1, p. 606). Although he conceived of social science as explaining human behavior in terms of causal laws, he warned against the fatalism of full predictability. "Social laws are hypothetical, and statistically-based generalizations by their very nature admit of exceptions" (Copleston, 1966, p. 101; see also Mill, [1843] 1893, VI, 5, 1, p. 596). Empirically confirmed instrumental knowledge about human behavior has greater predictive power when it deals with collective masses than when we are dealing with individual agents.

Mill's positivism is obvious throughout his work on experimental inquiry.[5] Based on the work of Auguste Comte, he defined matter as the "permanent possibility of sensation" (Mill, 1865b, p. 198) and believed that nothing else can be said about metaphysical substances.[6] With Hume and Comte, Mill insisted that metaphysical substances are not real and only the facts of sense phenomena exist. There are no essences or ultimate reality behind sensations, therefore Mill (1865a, 1865b) and Comte ([1848] 1910) argued that social scientists should limit themselves to particular data as a factual source out of which experimentally valid laws can be derived. For both, this is the only kind of knowledge that yields practical benefits (Mill, 1865b, p. 242); in fact, society's salvation is contingent on such scientific knowledge (p. 241).[7]

Mill's philosophy of social science is built on a dualism of means and ends. Citizens and politicians are responsible for articulating ends in a free society and science is responsible for the know-how to achieve them. Science is amoral, speaking to questions of means but with no wherewithal or authority to dictate ends. Methods in the social sciences must be disinterested regarding substance and content, and rigorously limited to the risks and benefits of possible courses of action. Research cannot be judged right or wrong, only true or false. "Science is political only in its applications" (Root, 1993, p. 213). Given his democratic liberalism, Mill advocates neutrality "out of concern for the autonomy of the individuals or groups" social science seeks to serve. It should "treat them as thinking, willing, active beings who bear responsibility for their choices and are free to choose" their own conception of the good life by majority rule (Root, 1993, p. 19).

Value Neutrality in Max Weber

When twenty-first-century mainstream social scientists contend that ethics is not their business, they typically invoke Weber's essays written between 1904 and 1917. Given Weber's importance methodologically and theoretically for sociology and economics, his distinction between political judgments and scientific neutrality is given canonical status.

Weber distinguishes value freedom from value relevance. He recognizes that in the discovery phase, "personal, cultural, moral, or political values cannot be eliminated; ... what social scientists choose to investigate ... they choose on the basis of the values" that they expect their research to advance (Root, 1993, p. 33). But he insists that social science be value free in the presentation phase. Findings ought not to express any judgments of a moral or political character. Professors should hang up their values along with their coats as they enter their lecture halls.

"An attitude of moral indifference," Weber ([1904] 1949b) writes, "has no connection with scientific objectivity" (p. 60). His meaning is clear from the value-freedom/value-relevance distinction. For the social sciences to be purposeful and rational, they must serve the "values of relevance."

> The problems of the social sciences are selected by the value relevance of the phenomena treated. ...The expression "relevance to values" refers simply to the philosophical interpretation of that

specifically scientific "interest" which determines the selection of a given subject matter and problems of empirical analysis. [Weber, (1917) 1949a, pp. 21–22]

Whereas the natural sciences, in Weber's ([1904] 1949b, p. 72) view, seek general laws that govern all empirical phenomena, the social sciences study those realities that our values consider significant. Whereas the natural world itself indicates what reality to investigate, the infinite possibilities of the social world are ordered in terms of "the cultural values with which we approach reality" ([1904] 1949b, p. 78). However, even though value relevance directs the social sciences, as with the natural sciences, Weber considers the former value free. The subject matter in natural science makes value judgments unnecessary, and social scientists by a conscious decision can exclude judgments of "desirability or undesirability" from their publications and lectures ([1904] 1949b, p. 52). "What is really at issue is the intrinsically simple demand that the investigator and teacher should keep unconditionally separate the establishment of empirical facts ... and his own political evaluations" (Weber, [1917] 1949a, p. 11).

Weber's practical argument for value freedom and his apparent limitation of it to the reporting phase have made his version of value neutrality attractive to twenty-first-century social science. He is not a positivist such as Comte or a thoroughgoing empiricist in the tradition of Mill. He disavowed the positivists' overwrought disjunction between discovery and justification, and he developed no systematic epistemology comparable to Mill's. Nevertheless, Weber's value neutrality reflects the Enlightenment's subject-object dichotomy in a fundamentally similar fashion. In the process of maintaining his distinction between value relevance and value freedom, he separates facts from values and means from ends. He appeals to empirical evidence and logical reasoning rooted in human rationality. "The validity of a practical imperative as a norm," he writes, "and the truth-value of an empirical proposition are absolutely heterogeneous in character" (Weber, [1904] 1949b, p. 52). "A systematically correct scientific proof in the social sciences" may not be completely attainable, but that is most likely "due to faulty data" not because it is conceptually impossible ([1904] 1949b, p. 58).[8] For Weber, as with Mill, empirical science deals with questions of means, and his warning against inculcating political and moral values presumes a means-ends dichotomy (see Weber, [1917] 1949a, pp. 18–19, [1904] 1949b, p. 52).

As Michael Root (1993) concludes, "John Stuart Mill's call for neutrality in the social sciences is based on his belief" that the language of science "takes cognizance of a phenomenon and endeavors to discover its laws" (p. 205). Max Weber likewise "takes it for granted that there can be a language of science—a collection of truths—that excludes all value-judgments, rules, or directions for conduct" (Root, 2003, p. 205). In both cases, scientific knowledge exists for its own sake as morally neutral. For both, neutrality is desirable "because questions of value are not rationally resolvable" and neutrality in the social sciences is presumed to contribute "to political and personal autonomy" (Root, 1993, p. 229). In Weber's argument for value relevance in social science, he did not contradict the larger Enlightenment ideal of scientific neutrality between competing conceptions of the good.

Institutional Review Boards

In an academic world of value-free social science, codes of ethics for professional and academic associations are the conventional format for moral principles. By the 1980s, each of the major scholarly associations had adopted its own code for directing an inductive science of means toward majoritarian ends. And institutional review boards (IRBs) likewise embody the same agenda of instrumentalist, neutral social science. In terms of the IRBs' scope, assumptions, and procedures, data that are internally and externally valid are the coin of the realm, experimentally and morally. Scientific research is presumed to benefit society by uncovering facts about the human condition. The guidelines entailed by IRB policy themselves establish the ends by which the scientific study of society is evaluated as moral.

In 1978, the U.S. National Commission for the Protection of Human Subjects in Biomedical and Behavioral Research was established. As a result, three principles, published in what became known as the Belmont Report, were developed as the moral standards for research involving human subjects: respect for persons, beneficence, and justice.

1. The section on respect for persons reiterates the codes' demands that subjects enter the research voluntarily and with adequate information about the experiment's procedures and possible consequences. On a deeper level, respect for persons incorporates two basic ethical tenets: "First, that individuals should be treated as autonomous agents, and second, that persons with diminished autonomy [the immature and incapacitated] are entitled to protection" (University of Illinois, 2006, n.p.).

2. Under the principle of beneficence, researchers are enjoined to secure the well-being of their subjects. Beneficent actions are understood in a double sense as avoiding harm altogether, and if risks are involved for achieving substantial benefits, minimizing as much harm as possible:

> In the case of particular projects, investigators and members of their institutions are obliged to give forethought to the maximization of benefits and the reduction of risks that might occur from the research investigation. In the case of scientific research in general, members of the larger society are obliged to recognize the longer term benefits and risks that may result from the improvement of knowledge and from the development of novel medical, psychotherapeutic, and social procedures. [University of Illinois, 2006, n.p.]

3. The principle of justice insists on fair distribution of both the benefits and burdens of research. An injustice occurs when some groups (e.g., welfare recipients, the institutionalized, or particular ethnic minorities) are overused as research subjects because of easy manipulation or their availability. And when research supported by public funds leads to "therapeutic devices and procedures, justice demands that these not provide advantages only to those who can afford them" (University of Illinois, 2006, n.p.).

These principles reiterate the basic themes of value-neutral experimentalism—individual autonomy, maximum benefits with minimal risks, and ethical ends exterior to scientific means. The authority of IRBs was enhanced in 1989 when Congress passed the National Institutes of Health Revitalization Act and formed the Commission on Research Integrity. The emphasis at that point was on the invention, fudging, and distortion of data. Falsification, fabrication, and plagiarism continue as federal categories of misconduct, with a new report in 1996 adding warnings against unauthorized use of confidential information, omission of important data, and interference (that is, physical damage to the materials of others).

With IRBs, the legacy of Mill, Comte, and Weber comes into its own. Value-neutral science is accountable to ethical standards through rational procedures controlled by value-neutral academic institutions in the service of an impartial government. Consistent with the way anonymous bureaucratic regimes become refined and streamlined toward greater efficiency, the regulations rooted in scientific and medical experiments now extend to humanistic inquiry. Protecting subjects from physical harm in laboratories has grown to encompass human behavior, history, and ethnography in natural settings. In Jonathon Church's metaphor, "a biomedical paradigm is used like some threshing machine with ethnographic research the resulting chaff" (2002, p. 2). Whereas Title 45/Part 46 of the Code of Federal Regulations (45 CFR 46) designed protocols for research funded by seventeen federal agencies, at present most universities have multiple project agreements that consign all research to a campus IRB under the terms of 45 CFR 46.

While this bureaucratic expansion has gone on unremittingly, most IRBs have not changed the composition of their membership. Medical and behavioral scientists under the aegis of value-free neutrality continue to dominate. And the changes in procedures have generally stayed within the biomedical model also. Expedited review under the Common Rule, for social research with no risk of physical or psychological harm, depends on enlightened IRB chairs and organizational flexibility. Informed consent, mandatory before medical experiments, is simply incongruent with interpretive research not on human subjects but with other human beings. Despite technical improvements, "[i]ntellectual curiosity remains actively discouraged by the IRB. Research projects must ask only surface questions and must not deviate from a path approved by a remote group of people. ... Often the review process seems to be more about gamesmanship than anything else. A better formula for stultifying research could not be imagined" (Blanchard, 2002, p. 11).

In its conceptual structure, IRB policy is designed to produce the best ratio of costs to benefits. IRBs ostensibly protect the subjects who fall under the protocols they approve. However, given the interlocking utilitarian functions of social science, the academy, and the state that Mill identified and promoted, IRBs in reality protect their own institutions rather than subject populations in society at large (see Vanderpool, 1996, chaps. 2–6).[9]

The Current Crisis

Underneath the pros and cons of administering a responsible social science, the structural deficiencies in its epistemology have become transparent (Jennings, 1983, pp. 4–7). A positivistic philosophy of social inquiry insists on neutrality regarding definitions of the good, and this worldview has been generally discredited. The Enlightenment model, setting the subject at odds with the objective world, is bankrupt. Reworking professional codes of ethics so they are more explicit and less hortatory will make no fundamental difference. Requiring ethics workshops for graduate students and faculty is of marginal significance. Strengthening government policy is desirable but not transformative. Refining the IRB process and exhorting IRBs to account for the pluralistic nature of academic research are insufficient.

Certainly, levels of success and failure are open to dispute even within the social science disciplines themselves. More unsettling for the empiricist mainstream than disappointing performance is the recognition that neutrality is not pluralistic but imperialistic. Reflecting on past experience, disinterested research under presumed conditions of value freedom is increasingly seen as de facto reinscribing the agenda in its own terms. Empiricism is procedurally committed to equal reckoning, regardless of how research subjects may constitute the substantive ends of life. But experimentalism is not a neutral meeting ground for all ideas; rather, it is a "fighting creed" that imposes its own ideas on others while uncritically assuming the very "superiority that powers this imposition." In Foucault's (1979, pp. 170–195) more decisive terms, social science is a regime of power that helps maintain social order by normalizing subjects into categories designed by political authorities (see Root, 1993, chap.7). A liberalism of equality is not neutral but represents only one range of ideals, and is itself incompatible with other goods.

This noncontextual, nonsituational model that assumes "a morally neutral, objective observer will get the facts right" ignores "the situatedness of power relations associated with gender, sexual orientation, class, ethnicity, race, and nationality." It is hierarchical (scientist-subject) and biased toward patriarchy. "It glosses the ways in which the observer-ethnographer is implicated and embedded in the 'ruling apparatus' of the society and the culture." Scientists "carry the mantle" of university-based authority as they venture out into "local community to do research" (Denzin, 1997, p. 272; see also Ryan, 1995, pp. 144–145). There is no sustained questioning of expertise itself in democratic societies that belong in principle to citizens who do not share this specialized knowledge (see Euben, 1981, p. 120).

A Social Science Ethics of Resistance

Over the past decade, a social ethics of resistance has made a radical break with rationalist presumption of Western canonical ethics. Rather than searching for neutral principles to which all parties can appeal, ethics is understood to rest on a complex view of moral judgments as integrating various perspectives into an organic whole—everyday experience, beliefs about the good, and feelings of approval and shame. This is a philosophical approach that situates the moral domain within the general purposes of human life that people share contextually and across cultural, racial, and historical boundaries. Ideally, it engenders a new occupational role and normative core for social science research.

Within a social ethics of resistance, the mission of social and cultural research is interpretive sufficiency. In contrast to an experimentalism of instrumental efficiency, this paradigm seeks to open up the human world in all its dynamic dimensions. The thick notion of sufficiency supplants the thinness of the technical, exterior, and statistically precise received view. Rather than reducing social issues to financial and administrative problems, social science research helps people come to terms with their everyday experiences themselves.

Interpretive sufficiency means taking seriously lives that are loaded with multiple interpretations and grounded in cultural complexity (Denzin, 1989, pp. 77, 81). How the moral order works itself out in community formation is the issue, not first of all what researchers or funding agencies consider virtuous. The challenge for those writing culture is not to limit their moral perspectives to their own generic and neutral principles, but to engage the same moral space as the people they study. In this perspective, research strategies are not assessed, first of all in terms of "experimental robustness," but for their "vitality and vigor in illuminating how we can create human flourishing" (Lincoln & Denzin, 2000, p. 1062).

Reinventing Power

Thus, a basic norm for interpretive research is enabling the humane transformation of the multiple spheres of community life. To accomplish that revolution, Paulo Freire speaks of the need to reinvent the meaning of power:

> For me the principal, real transformation, the radical transformation of society in this part of the century demands not getting power from those who have it today, or merely to make some reforms, some changes in it. ... The question, from my point of view, is not just to take power but to reinvent it. That is, to create a different kind of power, to deny the need power has as if it were metaphysics, bureaucratized, anti-democratic. [quoted in Evans, Evans, & Kennedy, 1987, p. 229]

Certainly oppressive power blocs and monopolies—economic, technological, and political—need the scrutiny of researchers and their collaborators. Given Freire's political-institutional bearing, power for him is a central notion in social analysis. But, in concert with him, qualitative research refuses to deal with power in cognitive terms only. The issue is how people can empower themselves instead.

The dominant understanding of power is grounded in non-mutuality; it is interventionist power, exercised competitively and seeking control. In Freire's alternative, power is relational, characterized by mutuality rather than sovereignty. Power from this perspective is reciprocity between two subjects, a relationship not of domination, but of intimacy and vulnerability—power akin to that of Alcoholics Anonymous, in which surrender to the community enables the individual to gain mastery. As understood so clearly in the indigenous Kaupapa Maori approach to research, "the researcher is led by the members of the community and does not presume to be a leader, or to have any power that he or she can relinquish" (Denzin, 2003, p. 243).

Dialogue is the key element in an emancipatory strategy that liberates rather than imprisons us in manipulation or antagonistic relationships. Although the control version of power considers mutuality weakness, the empowerment mode maximizes our humanity and thereby banishes powerlessness. In the research process, power is unmasked and engaged through solidarity as a researched-researcher team. There is certainly no monologic "assumption that the researcher is giving the group power" (Denzin, 2003, p. 243). Rather than play semantic games with power, researchers themselves are willing to march against the barricades.

In Freire's (1973) terms, the goal is conscientization, that is, a critical consciousness that directs the ongoing flow of praxis and reflection in everyday life. In a culture of silence, the oppressor's language and way of being are fatalistically accepted without contradiction. But a critical consciousness enables us to exercise the uniquely human capacity of "speaking a true word" (Freire, 1970b, p. 75). Under conditions of sociopolitical control, "the vanquished are dispossessed of their word, their expressiveness, their culture" (1970b, p. 134). What is nonnegotiable in Freire's theory of power is participation of the oppressed in directing cultural formation. If an important social issue needs resolution, the most vulnerable will have to lead the way.[10] Through conscientization the oppressed gain their own voice and collaborate in transforming their culture

(Freire, 1970a, pp. 212–213). Therefore, research is not the transmission of specialized data but, in style and content, a catalyst for critical consciousness. Without what Freire (1970b, p. 47) calls "a critical comprehension of reality" (that is, the oppressed "grasping with their minds the truth of their reality"), there is only acquiescence in the status quo.

The resistance of the empowered is more productive at the interstices—at the fissures in social institutions where authentic action is possible. Effective resistance is nurtured in the backyards, the open spaces, voluntary associations, among neighborhoods, schools, and interactive settings of mutual struggle without elites. Because only nonviolence is morally acceptable for sociopolitical change, there is no other option except an educational one—having people's movements gain their own voice and nurturing a critical conscience through dialogic means. People-based development from below is not merely an end in itself, but a fundamental condition of social transformation.

Transforming the IRB

Interpretive sufficiency as a philosophy of social science fundamentally transforms the IRB system in form and content. As with IRBs, it emphasizes relentless accuracy, but understands it as the researcher's authentic resonance with the context and the subject's self-reflection as a moral agent. In an indigenous Maori approach to knowledge, for example, "concrete experience is the criterion of meaning and truth," and researchers are "led by the members of the community to discover them" (Denzin, 2003, p. 243). However, because the research-subject relation is reciprocal, the IRBs' invasion of privacy, informed consent, and deception are nonissues. In an ethics of resistance, conceptions of the good are shared by the research subjects, and researchers collaborate in bringing these definitions into their own. "Participants have a co-equal say in how research should be conducted, what should be studied, which methods should be used, which findings are valid and acceptable, how the findings are to be implemented, and how the consequences of such actions are to be assessed" (Denzin, 2003, p. 257).

Interpretive sufficiency transcends the current regulatory system governing research on human subjects. Therefore, it recommends a policy of strict territorialism for the IRB regime. Given its roots historically in biomedicine, and with the explosion in both genetic research and privately funded biomedical research, 45 CFR 46 should be confined to medical, biological, and clinic studies and the positivist and postpositivist social science that is epistemologically identical to them. Research methodologies that have broken down the walls between subjects and researchers ought to be excluded from IRB oversight. As Denzin observes:

> Performance autoethnography, for example falls outside this [IRB] model, as do many forms of participatory action research, reflexive ethnography, and qualitative research involving testimonies, life stories, life-history inquiry, personal narrative inquiry, performance autobiography, conversation analysis, and ethnodrama. In all of these cases, subjects and researchers develop collaborative, public, pedagogical relationships. [2003, p. 249]

Because participation is voluntary, subjects do not need "to sign forms indicating that their consent is 'informed.'" Confidentiality is not an issue, "for there is nothing to hide or protect. Participants are not subjected to pre-approved procedures, but "acting together, researchers and subjects work to produce change in the world" (Denzin, 2003, pp. 249–250).

Given their different understanding of human inquiry, the review of their research protocols ought to be given to peers in academic departments or units familiar with these methodologies. The Oral History Association (OHA), for example, was excluded from IRB policy on September 22, 2003, in a letter from the Office for Human Research Protection (OHRP): "Oral history interviewing activities, in general, are not designed to contribute to generalizable knowledge and, therefore, do not involve research a defined by Department of Health and Human Services (HHS) regulations at 45 CFR 46.102d."

The OHA had argued that the regulations inscribed in the Common Rule were inconsistent with oral history methodology and inhibited critical inquiry. The IRB regulatory system is "based on a definition of research far removed from historical practice. Moreover, historians are acutely aware of the ethical dimensions of [their] work and have well-developed professional standards governing oral history interviewing" (Shopes, 2000. p. 8; cf. Shopes and Ritchie, 2004). Against the background of the American Historical Association's "Standards of Professional Conduct" adopted on January 6, 2005, the OHA has codified a set of principles and responsibilities for guiding its own work in lieu of submitting research protocols for IRB review. Ambiguities in interpretation remain, given historical research and interviews designed for generalizable knowledge. Three years after the ruling by the OHRP, studies indicated that most university IRBs had not yet formally implemented the oral history exclusion (Townsend, 2006).[11] Despite the limited gains, and even though the IRBs' canon of rationalist knowledge is not contradicted, OHA's exclusion represents an important challenge to the "mission creep" of IRB bureaucracy (Gunsalus et al., 2005).

Conclusion

As Guba and Lincoln (1994) argue, the issues in social science ultimately must be engaged at the worldview level. "Questions of method are secondary to questions of paradigm, which we define as the basic belief system or worldview that guides the investigator, not only in choices of method but in ontologically and epistemologically fundamental ways" (Guba & Lincoln, 1994, p. 105). The conventional view, with its extrinsic ethics, gives us a truncated and unsophisticated paradigm that needs to be conceptually transformed. This historical overview of theory and practice points to the need for an entirely new model of research ethics in which human action and conceptions of the good are interactive.

When rooted in a positivist worldview, explanations of social life are considered incompatible with the renderings offered by the participants themselves. In problematics, lingual form, and content, research production presumes greater mastery and clearer illumination than the nonexperts who are the targeted beneficiaries. Protecting and promoting individual autonomy have been the philosophical rationale for value neutrality since its origins in Mill. But the incoherence in that view of social science is now transparent. By limiting the active involvement of rational beings or judging their self-understanding to be false, empiricist models contradict the ideal of rational beings who "choose between competing conceptions of the good" and make choices "deserving of respect." The verification standards of an instrumentalist system "take away what neutrality aims to protect: a community of free and equal rational beings legislating their own principles of conduct" (Root, 1993, p. 198). A social ethics of resistance escapes this contradiction by reintegrating human life with the moral order.

Notes

1. For a more detailed essay on value-free experimentalism, though with a different orientation, see Christians (2005, pp. 130–164).

2. Michael Root (1993) is unique among philosophers of the social sciences in linking social science to the ideals and practices of the liberal state on the grounds that both institutions "attempt to be neutral between competing conceptions of the good" (p. xv). Root's interpretations of Mill and Weber are crucial to my own formulation. As will be seen, neutrality is the common linkage among IRB conceptions of science, the university structure, and the state apparatus.

3. Although committed to what he called "the logic of the moral sciences" in delineating the canons or methods for induction, Mill shared with natural science a belief in the uniformity of nature and the presumption that all phenomena are subject to cause-and-effect relationships. His five principles of induction reflect a Newtonian cosmology.

4. In his *A System of Logic*, Mill ([1843] 1893) combines the principles of French positivism (as developed by August Comte) and British empiricism into a single system.

5. For an elaboration of the complexities in positivism—including reference to its Millian connections—see Lincoln and Guba (1985, pp. 19–28).

6. Mill's realism is most explicitly developed in his *Examination of Sir William Hamilton's Philosophy* (1865b). Our belief in a common external world, in his view, is rooted in the fact that our sensations of physical reality "belong as much to other human or sentient beings as to ourselves" (p. 196; see also Copleston, 1966, p. 306, n. 97).

7. Mill (1969) specifically credits to Comte his use of the inverse deductive or historical method: "This was an idea entirely new to me when I found it in Comte; and but for him I might not soon (if ever) have arrived at it" (p. 126). Mill explicitly follows Comte in distinguishing social statics and social dynamics. He published two essays on Comte's influence in the *Westminster Review*, which were reprinted as *Auguste Comte and Positivism* (Mill, 1865a; see also Mill, 1969, p. 165).

8. The rationale for the Social Science Research Council (SSRC) in 1923 is multilayered, but in its attempt to link academic expertise with policy research, and in its preference for rigorous social scientific methodology, the SSRC reflects and implements Weber.

9. For a sociological and epistemological critique of IRBs, see Denzin (2003, pp. 248–257).

10. Because of his fundamental commitment to dialogue, empowering for Freire avoids the weaknesses of monologic concepts of empowerment in which researchers are seen to free up the weak and unfortunate (summarized by Denzin [2003, pp. 242–245] citing Bishop, 1998). Although Freire represents a radical perspective, he does not claim "as more radical theorists" do that "only they and their theories can lead" the researched into freedom (Denzin, 2003, p. 246, citing Bishop, 1998).

11. This specific evidence regarding OHA in 2006 is consistent with Denzin and Lincoln's conclusion regarding twenty years of debate over IRBs: "Institutional review boards appear, at least on some campuses, to be less, rather than more, sensitive to new epistemological concerns in the field, and more, rather than less, sensitive to newer forms of inquiry, including action research and participatory action research" (2001, p. xlv).

References

Bishop, R. (1998). Freeing ourselves from neo-colonial domination in research: A Maori approach to creating knowledge. *International Journal of Qualitative Studies in Education, 11*(2), 199–219.

Christians, C. G. (2005). Ethics and politics in qualitative research. In N. K. Denzin & Y. Lincoln (Eds.), *The Sage handbook of qualitative research*, 3rd ed. (pp. 139–164). Thousand Oaks, CA: Sage.

Church, J. T. (2002). Should all disciplines be subject to the common rule? Panel, U. S. Department of Health and Human Services. Available online at http://www.aaup.org/publications/Academe/02mj/02mjftr.htm. Accessed December 17, 2006.

Comte, A. (1910). *A general view of positivism* (J. H. Bridges, Trans.). London: Routledge. (Original work published 1848; subsequently published as the first volume of *Positive philosophy*, 2 vols. [H. Martineau, Trans.]. London: Trübner, 1853.)

Copleston, F. (1966). *A history of philosophy*, vol. 8. Garden City, NY: Doubleday.

Denzin, N. K. (1989). *Interpretive biography*. Newbury Park, CA: Sage.

Denzin, N. K. (1997). *Interpretive ethnography: Ethnographic practices for the 21st century*. Thousand Oaks, CA: Sage.

Denzin, N. K. (2003). *Performance ethnography: Critical pedagogy and the politics of culture*. Thousand, Oaks, CA: Sage.

Denzin, N. K., & Lincoln, Y. S. (2001). *The American tradition of qualitative research*, vol. 1. Thousand Oaks, CA: Sage.Descartes, R. (1916). *Discourse on method* (J. Veitch, Trans.). London: J. M. Dent & Sons, Ltd. (Original work published 1637.)

Euben, J. P. (1981). Philosophy and the professions. *Democracy, 2*(2), 112–127.

Evans, A. F., Evans, R. A., & Kennedy, W. B. (1987). *Pedagogies for the nonpoor*. Maryknoll, NY: Orbis.

Foucault, M. (1979). *Discipline and punish: The birth of the prison* (A. Sheridan, Trans.). New York: Random House.

Freire, P. (1970a). *Education as the practice of freedom: Cultural action for freedom*. Cambridge, MA: Harvard Educational Review/Center for the Study of Development.

Freire, P. (1970b). *Pedagogy of the oppressed*. New York: Seabury.

Guba, E. G., & Lincoln, Y. S. (1994). Competing paradigms in qualitative research. In N. K. Denzin & Y. S. Lincoln (Eds.), *Handbook of qualitative research* (pp. 105–117). Thousand Oaks, CA: Sage.

Gunsalus, C. K., Bruner, E. M., Burbules, N. C., Dash, L., Finkin, Goldberg, J. P, Greenough, W. T., Miller, G. A., Pratt, M. G., Iriye, M., & Aronson, D. (2005). Improving the system for protecting human subjects: Counteracting IRB "mission creep." Available online at http://www.law.uiuc.edu/conferences/whitepaper/papers/SSRN-id902995.pdf Accessed February 15, 2007.

Lincoln, Y. S., & Denzin, N. K. (2000). The seventh moment: Out of the past. In N. K. Denzin and Y. S. Lincoln (Eds.), *Handbook of Qualitative Research*, 2nd ed. (pp. 1047–1065). Thousand Oaks, CA: Sage.

Lincoln, Y. S., & Guba, E. G. (1985). *Naturalistic inquiry*. Beverly Hills, CA: Sage.

Mill, J. S. ([1865a] 1907). *Auguste Comte and positivism*. London: Kegan Paul, Trench, Trubner & Co.

Mill, J. S. (1865b). *Examination of Sir William Hamilton's philosophy and of the principal philosophical questions discussed in his writings*. London: Longman, Green, Roberts & Green.

Mill, J. S. (1893). *A system of logic, ratiocinative and inductive: Being a connected view of the principles of evidence and the methods of scientific investigation*, 8th ed. New York: Harper & Brothers. (Original work published 1843.)

Mill, J. S. (1957). *Utilitarianism*. Indianapolis: Bobbs-Merrill. (Original work published 1861.)

Mill, J. S. (1969). *Autobiography*. Boston: Houghton Mifflin. (Original work published posthumously 1873.)

Mill, J. S. (1978). *On liberty*. Indianapolis: Hackett. (Original work published 1859.)

Root, M. (1993). *Philosophy of social science: The methods, ideals, and politics of social inquiry*. Oxford: Blackwell.

Ryan, K. E. (1995). Evaluation ethics and issues of social justice: Contributions from female moral thinking. In N. K. Denzin (Ed.), *Studies in symbolic interaction: A research annual*, vol. 19 (pp. 143–151). Greenwich, CT: JAI.

Shopes, L. (2000). Institutional review boards have a chilling effect on oral history. *Perspectives online*. Available online at http://www.theaha.org/perspectives/issues/2000/0009/0009vie1.cfm. Accessed December 17, 2006.

Shopes, L., & Ritchie, D. (2004). Exclusion of oral history from IRB review: An update. *Perspectives online*. Available online at http://www.historians.org/Perspectives/Issues/2004/0403new1.cfm. Accessed December 17, 2006.

Townsend, R. B. (2006). Oral history and review boards: Little gain and more pain. *American historical association perspectives*. Available online at http://www.historians.org/perspectives/issues/2006. Accessed December 17, 2006.

University of Illinois at Urbana-Champaign, Institutional Review Board. (2006). Part II: Fundamental guidelines. A. Ethical principles. In *Investigator handbook: For the protection of human subjects in research*. Available online at http://www.irb.uiuc.edu. Accessed December 17, 2006.

Vanderpool, H. Y. (Ed.). (1996). *The ethics of research involving human subjects: Facing the 21st century*. Frederick, MD: University Publishing Group.

Weber, M. (1949a). The meaning of ethical neutrality in sociology and economics. In E. A. Shils & H. A. Finch (Eds. & Trans.), *The methodology of the social sciences* (pp. 1–47). New York: Free Press. (Original work published 1917.)

Weber, M. (1949b). Objectivity in social science and social policy. In (E. A. Shils & H. A. Finch, Eds. & Trans.), *The methodology of the social sciences* (pp. 50–112). New York: Free Press. (Original work published 1904.)

Chapter 2

Ethics and the Broader Rethinking/ Reconceptualization of Research as Construct

Yvonna S. Lincoln
Texas A&M University, College Station

Gaile S. Cannella
Arizona State University, Tempe

Any thoughtful discussion of research ethics will undoubtedly bring mention of research review (e.g., by institutional review boards in the United States, by various committees or boards with differing names in other locations), contemporary issues related to research ethics and regulation, and the startling differences between what is considered ethical practice for qualitative research and what counts as ethical practice for conventional research (usually governed only by federal guidelines and regulations). Further, an ongoing tension exists between what current federal administrations regard as the "gold standard" for research design and what are, contradictorily, growing perceptions and practices among researchers surrounding research ethics.

Although frequently conflated, there are, in reality and in practice, two separate discussions that should be ongoing. The first revolves about the regulatory environment enjoying currency at the moment, at national and international levels as well as at campus and individual researcher levels. Understandably, individual researchers feel an immediate threat regarding the conduct of their own work from legislated regulatory practices, especially with pressures to complete dissertation research and compile large numbers of publications. The second discussion can, and should, be around a broader conceptualization of research ethics and the undergirding philosophies and theories that support systems of ethical behavior in the conceptualization and conduct of research.

This second discussion is not nearly as common as the first, yet it is much more important if recognizing that the practice of research involves relationships, knowledge creation and exclusion, and usually the construction of privilege. We (as researchers) appear very open and willing to discuss the problems with regulation as imposed by state rules and unfair forms of implementation; however, this broader discussion of ethics is much less visible. In this chapter, we focus on the questions: What are people not talking about that should be part of our conversations? What do these silences mean for research as an ethical construct?

The Ethical Practice of Research in Contemporary Times

Ethics and the Historical Conceptualization of Research as Construct

Ethics as a field of concern has a rather brief history in the arena of research with human subjects, dating from the Nuremberg Trials and the documented horrors of experiments otherwise respectable scientists performed on living—and often unanesthetized—inmates of Nazi concentration camps. Most of the Nazis' victims were Jewish prisoners, rounded up and sent in cattle cars to work camps, death camps, and holding camps. The Helsinki Protocols, a statement of principles regarding the ethical and humane treatment of human subjects, was a first attempt to draft a set of guidelines for biomedical experiments with humans. Later revelations regarding the Tuskegee syphilis studies, the Miltown experiments, and CIA experiments with LSD on servicemen fueled the concern that human beings were being used as "guinea pigs," with little concern for whether the subjects recognized they were taking part in experiments.

Prior to the Nuremberg Trials, researchers were guided by their own personal research ethics and a history of science that claimed for researchers a philosophical as well as experimental objectivity, the purpose of which was to warrant a value neutrality vis-à-vis results of inquiries. Research was socially constructed as a massive struggle between a secretive "Mother Nature" and a curious scientist, eager to pry from nature her deepest secrets. The nature of the struggle itself, sometimes posed as faintly life and death, obligated scientists to pursue nature's truth utilizing whatever means came to hand (Merchant, 1980; Schaef, 1981). The ethics of how scientists came to know were considered far less important than the possibility of actually wresting from Nature the secrets of the universe.

The construction of the physical and natural world—and by extension the human world—as an all-powerful "Nature," a "mother" figure, from whom one forced or pried secrets, and from whom one reaped the vast rewards of a natural bounty, was a Romantic and Enlightenment myth, fueled by the extensive leaps in science of the seventeenth, eighteenth, and nineteenth centuries and the Industrial Revolution. In this construction of the physical and natural world as female, however, lay the seeds of another and far more insidious set of constructions. As Karen Horney pointed out:

> Mother goddesses are earthy goddesses, fertile like the soil. ... It was this life-creating power of woman, an elemental force, that filled man with admiration. And this is exactly the point where problems arise. For it is contrary to human nature to sustain appreciation without resentment toward capabilities which one does not possess. Thus a man's minute share in creating new life became, for him, an immense incitement to create something new on his part. He has created values of which he might well be proud. State, religion, art, *and science* are essentially his creations, and our entire culture bears the masculine imprint. [Horney, 1967, p. 115; emphasis added]

Whatever its origin—and some might disagree with the attribution of the creation and emergence of science to a dread of women or to an envy of feminine fecundity—the rise of science is clearly the cognitive and social product of men, and a specific class of men: those wealthy enough to create their own laboratories, to purchase the goods and materials necessary for carrying out experiments, and the leisure to engage in such work. Consequently, as Horney points out, science itself bears the marks of a social construction that is masculine in its bearing and assumptions. Objectivity is one such characteristic of this social construction, one that makes possible the assumption that scientists can pose questions to nature and that nature will either answer back, or can be forced to answer, with Truth, and is therefore ethical. The values of the scientist, if objectively controlled, are believed to be independent of the ongoing "conversation" between the experiment and Nature. In fact, once set into motion, the experiment "operates" on Nature with presumed neutrality, free of the scientist's influence or biases, until complete, that is, until the operation is over and the experiment itself delivers some set of findings.

Research Ethics and Academic Illusions

Such illusions as objectivity, freedom from value impingement on the research process, and that conducting research is itself an ethical activity (that would save the world) continue unabated in some circles to the present moment. As an example, the illusions of objectivity, freedom from values (i.e., embedded in practices like randomized field experiments), and ethical treatment of subjects (usually schoolchildren, in the newest incarnation) are being reinscribed contemporarily in the United States via the National Research Council's (NRC) (2002) description of what constitutes scientific research in education. The imposition of notions of truth, quality, and salvation further construct academic illusions that research is an inherently ethical activity.

Truth Speech. The NRC's report may be seen as a legitimating discourse, a form of "truth speech,"[1] one function of which is to legitimize some forms of research and delegitimize others (Baez & Boyles, 2006; Cannella & Lincoln, 2004a, 2004b; Lincoln & Cannella, 2004; Popkewitz, 2004; St. Pierre, 2004). An additional purpose of the report is to circumscribe and delimit what is considered normal, natural, and acceptable while at the same time defining the not-normal, the not-acceptable as pathological (Baez & Boyles, 2006). Discourse is one form of cognitive restraint, binding the minds of speakers and hearers alike. When words disappear from the routine lexicon of science, they cease to represent forms of research. Thus, when the NRC declares that *x* is research, but that other practices are scholarship—and not *science*—the practitioners of such inquiries are cast into scientific lexical oblivion.

Quality Illusions. Another form of legitimation, as well as pathologizing, are the systems of publication built by scientific communities. Journals and their editors pride themselves on rejection rates, the number of articles not accepted for publication, ostensibly because they are of insufficient quality to merit their appearance in a first-ranked journal. Although it is no doubt true that submissions are frequently turned down for various reasons related to inappropriate designs, ill-framed or hackneyed research questions, badly conceptualized research reviews or lack of analytic clarity, it is also the case that articles are rejected because of paradigmatic or methodological reasons. That is, the reviewers do not agree that the paradigmatic framework chosen is appropriate or worthwhile, or reviewers do not support some set of methods, often qualitative. Consequently, the community of social scientists has broad, if subtle, powers to shape and frame the discourse that appears in print, and such discretion is frequently exercised. Work from interpretive social scientists will be sent to conventional inquirers for evaluation and review. The upshot is that authors can never be completely responsive to reviewers' criticisms as reviewers would like, and the piece is subsequently rejected (C. Stanley, personal correspondence, February 9, 2006). This review process reinscribes the illusion that research, if conducted following all the rules for objectivity and quality, is a practice of ethics (requiring no further critique) that will save the world.

Salvation/Rescue. Still another form of academic illusion that has taken hold in the academy, that interconnects Christian missionary imperatives with modernist notions of scientific progress and even the somewhat postmodern inclination to eliminate oppression, is the persistent Western construction that our role is to rescue or save others. Impulses to represent the voices of others and to liberate the "less fortunate" are deeply embedded in both Western science and Western religious traditions, in which unbelievers are assumed to be living in a spiritual as well as material darkness. Indeed, in some instances, the lingering effects of colonialism as well as the emerging effects of late capitalism, globalization, and transcorporatization on those identified (by the "First World") as "less well-developed peoples" have led—and are leading—to systematic oppression and reconstitution of forms of Othering. Further, using discourses of progress, the expansion of trade and manufacturing has spread pollution to previously cleaner environments and has resulted in the patenting of cultural knowledge, clearly ethical issues related to research in both the physical and social worlds (although these dualistic constructions should also be placed under erasure). Additionally, the "research missionary"—whether in the guise of the objective scientist merely seeking what works, the community partner who would reflexively represent/interpret others, or the critical theorist wishing to liberate the oppressed—emerges from many philosophical perspectives that ethically legitimate themselves through notions of representation and rescue.

Ethics and Our Need for Ontological Transformation

Academia Rethinking the Purposes (and Warrant) of Research

Attending to the postmodern turn over the past twenty-five years, scholars in a variety of fields have certainly embraced diverse ontological and epistemological positions regarding research. Challenges to modernist grand narratives have themselves resulted in differing purposes for research and beliefs regarding researcher power and the imposition of results. Constructivist, feminists, postmodern criticalists, and a range of other researchers concerned with voice, power, interpretation, and representation have struggled with the ethics of research, whether labeled as such or not, as they have discussed researcher as instrument, reflexivity, participant member check, and multivoiced interpretations of results, just to name a few. There is no doubt that these scholars will continue to struggle with the ethical issues that surround their challenges to the will to truth (and with the recent attempts by conservatives to discredit their work). Further, as contemporary government constructions of research appear to be narrowing ethical regulations, questions regarding the role of "rogue scientists and quirky religious" groups in the control of ethical impositions are required (Smith, 2005, p. 100).

Individual scholars are themselves in the position to acknowledge positions from which the ethical practice of research is being constructed (Cannella & Lincoln, 2006). First, new forms of capitalist imperialism are legitimating knowledges based on the ways that market perspectives are benefited. All human activity is being interpreted through the lens of hypercapitalism (Cannella & Viruru, 2004; Chomsky, 1999; Horwitz, 1992). This broad-based interpretation imposes a free market (although the market is never actually free or equitable), entrepreneurial imperative over research activities.[2] This patriarchal hypercapitalism literally functions to construct a research 'ethics' that privileges privatization, corporatization, and profiteering.

Further, legislated regulation of research (ethics) practices are highly influenced by new colonialist practices imposed by contemporary hypercapitalism. Although regulations are, however well intended, designed (on the surface) to protect human subjects, research that receives high levels of funding is rarely ever rejected on ethical grounds; regulation is very often associated with avoiding legal problems for the investigator or institution responsible for the research, and researchers often function as if regulatory approval eliminates the possibility of future ethical problems.

Clearly, from within contemporary individualistic practices of research (no matter the paradigm), ethics are the responsibility of the researcher. As mentioned earlier, qualitative and critical scholars have been struggling with notions of research ethics for quite some time (and will continue to do so). These struggles have ranged from the recognition of the problem with voyeurism (Walkerdine, 1997) to attempts to propose a reflexive ethics that would require moral and circumstantial self-examination throughout the process (Guillemin & Gillam, 2004). We have discussed a Foucaultian perspective that challenges each of us as researchers to counter the power orientations within ourselves (Deleuze & Guattari, 1983) by constructing a genealogy of the self that would examine our axes of truth, ontology, and power to unveil the circumstances in which thought is concerned with moral/ethical conduct, the ethical rules and obligations that construct the self, how one invisions ethical possibilities, and how one reshapes the self (Cannella & Lincoln, 2006; Foucault, 1985, 1986; Rabinow, 1994). As we practice research within the "master's house" (Lorde, 1984, p. 112), a dwelling place that is individualistic and privileges rational self-examination, we can use some of the master's tools to contest and revise our own individual practices. Ultimately, however, the ethical practice of research may involve a radical reconceptualization.that would reject major components of most forms of research as we have known them, whether positivist, constructivist, or critical.

Indigenous and postcolonial scholars are challenging the ethical practice of research in ways that are resulting in new forms of critique and that may result in the elimination, or at least revision, of particular perspectives and methodologies. Examples of these challenges include critique of the unexamined belief in the legitimacy of attempts to "know" others (Dirks, 2001, p. 44); the imposition of the Eurocentric error, European inaccuracies and interpretations that have constructed the Other as artifacts, as "those" to be represented, as exotic, as those who would be research subjects or collaborative partners, and so forth (Jaimes, 1992); the creation of ethnographic fictions and even entire groups of people as ethnographic subjects (Subba & Som, 2005); and ways that the intrinsic focus on language through research privileges particular ways of being in the world (Loomba, 1998; Viruru & Cannella, 2006).

For some, this academic rethinking has combined with community activisms in ways that are creating possibilities for dialogue across research practices and ethical systems. To illustrate, feminist communitarianism (Christians, 2005) involves community participants in determining problems, methods, and in data collection with the assumption that "the community is ontologically and axiologically prior to persons" (p. 150). Rather than formal consensus, ethical practices of care, understanding, and multiplicity of interpretive voices are assumed (Benhabib, 1992; Denzin, 1997; Reinharz, 1993). Another example is the Kaupapa Maori approach that positions researchers within Maori metaphoric discourse and requires an ethical examination of research power that addresses initiation, accountability, legitimation, representation, and benefits (Bishop, 2005). Yet, even these dialogic possibilities can be critiqued for ways that they reinscribe power differentials across race, gender, and other forms of privilege, or for ways that particular dominant forms of interpretation (e.g., masculine, economic) are actually reconstituted through attempts to deconstruct them (see, for example, Escobar [1992, 1995] and Roucheleau [1994] for critiques of participatory action research).

Reconceptualizing Research from a Radical Ethical Perspective

In "Feminisms from Unthought Locations: Indigenous Worldviews, Marginalized Feminisms, and Revisioning an Anti-Colonial Social Science," Cannella and Manuelito (in press) propose that social science itself should be radically revisioned in ways that are egalitarian, anticolonial, and embedded within a nonviolent revolutionary ethical consciousness (hooks, 2000). This egalitarian social science would embody a concern for the ethics of our relationships with each other and our surroundings. This rethinking, reconceptualizing, and reconstructing would challenge the boundaries of the disciplines as well as the dualistic perspectives imposed by categorizations like physical/social and oppressor/oppressed.

An ethical, egalitarian social science would not accept the assumptions that human beings have the ability or "right" to define, know, or judge the minds or ways of being of others (even those identified as children, or poor, or uneducated, or underdeveloped). Notions of individual/groups as subject(s) of research (even to hear the "voices" of participants) would be called into question. The purposes of research would no longer be to represent or "know" others, but rather to examine and change the systems and discourses within which we function. Although avoiding the simplicities of "identity politics" or dualistic deconstructions—rather than reinscribing traditionally dominant power, discourses, and foundations of research (which could be read as white, male, capitalist)—identification would be with females, people of color, and border bodies that challenge time and space. This notion of radically reconceptualizing research would/should become the broader ethical question, a question that would include discussions of the ethical practice of research but also ethical conceptualizations of research—of its foundations, purposes, methods, and forms of interpretation (Cannella, 2006).

Ethics should almost always be recognized as essentializing, as a construction that must always be contested because of its tendency to reinscribe enlightened modernisms and truth orientations toward morality. However, the need for ethics as a major component of the construction of research cannot be avoided unless we yield to the notion that research should construct power matrices. The need for a reflexive ethics that is critical of itself while at the same time acknowledging the ethical orientations that underlie the questions the research chooses to explore as well as methodologies and interpretations cannot be denied. A reflexive, critical ethics could include a concern for: transformative egalitarianism, attention to the problems of representation, and continued examination of power orientations (however unintended, and even within one's own research purposes and practices). The conceptual focus of research in such a reconceptualized ethical, egalitarian social science could be to: examine and challenge social systems; explore egalitarian systems that would support social justice; and construct a nonviolent revolutionary ethical consciousness.

Examine and Challenge Social (and Therefore Science) Systems

The ethical purposes of research could be rethought to reveal and actively challenge social systems, discourses, and institutions that are oppressive and that perpetuate injustice and inequity (even if those systems are represented in disciplinary knowledge). These social systems would be understood as contemporary, yet both historical and changing, as even embedded within the social and physical science disciplines that have been created to perpetuate them. Rather than naming and "saving" oppressed groups, ways of making systems obviously visible in society would be explored continually attending to the presence of the Eurocentric/American error (Jaimes, 1992) and problems of distribution, recognition, and representation as intersecting issues (Fraser & Naples, 2004). Further, rethinking social/physical science and therefore purposes of, and ethical practices in, research would involve acknowledging that the politics of recognition have overshadowed issues of distribution and maintained representative power for the already privileged (whether as researchers, politicians, or religious leaders, to name a few). Illustrative egalitarian social science activities can already be found in contemporary practice. The following are examples of questions that have been or could be explored:

> How are particular groups represented in standardized examinations required of school children? (Viruru, 2006)

> How does an imperialist discourse currently overshadow Mexican immigrant children? (Miller, 2006)

> How do elite groups define problems (e.g., violence, achievement, accountability, quality) in ways that maintain matrices of power? (Collins, 1998)

> How are past practices like racial segregation played out in contemporary debt bondage imposed on 'illegal" immigrants (as human beings, adults, or children)? (Collins, 2005)

> How does our research with/for particular groups of people limit the unthought spaces that they could potentially inhabit as human beings (as they are constructed as "child")?

> How are groups being used politically to perpetuate power within systems?

> How are dominant (and/or market) constructions of science silencing (and oppressing) particular groups of people? How do these issues cross disciplinary boundaries (e.g., related to infant mental health in the United States; knowledge ownership that patents "intellectual commons")?

Support Egalitarian Struggles for Social Justice

Research within a reconceptualized, ethical social science would support knowledges that have been discredited by dominant power orientations in ways that are transformative in the complex struggle for social justice. Further, this struggle would always recognize the contemporary complexity of matrices of domination as illustrated through racism, sexism, classism, and other forms of imposed privilege (rather than simply revealing knowledge or assuming the appropriateness of representation) (Collins, 2000). Although the decolonial component would revision the oppressive stance of research as construct, the egalitarian component would go beyond countering domination, to construct unthought ways of being. New positions would be generated from which diverse forms of knowledge and human possibilities could be constructed, appreciated, and practiced. Multiple and even contradictory epistemologies could engage equitably and with caring support. The following are examples of research questions:

> Are there ways that discursive spaces can be generated for the diversity of noncapitalist economic activities (or as examples, for the diversity of activities that do not separate adult and child, or for ways of constructing diverse identities, etc.)? (Gibson-Graham, 2006)

> How can we enlarge the research (or gender, or religious, or childhood) imaginary to reveal the possibilities that our preoccupations have obscured?

Nonviolent Revolutionary Ethical Consciousness

Collins (2005) has reminded us of the importance of living in honest embodied selves, a complex conceptualization of the ethical body (that would not separate the mental from the physical). Further, the notion of a nonviolent revolutionary consciousness, as proposed by hooks (2000) combines an ethical self with an awareness that is activist, critical, and multiple. Social science generated through this revolutionary ethical consciousness would continuously examine itself as both contingent and of great importance; as contradicting the multiple and the singular or the complex and the simple; and as a concerned, activist morality that always examines itself. Research would be conceptualized in ways that are transparent, public, and reflexive. Examples of research questions could include:

Can we cultivate ourselves as those who can desire and inhabit unthought spaces regarding research (or childhood, or political possibilities, or diverse views of the world)?

Can we construct methods that privilege life-force, body knowledge, the unsettling of our dualisms so that bodies matter? (Butler, 2004)

Through this receptualization, some of our research practices can be transformed and/or extended; many must be eliminated. Others will emerge as we struggle together to hear, respect, and support each other and the collective environment that surrounds us all (Cannella, 2006).

Final Comments

Conceptualizing a different social science and consequently a research ethics as "not only a code of good conduct but a way of being that involves every aspect of one's soul" (Davidson, 1996, p. 123) requires that we reconsider the content of our research training, modeling, and the ways that we demonstrate what's important about ethical research practices to other researchers and to our graduate students, as well as to the public in general.

We will not engage in ethical conversations about ourselves, the ways we understand and think about research, or the ethical practice of research within systems of interconnected power unless we purposely create spaces for those conversations—unless those spaces are multiple and central to our way of being as researchers. Although critical qualitative researchers at times do illustrate how research should be reconceptualized and/or how our methods of data collection are (or can be) forms of engagement that require an ethical research self (as with the use of reflexivity for both data construction and emergent analysis of the ethical self [Guillemin & Gillam, 2004]), the students to whom we teach research methods are often not made aware of these ethical struggles. Further, these students must be part of our attempts to both reconceptualize an ethical social science as construct and the focus for research within that construct as well as our ethical struggles within research as contemporarily practiced.

Finally, living daily within modernist, colonialist, patriarchal, and hypercapitalist conceptualizations of research, the public has certainly not had the opportunity to be exposed to research practices that place ethics and concern for others at the forefront—or that challenges the "will to know others" that has been accepted without question by diverse forms of research (whether qualitative or quantitative). We must, therefore, place our ethical struggles at the center in ways that facilitate dialogue and understanding while at the same time rebutting attempts to discredit qualitative and/or critical inquiry as not rigorous or informative—if our concern for research ethics is placed at the forefront, all other issues will perhaps be transformed themselves.

Notes

1. We mean "truth speech" in the same dichotomizing way "hate speech" is meant—that is, as a denotation of what is pathological, and an implication of what is, by contrast, normal, acceptable.

2. There are those who even proudly label universities as entrepreneurial (usually after receiving financial donations to do so), seemingly without recognizing the ethical issues underlying such categorizations and resultant practices.

References

Baez, B., & Boyles, D. (2006). The elusive science of education. Paper presented at the 69th annual meeting of the American Educational Research Association, San Francisco, April 7–11.

Benhabib, S. (1992). *Situating the self: Gender, community and postmodernism in contemporary ethics.* Cambridge: Polity.

Bishop, R. (2005). Freeing ourselves from neocolonial domination in research: A Kaupapa Máori approach to creating knowledge. In N. K. Denzin & Y. S. Lincoln (Eds.), *Handbook of qualitative research*, 3rd ed. (pp. 109–138). Thousand Oaks, CA: Sage.

Butler, J. (2004). *Undoing gender.* New York: Routledge.

Cannella, G. S. (2006). Childhood studies and ethical practices: Proposing that we reconceptualize social science research. Paper presented at the 14th annual conference on Reconceptualizing Early Childhood Education, Rotorua, New Zealand, November 30–December 3.

Cannella, G. S., & Lincoln, Y. S. (2004a). Dangerous discourses II: Comprehending and countering the redeployment of discourses (and resources) in the generation of liberatory inquiry. *Qualitative Inquiry, 10*(2), 165–174.

Cannella, G. S., & Lincoln, Y. S. (2004b). Epilogue: Claiming a critical social science—Reconceptualizing and redeploying research. *Qualitative Inquiry, 10*(2), 298–309.

Cannella, G. S., & Lincoln, Y. S. (2006). Predatory vs. dialogic ethics: Constructing an illusion or ethical practice as the core of research methods. *Qualitative Inquiry, 12*(6), 1–21.

Cannella, G. S., & Manuelito, K. D. (In press). Feminisms from unthought locations: Indigenous worldviews, marginalized feminisms and revisioning an anti-colonial social science. In N. K. Denzin, Y. S. Lincoln, & L. T.-Smith (Eds.), *Handbook of critical and indigenous methodologies.* Thousand Oaks, CA: Sage.

Cannella, G. S., & Viruru, R. (2004). *Childhood and (post)colonization: Power, education and contemporary practice.* London: Routledge.

Chomsky, N. (1999). *Profit over people: Neoliberalism and global order.* New York: Seven Stories Press.

Christians, C. G. (2005). Ethics and politics in qualitative research. In N. K. Denzin & Y. S. Lincoln (Eds.), *Handbook of qualitative research*, 3rd ed. (pp. 139–164). Thousand Oaks, CA: Sage.

Collins, P. H. (1998). The tie that binds: Race, gender and US violence. *Ethnic and Racial Studies, 21*(5), 917–938.

Collins, P. H. (2000). *Black feminist thought: Knowledge, consciousness, and the politics of empowerment.* New York: Routledge.

Collins, P. H. (2005). *Black sexual politics: African Americans, gender, and the new racism.* New York: Routledge.

Davidson, A. (1996). Ethics as ascetics: Foucault, the history of ethics, and ancient thought. In G. Gutting (Ed.), *The Cambridge companion to Foucault* (pp. 115–140). Cambridge: Cambridge University Press.

Deleuze, G., & Guattari, F. (1983). *Anti-Oedipus, capitalism, and schizophrenia.* Minneapolis: University of Minnesota.

Denzin, N. K. (1997). *Interpretive ethnography: Ethnographic practices for the 21st century.* Thousand Oaks, CA: Sage.

Dirks, N. (2001). *Casts of mind: Colonialism and the making of modern India.* Princeton, NJ: Princeton University Press.

Escobar, A. (1992). Culture, economics, and politics in Latin American social movements theory and research. In A. Escobar & S. Alvarez (Eds.), *The making of social movements in Latin America* (pp. 62–85). Boulder, CO: Westview.

Escobar, A. (1995). *Encountering development: The making and unmaking of the Third World.* Princeton, NJ: Princeton University Press.

Foucault, M. (1985). *The use of pleasure: History of sexuality,* vol. 2, Robert Hurley (Trans.). New York: Pantheon.

Foucault, M. (1986). *The care of the self: History of sexuality,* vol. 3, R. Hurley (Trans.). New York: Pantheon.

Fraser, N., & Naples, N. A. (2004). To interpret the world and to change it: An interview with Nancy Fraser. *Signs: Journal of Women in Culture and Society, 29*(4), 1103–1124.

Gibson-Graham, J. K. (2006). *The end of capitalism (as we knew it).* Introduction to the New Edition: Ten Years On. Minneapolis: University of Minnesota Press.

Guillemin, M., & Gillam, L. (2004). Ethics, reflexivity, and "ethically important moments" in research. *Qualitative Inquiry, 10*(2), 261–280.

hooks, b. (2000). *Feminism is for everybody: Passionate politics.* Cambridge, MA: South End Press.

Horney, K. (1967). *Feminine psychology: Previously uncollected essays,* Harold Kelman (Ed.). New York: W.W. Norton Co. (Norton Library).

Horwitz, M. (1992). *The transformation of American law, 1870–1960.* Cambridge, MA: Harvard University Press.

Jaimes, M. A. (1992). La raza and indigenism: Alternatives to autogenocide in North America. *Global Justice, 3*(2–3), 4–19.

Lincoln, Y. S., & Cannella, G. S. (2004). Dangerous discourses: Methodological conservatism and governmental regimes of truth. *Qualitative Inquiry, 10*(1), 5–14.

Loomba, A. (1998). *Colonialism/postcolonialism.* London: Routledge.

Lorde, A. (1984). *Sister outsider.* Freedom, CA: Crossing Press.

Merchant, C. (1980). *The death of nature: Women, ecology and the scientific revolution.* London: Wildwood Press.

Miller, L. L. (2006). Dismantling the imperialist discourse shadowing Mexican immigrant children. *International Journal of Educational Policy, Research, & Practice; Reconceptualizing Childhood Studies, 7*(1), 35–58.

National Research Council (2002). *Scientific research in education.* Committee on Scientific Principles for Education Research, R. J. Shavelson & L. Towne, Eds. Center for Education. Division of Behavioral and Social Sciences and Education. Washington, DC: National Academy Press.

Popkewitz, T. S. (2004). Is the National Research Council Committee's report on scientific research in education scientific? On trusting the manifesto. *Qualitative Inquiry, 10*(1), 62–78.

Rabinow, P. (1994). *Michel Foucault: Ethics, subjectivity, and truth.* New York: The New York Press.

Reinharz, S. (1993). *Social research methods: Feminist perspectives.* New York: Elsevier.

Rocheleau, D. E. (1994). Participatory research and the race to save the planet: Questions, critique, and lessons from the field. *Agriculture and Human Values, 11*(2–3), 4–25.

Schaef, A. W. (1981). *Women's reality: An emerging female system in the white male society.* Minneapolis: Winston Press.

Smith, L.T. (2005). Researching the native in the age of uncertainty. In N. K. Denzin & Y. S. Lincoln (Eds.), *Handbook of qualitative research*, 3rd ed. (pp. 85–107). Thousand Oaks, CA: Sage.

St. Pierre, E. A. (2004). Refusing alternatives: A science of contestation. *Qualitative Inquiry, 10*(1), 130–139.

Subba, T. B., & Som, S. (2005). *Between ethnography and fiction: Verrier Elwin and the tribal question in India.* New Delhi: Orient Longman.

Viruru, R. (2006). Postcolonial technologies of power: Standardized testing and representing diverse young children. *International Journal of Educational Policy, Research, & Practice; Reconceptualizing Childhood Studies, 7*(1), 49–70.

Viruru, R., & Cannella, G. S. (2006). A postcolonial critique of the ethnographic interview: Research analyzes research. In N. K. Denzin & M. D. Giardina (Eds.), *Qualitative inquiry and the conservative challenge* (pp. 175–192). Walnut Creek, CA: Left Coast Press.

Walkerdine, V. (1997). *Daddy's girl: Young girls and popular culture.* Cambridge, MA: Harvard University Press.

Chapter 3 | The Pressing Need for Ethical Education

A Commentary on the Growing IRB Controversy

Thomas A. Schwandt
University of Illinois, Urbana-Champaign

Three Episodes in the Ethics of Scientific Investigations

Episode 1: In April 2003, the Center for Advanced Study at the University of Illinois at Urbana-Champaign, with the support of the Colleges of Law and Liberal Arts and Sciences and the vice chancellor for research, held a conference on "Human Subject Protection Regulations and Research Outside the Biomedical Sphere." Conference papers and panels explored the questions "Who are we seeking to protect, from what, and why?" in the context of the kinds of investigations conducted by oral historians, journalists, ethnographers, educational researchers, and others in the social sciences and the humanities. Following the conference, a multidisciplinary group of scholars at the University of Illinois at Urbana-Champaign produced an Illinois White Paper that diagnosed the causes and consequences of "mission creep" in universities' systems of research self-regulation (i.e., institutional review boards or IRBs). In that paper, they argued that the current system was in crisis because the workload of review boards has expanded beyond their ability to handle it effectively:

> Mission creep is caused by rewarding wrong behaviors, such as focusing more on procedures and documentation than difficult ethical questions; unclear definitions [e.g., risk, harm, research], which lead to unclear responsibilities; efforts to comply with unwieldy federal requirements even when the research is not federally funded; exaggerated precautions to protect against program

shutdowns; and efforts to protect against lawsuits. [College of Law, n.d., p. 2]

The authors of the Illinois White Paper recommended removing some activities from IRB review, developing sets of cases organized by different research methodologies—illustrating risk, harm, matters of confidentiality and anonymity, and so forth associated with such methodologies—to guide IRB decision making, and issuing a distributed model of research review that involved multiple tracks or pathways and different degrees of intensity relative to the level and types of risk as well as the vulnerability of the participants involved.

Episode 2: In April 2006, I attended Bio2006 in Chicago—a conference dedicated exclusively to the rapidly expanding field of biotechnology, a field that boasts of USD$20 billion in public and private financing in 2005. The Bio conferences are annual affairs of the world's largest biotech association with 1,100 member companies and organizations including large pharmaceutical companies like Abbott and Bayer and smaller start-up firms run by entrepreneurial scientists whose work often begins in university laboratories and medical clinics. The 20,000 people who attended the conference and its extensive exhibits focused on the growth of the industry in fields like proteomics (the large-scale study of proteins, instrumental in the development of biomarkers), genomics, and stem cell research. Exhibits and presentations addressed clinical trial research services, global compliance services, the construction of pharmaceutical outsourcing facilities, technologies for regenerative medicine, targeted individualized cancer therapies, and intellectual property rights, technology transfer, and patent law.

Episode 3: I am currently codirecting the research study of a Ph.D. student in special education. She proposes to study the ways in which young children without disabilities understand, construct, and make sense of their peers who have disabilities. The study will take place in classrooms in Cyprus. Because the study involves work with especially vulnerable human subjects, it was subject to a full review by the IRB. Her initial plans to videotape peer interactions were dropped after a consultation with an

IRB representative, prior to filing the necessary forms, indicated that such a procedure would raise a rather big red flag with the IRB. The researcher submitted the necessary forms and indicated that part of her methodology would involve "informal conversations with children"—a fairly common approach in fieldwork in which the researcher uses the occasion of informal interaction and conversation with children in the normal course of their day together in the classroom (rather than a "formal" interview) as an opportunity to generate potentially relevant data.

The IRB found this procedure problematic on several counts. First, it held that it would be difficult to maintain confidentiality if the researcher spoke with children informally and that there could be no guarantee of confidentiality when the researcher spoke with children in groups. Second, the IRB expressed concern that it would be impossible for the researcher to know which children had received parental permission to participate in such conversations with the researcher if they were occurring naturally in the school. Third, the IRB held that even if the researcher did know which children had received parental permission, she would find it difficult to ask those children who had not received permission not to participate in the conversation.

After discussing these concerns with her research committee, and considering the difficulty one normally has in interviewing children, the researcher decided to drop this procedure from her study. In addition to these queries received from the IRB about the proposed study, some eleven other procedural items required attention including how the data would be kept secure when transported back to the United States; that consent letters for parents did not indicate that they could call the IRB collect if they so desired; that the consent letter did not indicate that participants would not be penalized if they declined to participate in the study; that IRB contact information was missing from the consent form; that the IRB web address was missing from the consent form making it impossible for participants to contact the IRB by e-mail if they so desired; and so on. Although there was a bit of an air of resignation among the three of us about these changes, none of us saw them as major impediments to the conduct of the study.

Commentary on the Episodes

Each of these episodes illuminates a different aspect of the current controversy surrounding ethically responsible scientific research. The first points to a profound institutional problem—perhaps even an organizational pathology—in the systems that universities have in place for the self-regulation of research practices. There seems to be widespread consensus that the current regulatory climate encourages a highly conservative approach on the part of IRBs in applying the Belmont Principles; that there is a strong tendency on the part of IRBs to interpret those principles in a manner most fitting high-risk biomedical clinical research; and that many IRBs often do not seem to display considered judgment of how different kinds of research procedures demand different ways of making sense of the risks and benefits of research or the vulnerability of research participants (Bosk & Devries, 2004). The system appears to have a very difficult time understanding differences in matters of informed consent, confidentiality, anonymity, risk, benefit, and harm for different kinds of research practices—on the one hand are practices devoted to studying the body and mind that primarily require touching, drugging, and cutting people; on the other hand are practices devoted to studying words and actions that primarily require watching and talking with people.

Episode 2 is a stark reminder that ethics of research—whether in the social, behavioral, or biomedical sciences—are not simply matters of the protection of human subjects but also about what constitutes socially responsible science. For the social-political scientist and the ethicist, Bio2006 was both a dream come true and a nightmare. It was a dream come true because it was such virgin territory for exploring the local and global social, political, economic, and moral implications of what is being discovered and invented as the industry moves from molecular antibodies to protein based drugs to regenerative medicine. It was a nightmare because the science in these areas is progressing so rapidly that it is outpacing our ability to simultaneously conceptualize and analyze these seemingly extra-scientific (i.e., moral and political) issues. A few of the complex legal, political, and moral questions that are involved in these developments include: Are current systems of governance adequate to regulate emergent biomedical technologies? Is expenditure of monies on biomedical research and drug therapies justified—is the money better spent on preventative health care programs? Are emerging technologies actually likely to close the current considerable gap in racial disparities in the health care system? What are the social consequences of medical care moving to personalized, direct, individualized patient medicine as a result of targeted therapies?

The third episode reveals the kind of difficulties involved in careful ethical analysis in the actual circumstances of a research case. Does videotaping these children in this study in Cyprus incur more than customary risk and exposure to harm? If the observational study is primarily concerned with identifying *patterns* or *types* of children's actions rather than the behavior of any single child, then how do we assess the risk of participation to any single individual? What expectations, norms, and values inform research practices in these cultural circumstances? What types and levels of risk are entailed in having conversations with children about their ways of interacting with peers with disabilities? Is this one of those cases of research most likely to have serious consequences and, hence, should it be subject to the most thorough kind of ethical review? How can we be sure that the researcher will conduct herself in an ethically and scientifically responsible way as the field study actually unfolds?

It seems fashionable of late for qualitatively inclined researchers to offer stories of the kind suggested by this episode; claim that a review board's oversight is more legalistic than ethically instructive, as well as seemingly ignorant of careful consideration of the kind of research involved; and then denounce the relevance of the entire process of prospective ethical review for the kind of research they do. Cases certainly call our attention to problems. The critical issue, however, is to identify the kinds of problems that are actually brought into view by such cases. For example, are these cases of unwanted ethical surveillance, overzealous review, an overworked review board, a review board more concerned about legal action than ethical guidance, a lack of understanding of specific research practices, or inappropriate understandings of risk and harm? In sum, stories from the field are valuable, but they require careful interpretation. Qualitative researchers, especially, surely realize that the question "What is this a case of?" cannot go unanswered. Moreover, in making inferences from cases, the principle of charity demands of us that we treat those charged with conducting IRB reviews as acting with intelligence, sincerity, and good faith until we are convinced by evidence and argument otherwise.

From the many cases of difficulties that qualitatively inclined researchers (as well as others) have had with garnering IRB approval for their research we learn some simple, profound, and often unsettling human truths. These include the facts that institutional mechanisms initially established to do good often become pathological over time; that well-intentioned people make mistakes in judgment; that, in the face of pressures to protect an institution, appeals to common sense are often given less weight than appeals to procedures; that exercising, defending, and explaining practical moral judgments is much harder to do than exercising, defending, and explaining that one followed the rules; and that the question of what constitutes research—a robust and never-ending debate within the university—cannot be decided by an IRB with any greater clarity and certainty than we can normally muster in other conversations we have about this matter in the university.

An interlocking set of problems surrounds the self-regulation of research within universities—problems surrounding the definition of research, the confusion of legal compliance with sound ethical review, ensuring ethical behavior in advance of what actually transpires in a given study, review board workload, defining and understanding the ethical demands and risks of various methodologies, and so on (e.g., Candilis, Lidz, & Arnold, 2006; Labott & Johnson, 2004; Sieber, Plattner, & Rubin, 2002). Addressing these problems within the academic community is itself an ethical obligation of being a member of such a community; it is part of our academic duty, so to speak. Efforts to deal with such problems effectively, however, are frustrated by the following kinds of responses to cases:

(1) "Get the IRB off our backs; it is unnecessary surveillance"—

This common response ignores the fact that some kind of prospective review of the ethics of research is, and will likely always be, a fact of academic life. How *best* to do such a review is an open question, but *whether* such a review should be done is not. Review and surveillance are not synonymous. We routinely engage in several kinds of prospective peer review in the university, and reviewing the ethics of our proposed research undertakings should be no exception. Furthermore, to paint the work of an IRB with the label of surveillance—as rhetorically useful as that might be to some on a given occasion—is to ignore what we as academics are doing in our work place. IRB committee work, meetings, and presentations about IRB review procedures and the like and the controversy that surrounds all of this, like many of the other activities we repeatedly engage in and lament as faculty—strategic planning committees, departmental reviews, annual merit reviews, curriculum reform, and so on—are all part of academic community–making, reflecting the pursuit of communally shared objectives (Bosk & DeVries, 2004). In other words, it is in such activities and discussions that we realize, and continually constitute, the very nature and aims of our practice. In the present case, that shared objective is treating those we study with respect and acting as ethically responsible investigators of natural and social phenomena. Serving on IRBs and participating in discussions of research ethics and the role of peer review of research in the academy is one aspect of the continual examination of the kind of community we have been, are, and hope to be (Bosk & DeVries, 2004).

(2) "IRB mission creep is the latest and most serious attack on the integrity and value of nonexperimental methods in the social sciences"—To be sure, IRB procedures were designed for attending specifically to the risks inherent in clinical experiments conducted in biomedical research, and, often, this is the research model that many IRB members understand best. Given this way of understanding research methodology, review board members often have a very difficult time fitting nonexperimental methodologies into their way of thinking about informed consent, benefit, and risk. As a result, nonexperimental researchers often are outraged when their projects are delayed by what seems a willfully obstructionist review process (Bosk, 2004). However, *ignorance of*

other research methodologies and the ethical problems they may (or may not) pose is not by definition equivalent to *condemnation* of these means of researching human life. If understanding of fieldwork methods is missing in the deliberations of an IRB, then the proper response is to get that kind of representation on review boards. Different kinds of research methodologies require different standards of review. To ensure that this point of view is represented in IRBs, nonexperimental and qualitatively inclined social scientists must take an active role in prospective ethical review (Haggerty, 2004).

(3) "Just learn how to play the game"— I have been guilty of this response at times in advising my own students on navigating IRB review. We publicly and privately complain about the onerous review process, but when it comes time to file the papers, we simply figure out what it is in terms of language and procedure that IRBs are looking for and then find ways to say it just so (see, e.g., Bosk, 2004). Obviously, behaving in this way sends, at best, a very cynical message about what academic community–making entails. More significantly, a major problem with such a strategy is that it encourages confusing technical compliance with IRB regulations with careful and sound substantive ethical review of one's research. Moreover, it creates the impression that ethical matters are dealt with once IRB approval has been granted.

(4) "I do just fine on my own in dealing with ethical problems; review boards should not exist for the kind of social research that I do. It is the biomedical researchers who should be monitored very carefully"—There are two basic flaws in this way of thinking. First, as Bosk and DeVries (2004) have argued,

> there is more than a whiff of hypocrisy in imposing obligations on ... physicians and medical researchers who cannot be trusted because their own self-interest makes unreliable their judgments of other's best interests ... while resisting those very same obligations for oneself because our work is harmless, our intentions good, and our hearts pure [p. 256].

Second, this individualistic response fundamentally ignores the idea of science as a socially embedded activity and science as a socially responsible community. As citizens, we place our trust not simply in individual investigators but in the enterprise of science itself, relying on the group to ensure that its members are competent and perform their investigations to high ethical standards: "What gives credence to claims for scientific autonomy is not some lofty sense of the moral rectitude of individual scientists, but rather the self-regulating and communal structure of science" (Frankel, 1994, p. 4). Rather than taking a holier-than-thou stance, we ought to focus on the adequacy of actual practices for ethical review in different research endeavors that, taken collectively, comprise the communal structure of scientific investigations undertaken in the research university.

(5) "There are no real risks in the kind of social research I do"—There can be little doubt that the risks of morbidity and mortality attendant upon biomedical research are generally greater than the risks involved in much sociological and behavioral research, and that the former are certainly more clearly specifiable and determinable as well as qualitatively different than the latter. Likewise, the specification of benefits in the case of biomedical research can often, at least in principle, be made more clearly. Hence, at least qualitatively, one can weigh up risks and benefits. However, to claim no real risk accompanies social and behavioral research is simply wrong. In fact, it is the difficulty in pinning down less tangible social, psychological, legal, and dignitary risks (Labott & Johnson, 2004) as well as specifying genuine benefits that actually *raises* the ethical stakes, so to speak, in sociobehavioral research. The complexity entailed in determining whether respondents who are interviewed or observed are experiencing inconvenience, guilt, shame, fear, embarrassment, boredom, anxiety, or frustration as a result of their participation in research; whether they are learning information about themselves or others that is unpleasant and potentially damaging of self-confidence and self-concept; whether they are in some way stigmatized as a result of participation; whether their confidence has been violated; whether a research participant's friends, family members, or colleagues experience negative consequences; and whether these circumstances pose risks greater than those associated with everyday living are matters not clearly definable and readily measurable.

Where Do We Go from Here?

As suggested earlier, problems in the system that universities have established for the ethical review of research in universities demand immediate attention. That current IRB practices fail to live up to our cherished ideals of assuring the public that university-based research is planned and conducted with the highest ethical awareness does not mean those practices (and those ideals) are not worth having. Addressing the organizational, administrative, and intellectual problems entailed in such practices requires more involvement of humanists and social and behavioral scientists in discussions of what constitutes legitimate and useful review (as, for example, took place at the Illinois conference mentioned above), and more involvement of these scholars on IRB review panels. This undertaking, however, is only half the task we face in the university.

The IRB controversy suggests that we ought to revisit how it is that we currently educate ourselves and our students about what protecting research participants from harm and what engaging in socially responsible science entail in the broadly conceived scientific enterprise. Unfortunately, discussion of the latter is often framed in adversarial terms, for example, value neutrality and objectivity *versus* advocacy and partisanship. More systematic and intellectually responsible investigations in this arena would avoid indoctrination into a particular way of thinking about scientific practice, focusing instead what we might learn about responsible and socially significant science from studies in the history, sociology, and philosophy of various kinds of scientific practices. Such studies would involve thoroughgoing exploration of how two fundamental issues in scientific research have been historically addressed within a given field of inquiry.

The two issues in question are these: (1) How have the engaged and the analytic (or the moral and the technical, if you like) orientations to reality been enacted and appraised within a given field of inquiry; what are the consequences of adopting one orientation versus the other; can and should they be combined and if so, how? (2) How are we to understand, within a given practice of inquiry, the intersection of the ethics and politics of research? How are issues of the power of the scientific enterprise, and the obligation and responsibility of scientists mutually implicated? How can we best simultaneously consider the ethics of research (i.e., the habits, obligations, and modes of thought that define ethically responsible inquiry) and the matter of political commitments and responsibilities? These kinds of explorations of science and society ought to be exercises in interdisciplinary education and not confined to courses within a discipline or field of study. The entwined moral, legal, and political problems attendant upon the role and purpose of both the biomedical and the sociobehavioral sciences in society demand joint exploration among practitioners of laboratory and clinical sciences, sociology, political science, law, and other professional fields.

When it comes to teaching research ethics, I suspect that many research universities are like my own—there are many courses in methods and methodologies, but few devoted solely to the matter of research ethics. Spending a class meeting or two on IRB regulations or discussing the standard methodology textbook treatment of anonymity, confidentiality, and informed consent is insufficient. A more complete approach to research ethics education would address the following matters:

First, understanding that researcher integrity or attention to proper scientific (i.e., methodical, logical, systematic, truth-seeking) conduct in the generation and evaluation of evidence, as well as authorship, allocation of credit, and awareness of error and negligence are as much part of the ethical obligation of researchers as is respect for persons, informed consent, and protecting research participants from harm (National Academy of Sciences, 1995).

Second, appreciating and understanding the complexity of ethical considerations involved in research. Consider, for example, the statement of the aim and scope of the *Journal of Empirical Research on Human Research Ethics* [http://www.csueastbay.edu/JERHRE/aim.html] and its elaboration of the interlocking sets of issues in communication, risk and benefit, theory and design of research, and the social, political and organizational circumstances of research that, taken together, constitute the ethical landscape of research.

Third, engaging in a case-based, casuistic approach to ethical reasoning in which students are led to explore simultaneously the standing ethical and normative commitments of the scientific practice they are preparing for and the particulars of individual cases. Instruction of this kind in ethical reasoning can help students grasp the fact that ethical principles and guidelines cannot literally be *applied to* practice. Behaving ethically in research is not a simple exercise in rule following. To be sure, there is an influential approach in moral reasoning called applied ethics that is

> modeled on a geometrical, deductive account of practical reasoning. The general approach is to take an abstract principle and apply it to a problem in a "top down" fashion, or to pick out features of a situation and ascertain whether they abide by a more general rule. Cases are resolved by subsuming them under principles that are crafted antecedent to experience. [Miller, 1996, p. 237]

However, there is considerable evidence indicating that researchers (and all professionals for that matter) do not and cannot behave as moral geometers following formal ethical decision-making rules in producing judgments of what it means to act well in professional practice (e.g., Polkinghorne, 2004). This is not simply the case, because, ethical guidelines "are typically mind-numbingly vague and general" and offer very little in the way of concrete guidance (Fowers, 2003, p. 424), as one psychologist noted in commenting on guidelines for his practice. Moral calculation demonstrating airtight conclusions is not an adequate description of what ethical reasoning in practice involves because ethical or moral reflection requires practical wisdom, and its skills of moral perception and deliberation, as well as the union of the emotive and cognitive (i.e., the engagement of the entire "self" of the ethical decision maker). Moreover, because ethical issues are fundamentally moral-practical matters, it is difficult to neatly separate ethical considerations from other practical considerations such as politics and law. I do not intend to develop and defend this account of virtue ethics and an Aristotelian view of practical reasoning here. However, I suspect that the vast majority of university-based instruction in research ethics often assumes by default a Kantian view of ethical choice and action as a matter of cool detached reason (versus virtue ethics, which views ethical action originating in a "more holistic blend of purpose, disposition, affect, cognition, and social engagement" [Fowers & Tjeltveit, 2003, p. 391]).

Perhaps one of the reasons we find ourselves in such a contentious and controversial situation regarding the ethical review of research is that we have done a poor job of educating graduate students in both a broad view of what constitutes responsible scientific research and research ethics. There is a pressing need for more a planned, integrated, and systematic approach to these matters in the academy. It ill behooves us to lose sight of this moral obligation we have as faculty while we are preoccupied with improving the processes whereby IRBs perform prospective ethical reviews of research.

References

Bosk, C. L. (2004). The ethnographer and the IRB: Comment on Kevin D. Haggerty, "Ethics Creep: Governing Social Science Research in the Name of Ethics." *Qualitative Sociology, 27*(4), 417–420.

Bosk, C. L., & DeVries, R. G. (2004). Bureaucracies of mass deception: Institutional Review Boards and the ethics of ethnographic research. *Annals, AAPSS, 595*(1), 256, 262.

Candilis, P. J., Lidz, C. W., & Arnold, R. M. (2006). The need to understand IRB deliberations. *IRB: Ethics & Human Research, 28*(1), 1–5.

College of Law, University of Illinois at Urbana-Champaign (n.d.). Improving the System for Protecting Human Subjects: Counteracting IRB "Mission Creep." The Illinois White Paper, Center for Advanced Study, University of Illinois at Urbana-Champaign. Available online at http://www.cas.uiuc.edu/documents/whitepaper.pdf. Accessed December 21, 2006.

Fowers, B. J. (2003). Reason and human finitude: In praise of practical wisdom. *American Behavioral Scientist, 47*(4), 415–426.

Fowers, B. J., & Tjeltveit, A. C. (2003). Introduction: Virtue obscured and retrieved—Character, community, and practices in behavioral science. *American Behavioral Scientist, 47*(4), 387–394.

Frankel, M. S. (1994). Science as a socially responsible community. Bloomington: The Poynter Center for the Study of Ethics and American Institutions, Indiana University. Available online at http://poynter.indiana. edu/publications.shtml. Accessed December 21, 2006.

Haggerty, K. D. (2004). Ethics creep: Governing social science research in the name of ethics. *Qualitative Sociology, 27*(4), 391–414.

Labott, S. M., & Johnson, T. P. (2004). Psychological and social risks of behavioral research. *IRB: Ethics and Human Research, 26*(3), 11–15.

Miller, R. B. (1996). *Casuistry and modern ethics.* Chicago: University of Chicago Press.

National Academy of Sciences, Committee on Science, Engineering, and Public Policy (1995). On being a scientist: Responsible conduct in research. Washington, DC: National Academy Press. Available online at http://www.nas.edu. Accessed December 21, 2006.

Polkinghorne, D. E. (2004). *Practice and the human sciences.* Albany: State University of New York Press.

Sieber, J. E., Plattner, S., & Rubin, P. (2002). How (not) to regulate social and behavioral research. *Professional Ethics Report, 15*(2), 1–4.

Chapter 4 | Qualitative Inquiry, Ethics, and the Politics of Evidence

Working within These Spaces Rather than Being Worked over by Them

Julianne Cheek
University of South Australia

Introduction

This chapter explores some of the spaces that have been created for, and are being created by, the confluence and at times collision between qualitative inquiry, ethics, and the politics of evidence and how we as a community of qualitative researchers can position ourselves to work within and on these spaces. The imprimatur to a large extent for the approach that I am adopting emanated from the very wide observation made by Zygmut Bauman (2000, p. 86) that "to *work* in the world (as distinct from being 'worked out and about' by it) one needs to know how the world works."

So, what are some observations about these spaces? First, we increasingly find ourselves in contexts that are replete with paradoxes. On the one hand, our worlds—for there are many that we simultaneously inhabit—have never been more uncertain, fragmentary and, in many ways, to use a term of Judith Butler (2004), "precarious." For example, if we work in the university system, we are faced with different forms of this uncertainty in the way that administrators and governments alike clamor for and constantly drive change in the quest for ensuring value for money and quality and excellence in education. This creates an environment in which I find myself constantly wondering where the next reform will come from and what form it will take. The paradox lies in the fact that this uncertainty derives from the quest on the part of these bodies to establish certainty with respect to measures and assurances of quality and excellence (the buzz words). The more we try to attain certainty, the more uncertain things become!

Delimited Spaces: Neoliberal and Neopositivist Boundaries

In Australia, for example, we have decided to go the route of a Research Quality Framework (RQF). This reflects the outworking of the steady rise of audit culture and the neoliberal-derived government agenda to ensure value for money in terms of investment in research (Cheek, 2006). Herein lies another paradox, of course, in that neoliberal-influenced governments would have us believe that the principles of the marketplace, competition, and enterprise are paramount. Yet, as Barry, Osborne, and Rose (1996, p. 10) pointed out some ten years ago, neoliberal thought is productive of a range of apparatuses and technologies designed to "*actively* create the conditions within which entrepreneurial and competitive conduct is possible." In other words, it is a form of bounded or delimited entrepreneurship or market.

It is this notion of bounded or delimited entrepreneurship or market that I think is particularly pertinent to this discussion. I think that one way of thinking about the spaces in which we find ourselves pushed and pulled in relation to qualitative inquiry, ethics, and evidence is as spaces in which we experience the paradox of delimited autonomy as researchers and scholars. We experience frustration and at times are perplexed as we rub up against the boundaries and as the boundaries themselves shift and change as they, too, are impacted on by the wider political context.

One of the major contemporary influences creating uncertainty and permeability in these boundaries with respect to the injection of new forms of enterprise and competitive rhetoric is a resurgence of neopositivist-influenced and -derived approaches to research. We now see new forms of combinations of methodological fundamentalism and understandings of evidence, ethics, and research inquiry emerging within these spaces as they are colonized by discourses such as the evidence-based movement and new and mutated understandings about and associated technologies of measures of both research and research outcomes. Influenced by and also influencing (for we must not forget the dynamic that is in operation here) are technologies providing the scaffolding for these spaces, and these technologies include ethics committees, review panels for both journals and funding schemes, and dissertation-examining panels. In these uncertain spaces, certainty is sought by new forms of surveillance of both researchers and researchers' activities. For example, research activity is both subject to and object of cascading levels of scrutiny and examination designed to compare, rank, and identify deficits. Certainty in terms of the quality and impact of research is sought with metrics emerging as one certain way to do so. By metrics, I mean the emergence of numerical measures of publication quality such as impact factor of journals and number of citations and amount of dollars gained for funding.

Recently, the United Kingdom, home of the Research Assessment Exercise (RAE), which has strongly influenced the RQF discussion in Australia, has flagged the demise of the RAE and its replacement by a metric base system of funding allocation for research performance that the UK chancellor, Gordon Brown, described as radically simplifying the process. A statement from the Treasury in March 2006 (it is interesting that it is this department issuing the directives and statements about measures of research quality and excellence) reported in the press declares:

> In May 2006, the government will launch a consultation on its preferred option for a metrics based system for assessing research quality and allocating QR funding ... the 2008 RAE should go ahead, incorporating a shadow metrics exercise alongside the traditional panel-based peer review system. ... However, if an alternative system is agreed and widely supported, and a clear majority of UK universities were to favour an earlier move to a *simpler* system, the government would be willing to consider that. [MacLeod, 2006; emphasis added]

At the same time, with a change of minister in Australia, the proposed RQF is undergoing review and one of the strong possibilities is a move toward a much more metrics-based system.

What is lost sight of in all this is the uncertain premises on which such touted certain metric measures are built.

For example, we know that supposed objective metrics such as citation rates and journal impact factors are influenced by assumptions both philosophical and technical that are not necessarily related to the scientific quality of the articles (Cheek, Garnham & Quan, 2006). Yet, although the impact factor "has serious limitations, is being misapplied and has unwanted consequences" (Bloch and Walter, 2001, p. 563), its use globally by governments, granting councils, and promotions and appointment committees is being promulgated. Indeed, some ethics committees are being colonized by such understandings to the extent that ethical research in terms of research that has benefit is being conflated with research that produces publications of high quality (read: high impact). Thus, a further delimited space of autonomy is produced for researchers. Within those spaces are material apparatuses that form part of an audit culture and reflect particular understandings of research and research outcomes.

These examples comprise one case of space that reflect and contribute to the tensions, contradictions, and hesitations (Denzin & Lincoln, 2005) that affect both qualitative research and those who carry out this research. We are seeing relentless colonization of spaces we occupy as qualitative researchers by new and refracted forms of "old" issues including the eternal quest for how to assess quality and establish impact of research, how to determine what is good and useful research, what constitutes evidence of impact and quality of research, and what ethical research is and how the ethics of research relates to this.

Working within and on These Spaces: Posing the Hard Questions to Know How These Spaces Work

So, how should we work in these spaces rather than being worked over them or as Bauman (2000) put it "worked out and about" by them? I think the starting point is to try to understand and to deeply think about how these spaces work and what these spaces are. This is part of the call for hesitation alluded to previously. In a very small and limited way, I have thus far attempted to show how we might do this in relation to some aspects of these spaces we as researchers find ourselves in. But understanding the spaces is not enough. What action are we going to take? What positions are we going to adopt? Importantly, what are positions that we might adopt?

To explore working within these spaces, the remainder of this chapter explores a number of questions that I think highlight the sorts of things that we might usefully look at. I have chosen these questions because they are ones that I don't have the/an answer for and because they are ones that are troubling and perplexing me. In this sense, I think that it is the *questions* that are actually the important thing more so than the answers. Posing these questions exposes the multiple, competing, and at times contradictory positions/spaces we find ourselves in. Indeed, the more that I think about these things, the less I am sure that I actually know!

That said, the only thing I am certain about is that now is the time for us to go further than just acknowledging that these spaces exist. We are working in what I consider to be uncertain, fragmented, and precarious times for qualitative researchers. In many ways, we have made many gains; at the same time, the paradox is that more than any other time I think we could find ourselves in a period of massive backlash in spaces that are potentially and actually hostile—for example, the "dangerous discourses" referred to by Lincoln and Cannella (2004) such as the return to high modernism, backlash against diverse forms of research, and direct government intervention and actions. And what is new about this is that some of these spaces are emerging *within* qualitative research itself as we seek to survive in this environment—I will elaborate on this in what follows:

Question One

How do we want excellence in qualitative research to be defined? The funding dollars we are granted, the changes our research influences among our participants, the types of papers that we write, something else, or all of the above? Is it possible that we will see the emergence of new forms of methodolatory within qualitative research as we grapple with demands to justify and provide "certain ways" to measure excellence and impact of our research? This is a really difficult space that I find myself in as I sit on panels to award funding, and members who have little understanding of qualitative research (but who vote nonetheless) ask me for guides or checklists to determine how to score or assess qualitative proposals. What are we going to do about this and how? Already there are the beginnings of a debate about this in the literature, but I think there is a need for a fuller and more robust debate about this issue and possibly the need for a more unified and consistent approach to this.

However, as I say this, I am aware that this is creating tensions for me in that once we do this will it preclude and exclude or marginalize other forms of qualitative research including emergent ones as well? If we think that we can avoid this, that this a passing phase—then we may need to think again—the trend toward metrics and the desire for certainty that I have alluded to in the spaces that I find myself make this impossible for me to ignore. My position as chair of one of these committees puts me in the position of being part of the scaffolding that is supporting these boundaries creating the spaces in which we operate. Yet, if we don't define excellence, then perhaps someone else will and then we really will be worked over in these spaces. In such a scenario, we run the risk of colonization of our spaces by metrics determined by others and the emergence of a form of politically correct qualitative research. However, if we do define excellence/ try to grapple with a metric-derived system for evaluating our research, then have we been worked over by these spaces anyway? I don't know the answer, but at the very least we need to be writing and speaking about these things.

Question Two

How, in what I believe is a fundamentally conservative context, do we keep the critical/risky edge on qualitative research that has been its hallmark and to some extent its contribution to many of our participants? If we are in spaces where metrics are going to become of increasing import, how can we ensure that radical and diverse politics and research is valued? As editors or editorial board members, what do we do in terms of the journals where we know we are more likely to be able to publish this type of work? Should they all have impact factors? Perhaps it is time for us as qualitative researchers to talk as much about processes and reviews as about methods and theories. When as individuals we publish, what things do we think about when deciding what and where to publish? Should we subvert the process by ensuring we inflate the impact factors of our journals, or do we ignore the whole thing, running the risk that our journals are only ever categorized as second or third tier? Does that matter? Or, put another way, how do we navigate/reconcile/transcend what it might be useful to think of as the politics of excellence and the criteria for visibility especially with respect to performance? Are excellence and visibility the same thing anyway?

Question Three

What does this mean in terms of the politicization of qualitative research and the qualitative research community itself? Do we need to be creating new forms of cooperative and collective communities of qualitative researchers that can take a stance on some of these issues and that can help isolated or less powerful researchers who are buffeted relentlessly in the spaces that they find themselves in and who seek support in these spaces? Do we need to become more strategic about this; if so, who and how? Is there a need for some form of championing of qualitative research; if so, in what contexts, by whom, and how? How do we identify "experts" and "expertise" in qualitative research if asked to for panels or government advisory committees? Or would this mean selling out on some of the very things that drew us to qualitative research in the first place?

Question Four

Is all of this challenging the very notion of qualitative research being an identifiable field and one that holds us together as a community? Is it qualitative research that we have in common, or has the term become so contested and diverse that it has almost lost meaning as some form of unifying or identifiable overarching construct? Are we seeing the possibility of the fracturing of what once we would have referred to as qualitative research into different forms and versions with different emphases, or combinations of emphases—such as on "purity" of method, explication of theoretical influences, a vehicle to gain funding, a way of producing dissertations, contributing to social justice—so that it might be argued that some forms/outworkings of qualitative research endeavors have more in common with other fields than with qualitative research per se. For example, do some forms of qualitative research that are funded run the risk of having to be reduced to atheoretical techniques that have more in common with traditional positivist notions of research and research methods than understandings of qualitative research as a philosophically and theoretically informed endeavor? Is the notion of qualitative research as something we can all understand no longer applicable in light of the spaces we find ourselves in and the different emphases in those spaces? Can we find some common ground that enables us to still think of qualitative research as a useful unifying concept, albeit one that is necessarily heterogeneous and importantly always open to contestation? Does it matter?

A Time to Hesitate

To conclude what has necessarily been an introductory look at these issues, I am convinced that there is a need to think deeply about the spaces we find ourselves in. Unless we better understand how we both are positioned and position ourselves in these spaces, there is the very real possibility that we will be worked over by the spaces rather than working in them and *importantly on them.* It is not so much the choices we make or the answers that we give that are my prime focus or concern. Rather, it is the *reasons* for those choices that need to be surfaced, made explicit, opened up to examination, and contested. This is a call to new forms of activism, ones that focus on tensions operating *within* the field (I struggled for the right word here) we have historically known as qualitative research as much as they do on forces or tensions operating on that field from without.

Thus, this is a call for hesitation with respect to how we think about the spaces we find ourselves in, how we work within these spaces, and how we might work on them. Otherwise, there is absolutely no doubt in my mind—the only certain statement I will make—that we will increasingly find ourselves worked over by them.

References

Barry, A., Osborne, T., & Rose, N. (Eds.). (1996). *Foucault and political reason: Liberalism, neo-liberalism, and rationalities of government.* Chicago: University of Chicago Press.

Bauman, Z. (2000). On writing: On writing sociology. *Theory, Culture, & Society, 17*(1), 79–90.

Bloch, S., & Walter, G. (2001). The impact factor: Time for change. *Australian and New Zealand Journal of Psychiatry, 35*(5), 563-568

Butler, J. (2004). *Precarious life: The power of mourning and violence.* London: Verso.

Cheek, J. (2006). The challenge of tailor-made research quality: The RQF in Australia. In N. K. Denzin & M. D. Giardina (Eds.), *Qualitative inquiry and the conservative challenge: Contesting methodological fundamentalism.* Walnut Creek, CA: Left Coast Press.

Cheek, J., Garnham, B., & Quan, J. (2006). What's in a number? Issues in providing evidence of impact and quality of research(ers). *Qualitative Health Research, 16*(3), 423–435.

Denzin, N. K., & Lincoln, Y. S. (2005). Preface. In N. K. Denzin & Y. S. Lincoln (Eds.), *Handbook of qualitative research*, 3rd ed. (pp. ix–xix). Thousand Oaks, CA: Sage.

Lincoln, Y. S., & Cannella, G. S. (2004). Dangerous discourses: Methodological conservatism and governmental regimes of truth. *Qualitative Inquiry, 10*(1), 5–14.

MacLeod, D. (2006). Research exercise to be scrapped. *Education Guardian.* Available online at http://education.guardian.co.uk/RAE/story/0,,1737082,00.html. Accessed April 24, 2006.

Part II

Indigenous Moral Ethics

Chapter 5 | Research Ethics for Protecting Indigenous Knowledge and Heritage

Institutional and Researcher Responsibilities

Marie Battiste
University of Saskatchewan

The term "research" is inextricably linked to European imperialism and colonialism. The word itself, "research," is probably one of the dirtiest words in the indigenous world's vocabulary.

—Linda Tuhiwai Smith, 1999

Introduction

Indigenous peoples around the world have lived in their natural contexts, acquiring and developing sustaining relationships with their environments, and passing this knowledge and experience to succeeding generations through their language, culture, and heritage. Their acquired knowledge embodies a great wealth of science, philosophy, oral literature, and art as well as applied skills that have helped sustain indigenous peoples and their land for millenniums. From their elders and within their spiritual connections, indigenous peoples have learned to heal themselves with the medicines of the earth that have been naturally part of their environment. They have observed the patterns in nature and learned how to live and flourish within them. This knowledge has been embedded in the collective community's oral and literacy traditions[1]; transmitted in the values, customs, and traditions; and passed on to each generation through their indigenous language as instructed by the Creator and their elders.

Eurocentric education and political systems and their assimilation processes have severely eroded and damaged indigenous knowledge, however. Unraveling the effects of generations of exploitation, violence, marginalization, powerlessness, and enforced cultural imperialism on Aboriginal knowledge and peoples has been a significant and often painful undertaking in the past century. Many individuals and organizations have thought this step important to the overall goal of healing the individuals and the nation. The Royal Commission Report on Aboriginal Peoples (RCAP) (1996) revealed the massive damage to all aspects of Aboriginal peoples' lives.

RCAP's conclusions and recommendations reflect a broad consensus of the distinguished 150 Canadian and Aboriginal scholars and the deliberations of fourteen policy teams composed of senior officials and diverse specialists in government and politics (vol. 5, pp. 296–305). The *Final Report* officially speaks to the neglect and avoidance of the on-going colonization of Aboriginal peoples in Canadian society. In more than 76,000 pages of transcripts, 356 research studies, five volumes of the *Report* (1996), and more than 400 recommendations, RCAP proposes a process to create a postcolonial agenda for transforming the traumatic relationship between Aboriginal peoples and Canadians and proposes solutions to these difficult problems. The *Report* notes how the false assumption of settler-invader superiority positioned Aboriginal students as inherently inferior, contaminating residential schools' objectives and systematically suppressing Aboriginal knowledge, languages, and cultures (vol. 1, pp. 251, 331–409). It argues that these ethnocentric and demeaning attitudes linger in policies that purport to work on behalf of Aboriginal people. It notes that although these false assumptions are no longer formally acknowledged, it does not lessen their contemporary influence and capacity to generate modern variants (vol. 1, pp. 249, 252–253). It proposes that the way of the future necessarily requires Canada to dispense with of all notions of assimilation and subordination and to develop a new relationship based on sharing, mutual recognition, respect, and responsibility.

Today, ten years after RCAP, Aboriginal people note that

little has changed. Indigenous peoples throughout the world still feel the tensions created by a modern conventional education system that has taught them not only to mistrust their own indigenous knowledge and elders' wisdom but also their own instincts. Indigenous elders are aware of the growing eroding environmental and land base that will require new ways of thinking and interacting with the earth and with each other. Indigenous peoples are also experiencing a growing awareness of the limitations of technological knowledge and its capacity to provide solutions to their health, environment, and biodiversity as we witness the undiscovered potential capacity of our own knowledge systems rapidly eroding and in need of urgent reform and action.

Mainstream educational institutions are also feeling the tensions and the pressures to make education accessible and relevant to Aboriginal people. With the rise in Aboriginal populations, especially in the northern territories and Prairie provinces, and with the expected future economy depending on a smaller number of employed people, there is pressure on conventional educational institutions to make Aboriginal populations more economically self-sufficient through education (Avison, 2004). In addition, educators are aware of the need to increase the diversity of the population they train as they seek to address the diversity that will exist in the population at large. As diversity is recognized, so, too, are questions about the processes for engendering inclusiveness, tolerance, and respect.

As an Mi'kmaq educator and professor at the University of Saskatchewan, and as a former classroom teacher and curriculum developer, principal, and education director, I have found public schools to be less receptive to the inclusion of indigenous languages and knowledge in the conventional curricula of educational institutions; as such, the work of developing Aboriginal languages and inclusive education remains primarily in First Nations schools. In 2004, the Council of Ministers of Education made Aboriginal education a priority, and the work of finding pedagogy, content, and inclusive processes in all the provinces and territories has begun (CMEC, 2006). Of late, the challenge is not so much finding receptivity to inclusion, but of ensuring that receptivity to inclusive diverse education is appropriately and ethically achieved and that the educators become aware of the systemic challenges for overcoming Eurocentrism, racism, and intolerance. The add-and-stir model of bringing Aboriginal education into the curricula, environment, and teaching practices has not achieved the needed change (RCAP, 1996), but rather continues to sustain difference and superiority of Eurocentric knowledge and processes. The challenge thus continues for educators to be able to reflect critically on the current educational system in terms of whose knowledge is offered, who decides what is offered, what outcomes are rewarded and who benefits, and, more importantly, how those are achieved in an ethically appropriate process.

This chapter discusses why indigenous knowledge is important for all peoples and its vitality and dynamic capacity to help solve contemporary problems. It addresses Eurocentric biases, the cultural misappropriations that are endangering indigenous peoples, and the benefits they may receive. It also provides an overview of the current regimes of ethics that impinge on indigenous knowledge. In concluding, I offer a process for Aboriginal communities to protect their knowledge, culture, and heritage, through a double-door process, calling to mind the actions taken internationally and regionally among indigenous communities to stop the erosion of our knowledge and heritage. I cite an example of an indigenous nation that has considered these ethical issues and discuss their one, albeit partial, solution.

The Mi'kmaq Grand Council of Mi'kma'ki (also known as Sante Mawio'mi within the seven districts of the Mi'kmaq Nation) has assigned the Mi'kmaw Ethics Watch (*Ethics' Eskinuapimk*) to oversee research processes that involve Mi'kmaw knowledge sought among Mi'kmaw people, ensuring that researchers conduct research ethically and appropriately within Mi'kma'ki (Mi'kmaq Nation territories). As a member of that working group who participated in the process of arriving at principles and guidelines for ensuring the protection of Mi'kmaq knowledge and now involved in enforcing these principles and guidelines, I offer, with permission from the Mi'kmaw Ethics Watch, a discussion of some of the principles and measures taken and the processes articulated in the protocols, together with an appendix of these principles and guidelines. This is a significant step toward ensuring Mi'kmaw peoples' self-determination and the protection of our cultural and intellectual property. The responsibility for educating both Aboriginal and non-Aboriginal people about these principles and guidelines is both a communal and personal responsibility of every indigenous person and among those using or taking up indigenous knowledge. Hence, in so understanding, I take on this task to continue to educate both Aboriginal and non-Aboriginal people to these minimum standards in approaching research in our communities in respectful inquiry and relations.

Indigenous Peoples and Knowledge

Indigenous knowledge is derived from indigenous peoples. Over 5,000 indigenous peoples live in seventy countries, with a world population of over 300 million peoples. In Canada, the Aboriginal population was 1.3 million in 2001, representing 4.4% of the total population (Statistics Canada, 2001). Aboriginal people continue to reside in small-populated communities in rural areas or in larger numbers in northern isolated areas in the territories. Over half live in urban areas, and the majority live in the north and prairie provinces (Statistics Canada, 2001). In Saskatchewan, this diversity is represented in an Aboriginal population with six First Nations languages, representing three language families, over 500,000 people, in seventy-five First Nations reserves. Métis are constitutionally recognized and constitute nearly twice the First Nations population. Together they represent, like the flora and fauna, a tremendous diversity of peoples, languages, cultures, traditions, beliefs, and values. Such diversity at the world level has been difficult to capture within a working definition. The International Labor Organization has defined indigenous peoples as

> Tribal peoples in independent countries whose social, cultural and economic conditions distinguish them from other sections of the national community, and whose status is regarded wholly or partially by their own customs or traditions or by special laws or regulations. [ILO, 1989, Article 1, Section A]

Indigenous people's epistemology is derived from the immediate ecology, their experiences, perceptions, thoughts, and memory, including experiences shared with others and from the spiritual world discovered in dreams, visions, and signs interpreted with the guidance of healers or elders. Most indigenous people hold various forms of holistic ideographic systems as partial knowledge meant to interact with the oral traditions. They are interactive, invoking the memory, creativity, and logic of the people. The most significant meanings quickly pass from family to family and to succeeding generations through dialogue, storytelling, and family and community rituals and legendary archetypes. Through analogies and in personal style, each person in tribal society models the understood harmony among humans and the environment within the stories, artistic expressions in crafts, clothing, and design. The personal and tribal experience with their immediate environment and with their personal and intense interaction with the spiritual world provide the core foundations for their knowledge. Many cultural manifestations of those diverse experiences are available today, although many have also been lost to environmental conditions, colonization, and neglect. Ideographs on petroglyphs, pictographs, birch bark, hides, trees, and other natural materials thus catalogued the deep structure of the knowledge of the two worlds in holistic meaningful ideas or visions. Finally, through oral tradition and appropriate rituals, traditions, ceremonies, and socialization, each generation transmitted the collective knowledge and heritage to the next.

All the products derived from the indigenous mind represent a wealth of knowledge, which is in a constant flux and dependent on the social and cultural flexibility and sustainability of each nation. Indigenous knowledge represents a complex and dynamic capacity of knowing, a knowledge that results from knowing one's ecological environment, the skills and knowledge derived from that place, knowledge of the animals and plants and their patterns within that space, and the vital skills and talents necessary to survive and sustain themselves within that environment. It is a knowledge that requires constant vigor to observe carefully, to offer those in story and interactions, and to maintain appropriate relationships with all things and all peoples.

Indigenous knowledge, then, is a dynamic knowledge constantly in use as well as in flux or change. It draws from the same source: the relationship within the global flux that needs to be renewed, kinship with the living world and life energies embodied in their land, and kinship with the spirit world. The natural context is itself a changing ecosystem that manifests itself in many indigenous sociocultural forms: stories, ceremonies, and traditions that can be explained in any number of disciplinary knowledge such as science, art, humanities, mathematics, physics, linguistics, and so forth. Within a functional system of family and community dynamics, indigenous knowledge is constantly shared, making all things interrelated and collectively developed and constituted. There is no singular author of indigenous knowledge and no singular method for understanding its totality.

Indigenous knowledge thus embodies a web of relationships within a specific ecological context; contains linguistic categories, rules, and relationships unique to each knowledge system; has localized content and meaning; and has customs with respect to acquiring and sharing of knowledge that implies responsibilities for possessing various kinds of knowledge. No uniform or universal indigenous perspective on indigenous knowledge exists—many do. Its unifying concept lies in its diversity. Each group holds a diversity that is not like another, although as Tewa educator Gregory Cajete (1995) has offered, there are unifying strands among indigenous nations that lie beyond the colonizing features of each group. These strands are related again to ecology, to place, and to the relationships embedded with that place (Battiste & McConaghy, 2005).

To acquire indigenous knowledge is to do so through extended conversations and experiences with elders, peoples, and places of Canada. Researchers with many years of field experience such as those anthropologists, ethnologists, and other academics can only give a dimension of the knowledge and some of the observed characteristics of that group of people. The fact that researchers focus their distinctive yet myopic disciplines around certain dimensions of culture and community limits their capacity to see the whole. Many social scientists have labored over discovering the exotic aspects of Aboriginal cultures, although private corporations and multinationals have only recently begun to see how these once-thought "primitive" and exotic cultures some of the literature discusses medicinal knowledge or botanical knowledge as belonging to traditional ecological knowledge and acknowledges it as being threatened and exploited, the same value has not been given to the breadth of knowledge in indigenous language, songs, stories, and kinship relationships. These elements of culture are internally threatened for loss of use, although not externally exploited. The tension around protecting indigenous knowledge ultimately surrounds the boundaries of what counts as knowledge in educational institutions and what does not, as the all-encompassing macro terms of "knowledge" make it difficult to legislate protection for it.

Efforts in Protecting Indigenous Knowledge

The Working Group on Indigenous Populations has been one of the largest attended gatherings in the United Nations of indigenous peoples. It has most recently achieved permanency status in the UN Permanent Forum on Indigenous Issues (UNESCO resolution 2000/22; available online at http://www.unhchr.ch/indigenous/ind_pfii.htm).

Dr. Erica Irene Daes (1993), former special rapporteur and chairperson of the Working Group on Indigenous Populations, reported that the heritage of indigenous people is not merely a collection of objects, stories, and ceremonies, but a complete knowledge system with its own languages and with its own concepts of epistemology, philosophy, and scientific and logical validity. She underscored the central role of indigenous peoples' own language, through which each people's heritage has traditionally been recorded and transmitted from generation to generation. She has urged legal reforms to recognize the unique and continuing links to the ecosystem, language, and heritage of the indigenous peoples. Reporting to the UN Sub-Commission on Prevention of Discrimination and Protection of Minorities, Daes emphasized that "such legal reforms are vital to a fair legal order because indigenous peoples cannot survive or exercise their fundamental human rights as distinct nations, societies, and peoples without the ability to conserve, revive, develop, and teach the wisdom they have inherited from their ancestors" (Daes, 1993, p. 13).

could become instrumental to their economic and social-political growth.

Indigenous peoples' knowledge of plant and animal behavior, as well as of their self-management of natural resources, has particularly inspired a new burgeoning field of involvement and interest among researchers and academicians worldwide. Much of this is still embedded in the hegemonic relations in society and is largely exploitative. Pharmaceutical companies are bypassing the multiple and expensive trials on plants by going directly to indigenous experts to ascertain how each plant is used, doing its tests on these derivatives, and then patenting the knowledge and products for mass consumption and financial gain. Delivering back a journal essay on the knowledge is not delivering benefit to the communities that have held that knowledge. This interest, and those of others seeking indigenous knowledge, has been the thrust of a new hot-button issue dealing with indigenous knowledge and intellectual and cultural property that has fueled a political confrontation of indigenous and non-indigenous peoples. The national and international communities are again faced with a new form of global racism that threatens many indigenous peoples, a racism in which cultural capital is used as a form of superiority over colonized peoples.

Using international and national funds, nation-states and multinational corporations have commodified the very productions of indigenous knowledge without indigenous peoples' collective consent, knowledge, or adequate compensation or consideration of the impact on the collective who have developed this knowledge. This seemingly normal practice of commodification of knowledge is evident in books, marketing, and institutional copyrights and is very much an on-going enterprise in modern capital systems, including education. This commodification of indigenous knowledge without consent, consideration, or compensation is another form of exploitation and marginalization of indigenous peoples.

The benefits of this commodification do not accrue to indigenous peoples per se; rather, they remain the profits of corporations and institutions or individuals' academic and personal gain. Often, the knowledge is acquired by less than ethical means and used in a manner that distorts or marginalizes it. Although

From a sociological perspective, although all peoples have knowledge, the transformation of knowledge into a political power base has been built on controlling the meanings and diffusion of knowledge. Some groups in society use knowledge and control of knowledge and its meanings to exercise power over other groups (Apple, 1982, 1993, 1996; Corson, 1997). This has been the case of controlling agents of education. They have linked these diffused meanings with economics, ensuring that some knowledge is diffused with rewards and others not. This ensures a cognitive imperialism around knowledge that positions some groups in power and others to be exploited and marginalized (Battiste, 1986).

The realization of the losses to indigenous peoples' cultures, languages, histories, and knowledge is not without repercussions for those seeking to redefine or restore indigenous poverty, which has been the overarching common experience of indigenous peoples. For indigenous people to be able to utilize their resources and talents to develop their economic potential has been recognized by many academics and countries as positive goals.

However, poverty need not and should not open the door to exploitation, whether from the inside or outside of Aboriginal communities. Individuals seeking to use indigenous knowledge have responsibilities to protect the collective aspects of the groups' knowledge. Culturally sensitive protocols and ethics are also not a superhighway for access to those individuals, however well intentioned, to take what appears necessary for other ends. It is not enough for corporations or universities to seek to include indigenous people in their research for their purposes, even when some benefits accrue to some of those individuals. Vetting research on indigenous knowledge or among indigenous peoples through a university ethics committee that does not consider protection issues for the collective may contribute to the further appropriation and continuing pillage of indigenous culture, heritage, and knowledge.

How indigenous peoples achieve economic and educational self-determination is an important issue today, and education has much to offer. However, research and education must examine not only the Eurocentric foundations of that inquiry, but also the partnerships of trust that will achieve equity. How can ethics processes and responsibilities in them ensure protection that the heritage and benefits will accrue to indigenous peoples for their knowledge and not only to the researcher and/or their institution? This will be the subject of the following section.

Indigenous knowledge and issues of principles and responsibility of the researcher dealing with sensitive knowledge and protection are fraught with both ambiguity and uncertainty for indigenous peoples. They are ambiguous when dealing with areas such as how communities can recover their languages where they have been eroded, or how schooling should be used to recover or teach Aboriginal heritage. For sure, Elders and community members must be part of those decisions. The role of indigenous knowledge and languages in any sphere must arise from the first principle that indigenous peoples must be the custodians of that knowledge. Schools cannot and should not be responsible for teaching Aboriginal knowledge in all its complexity and diversity, nor should they be solely responsible for reviving Aboriginal languages, even if they could. Indigenous knowledge is diverse and must be learned in the similar diverse and meaningful ways that the people have learned it for it to have the continuing vitality and meaning. Education must also respect the fact that indigenous knowledge can only be fully known from within community contexts and through prolonged discussions with each of these groups. This process must also acknowledge and respect the limitations placed on who can receive certain kinds of knowledge and in what contexts can it be shared widely.

The issues regarding what principles will guide the protection of indigenous communities and issues of cultural and intellectual property governing those decisions are at the cornerstone of a recent book entitled *Protecting Indigenous Knowledge and Heritage: A Global Challenge* (Battiste & Henderson, 2000). The universal losses among indigenous peoples and the current resource rush on indigenous knowledge require that a uniform and fair policy or set of practices be established and used by nation states and multinationals. This will guide research practices that seek to engage indigenous knowledge or protect communities' current resources, knowledge, ideas, expressions, trade secrets, and teachings from tourism and other forms of commodification. In addition, such guidelines must be part of every university or research institution. Indigenous peoples have a responsibility to be sensitive and inclusive, while also pressuring and ensuring universities protect the collective interests in indigenous knowledge. The need for protective practices intensifies within these institutions and the following section addresses some of the issues surrounding their research ethics and the vulnerabilities that are identified. Battiste and Henderson (2000) have asserted that the main principles for research policy and practice must be that indigenous people should control their own knowledge; that they do their own research; and that if others should choose to enter any collaborative relationship with indigenous peoples, the research should empower and benefit indigenous communities and cultures, not just researchers, their educational institutions, or society.

As discussions develop regarding the principles and ethics governing indigenous research, the issue of control or decision making reverberates with the single most important principle—indigenous peoples must control their own knowledge, a custodial ownership that is prescribed from the customs, rules, and practices of each group. This can only be achieved through the involvement of those groups that hold the custodial relationships with the knowledge. More often than not, this will not be the elected leader of that community (for example, the chief), but others whose responsibilities are directly related to the knowledge and teachings of the clan, family, or nation. Thus, the problem is how any research in the community can be vetted or controlled by the rightful owners. Although seemingly problematic, the inclusion of a local community voice seems necessary for arriving at the issue of control. First, inclusion necessarily requires that local indigenous peoples and nations become informed and aware of the research being done on, among, or with them. Second, they must train local people in the holistic understanding of issues, practices, and protocols for doing research. In so doing, they will build a capacity to do their own research and consequently utilize research for their own use and benefit, strengthening and revitalizing their communities, territories, and people while warding off the threats to their culture from those who seek to take their knowledge for benefits defined outside their community. Third, they must decide on processes that will ensure that principles of protection and use are developed, disseminated, and used as normative procedures in their territory.

RCAP Ethical Guidelines for Research in Canada

In 1993, RCAP, with the advice of Aboriginal and non-Aboriginal researchers, formulated a set of ethical guidelines to guide its research (RCAP, 1996, vol. 5, app. C). These guidelines emphasized that Aboriginal peoples have distinctive perspectives and understandings, which are derived from their knowledge, culture, and history, and which are embodied in Aboriginal languages. Those researching Aboriginal experiences must respect these perspectives and understandings. They must also observe appropriate protocol when communicating with Aboriginal communities. Finally, they must view the oral traditions and teachings of Aboriginal peoples as valuable research resources, along with documentary and other sources. Proficiency in Aboriginal languages should always be an issue in Aboriginal research projects.

In setting research priorities and objectives for community-based research, RCAP and its researchers were required to give serious and due consideration to the benefit of the communities concerned. Researchers were to consider the widest possible range of community interests and the impact of the research at the local, regional, and national levels. They were to identify potential conflicts of interest within the communities and employ problem-solving strategies before commencing their research and while their research was in progress. Whenever possible, the guidelines provided that the commission's research was to support the transfer of skills to individuals and to increase the capacity of the community to manage its own research.

The commission required informed and written or recorded consent be obtained from all individuals and groups participating in the research, with parents or guardians signing for children. Individuals and groups participating in the research were to be provided with information about the purpose and nature of the research activities, including expected benefits and risk. The degree of confidentiality maintained in the study was to be stated. No pressure was to be applied to induce participation, and participants were to be informed that they were free to withdraw from the research at any time.

In studies located principally in Aboriginal communities, researchers were to establish collaborative procedures to enable community representatives to participate in the planning, execution, and evaluation of research results. If the research might affect particular Aboriginal communities, similar consultations with appropriate leaders were to be sought. In research portraying community life or community-based studies, the multiplicity of viewpoints or cross-section of interests present within Aboriginal communities was to be represented fairly, including viewpoints specific to age and gender groups. Advisory groups convened to provide guidance on the conduct of research were not allowed to preempt the commission's guidelines. Above all, researchers were to accord fair treatment to all persons involved in the research activities.

The commission's researchers had an obligation to observe ethical and professional practices relevant to their respective disciplines; however, because of the ethnocentric and racist interpretations of past researchers, the existing body of research, which normally would provide a reference point for new research, was open to reassessment. Researchers had to disclose if Aboriginal knowledge or heritage or perspectives in any way challenged the Eurocentric assumptions brought to the subject by previous research or the design of the commission's research. They also had to disclose how they would resolve any conflicts and how they would portray conflicting Aboriginal knowledge, heritage, or perspectives.

The commission's ethical guidelines stated that reviews of research results were to be solicited both in the Aboriginal community and in the scholarly community prior to any publication. The guidelines provided that the commission was to maintain a policy of open public access to the final reports of the research activities. In cases in which scholarly and Aboriginal community responses were deemed useful, these reports were to be circulated in draft form. Research reports or parts of the reports were not to be published if there was reasonable grounds for thinking that publication would violate the privacy of individuals or cause significant harm to participating Aboriginal communities or organizations. The results of community research were to be distributed as widely as possible within participating communities, and reasonable efforts were to be made to present results in Aboriginal languages or nontechnical English where appropriate.

Procedural Duty to Inform and Seek Consent: The Single or Double-Door Approach

Indigenous peoples throughout the world are concerned about the global onslaught of their knowledge and culture. They seek protection at all levels and increasingly are becoming attuned to the political issues and questions facing them today. The issues associated with protecting indigenous knowledge are concerned with the structural inability of the law to give indigenous peoples' control of their humanity, heritage, and communities. The absence of protection of the humanity of indigenous peoples in local and international law is particularly disturbing (Battiste & Henderson, 2000). In the absence of clear guidelines at the national and international levels, each community must work to affect its own process.

This takes me to the work of the Mi'kmaw Ethics Watch among the Mi'kmaw Nation in Nova Scotia. Under the treaty authority of the Grand Council of Mi'kma'kik, the official treaty holders and residual beneficiaries of the Constitution of Canada Section 35 (1), the Mi'kmaw Eskinuapimk (Mi'kmaw Ethics Watch) oversee the research protocol and ethical research processes among the Mi'kmaw communities throughout the seven traditional districts of the Grand Council, which includes the maritime provinces of Newfoundland, New Brunswick, Nova

Scotia, Prince Edward Island, and Quebec. The Mi'kmaw Ethics Watch is to ensure that Mi'kmaw people and knowledge are protected within Mi'kma'ki territory, to the degree that research processes can ensure this capacity.

In the summer of 1999, discussions among elders and families about the issues of protection of Mi'kmaw heritage at the annual customary gathering of the Grand Council of Mi'kmaq at Chapel Island, Nova Scotia, led to a discussion within the Grand Council about protection issues facing the Mi'kmaw people. During the St. Ann Mission speeches, the Grand Captain of the Mi'kmaq, Alex Denny, announced the appointment of a group of Mi'kmaw community elders, leaders, and researchers to the task of considering the issues of protection of Mi'kmaw knowledge and heritage. They were to return the following year with an update and recommendations from their deliberations.

The group convened over the following year through various means including telephone, e-mail, and local community meetings to arrive at the identification of the central issues affecting their Mi'kmaw knowledge. Through further collaboration and consultation with elders, including more research and drafting sessions, a set of draft principles and guidelines were developed, largely drawn from the United Nations Principles and Guidelines for the Protection of Indigenous Heritage (Daes, 1993). At the conclusion of the St. Ann Mission in 2000, delegates of the assigned research and drafting committee presented their findings and recommendations in a drafted document at the traditional meeting of the Grand Council. In turn, the Grand Council announced the creation of an on-going committee to oversee the principles, guidelines, and protocols for the Grand Council. The name given to this group was the Ethics *Eskinuapimk*.

The name of the Mi'kmaw Ethics Watch (Ethics *Eskinuapimk*) derives from an ancient traditional role among Mi'kmaw people. At each major gathering involving the Grand Council, a person (or persons) was assigned responsibility for ensuring the safety of the Grand Council by watching the door of the wigwam. The person would ensure that those who entered had their wampum or protocols in place, had a reason and purpose for being there, and were told where they should seat themselves and how they should behave. This role was both normative and prohibitive. It maintained relations among the group and ensured the safety of the group inside as well as providing guidance for those outside seeking counsel among the elders and leaders. Each wigwam also had its own person who acted in this capacity such that normative relations were engendered and safety was assured everyone. In so adopting this term, the Grand Council seeks to provide researchers the manner and relationships necessary for a harmonious relationship and to protect Mi'kmaw people and their knowledge and heritage from exploitation.

The Mi'kmaw Ethics Watch[2] oversees the research protocols, on behalf of the Grand Council of Mi'kmaq, by receiving and assessing research proposals for the Grand Council, applying the principles and guidelines to the proposals, making comments on the omissions found or on the needed clarity of the proposals for addressing the protocols. They then return these comments and their assessments to the chairperson of the Mi'kmaw Ethics Watch, currently the director of the Mi'kmaq Research Institute at the University College of Cape Breton, now called Cape Breton University, who communicates this information to all the relevant parties.[3] The cycle of communication is then reenacted after the researchers respond to the comments, with final consensus made on the approval of the research or for the need to revise the proposal. When approval has been granted, a final letter of approval is then sent to the researcher(s) for their use in finalizing their research protocols within their own institutions.

The Mi'kmaw guidelines are divided into three sections: the first addresses the principles underlying Mi'kmaw authority and holds that the responsibility for Mi'kmaw knowledge, heritage, language, including their rights and obligations to exercise control to protect their cultural and intellectual properties and knowledge rests with Mi'kmaw people. The second section identifies the obligations and protocols and responsibilities for researchers seeking to conduct research among Mi'kmaw people, including research that involves collecting information from any Mi'kmaw person, regardless of topic. The final section deals with the obligations and responsibilities of the Mi'kmaw Ethics Watch (Ethics *Eskinuapimk*) and processes for dealing with these obligations through the Grand Council and Mi'kmaw communities. The Mi'kmaw Ethics Watch Principles and Guidelines as offered online at the Mi'kmaq College Institute at Cape Breton University (http://www.cbu.ca/cbu/pdfs/Ethics%20Watch%20G uidelines.pdf) offer prospective researchers help in how to derive their respectful inquiry. These may be useful to researchers as they begin the process of preparing for the ethics review process in the Mi'kmaw community and may require Mi'kmaw Ethics Watch approval.

Conclusion

Indigenous knowledge represents the protection and preservation of indigenous humanity. Such protection is not about preserving a dead or dying culture. It is about the commercial exploitation and appropriation of a living consciousness and cultural order. It is an issue of privacy and commerce. The use of indigenous knowledge for private or public profit by others under existing laws is a central issue. As each of the local communities becomes informed of the actual and potential threats to their communities, because of the destruction of their languages and cultures, the increased interest in renewal and restoration of indigenous cultures increases the need for protection from continued exploitation and expropriation. Although communities are developing these priorities for themselves, research standards that are not inclusive to indigenous communities that want to and should control their own knowledge are emerging but are not present in all institutions where research is being authorized. Indigenous peoples are in a precarious position, and their continued existence is threatened.

Indigenous knowledge offers Canada and other nation-states a chance to comprehend another view of humanity as they never have before. The nation-states should understand indigenous humanity and its manifestations without paternalism and without condescension. In practical terms, this means that indigenous peoples must be involved at all stages and in all phases of research and planning, as articulated in the United Nations Working Group's Guidelines and Principles in Protection of Indigenous Populations. These principles and protocols can offer each nation-state an opportunity to rededicate their peoples to protecting humanity; redressing the damage and losses of indigenous peoples to their language, culture, and properties; and enabling indigenous communities to sustain their knowledge for their future.

Much of the dialogue and discourse among educated Aboriginal educators and scholars in the last twenty-five years have focused attention on colonialism and oppression of peoples worldwide. It has been both a systemic and personalized process through education. We have been seeking an uncensored history that enables us to have a clear sense of our sociohistoric reality from which we can heal (Duran & Duran, 1995). Our journeys have led us to multiple ways to express ourselves and to give voice and imagery to our pain and anguish, our hopes and dreams, our strategies and alternatives, and our resistance and resilience. Many of us have come to realize that we do not have to be perceived through the Western lens to be legitimated. Yet, we are all too aware that what is defined as knowledge for schools and curricula is not yet sufficiently comparable with our conceptualization of knowledge. We must continue to find ways to have an influence through our participation in educational discourse, policy, and practice, in particular to identify and shape what is considered for schools texts as knowledge for those schools. We have become aware that we, indigenous peoples, must be actively part of the transformation of knowledge. As Elizabeth Minnick (1990) notes, it is not just knowledge and thought that needs to be changed, but also "preconscious cultural assumptions and habits that are fraught with emotion and reflect not only the ignorance but the systemically created and reinforced prejudices of the dominant culture" (p. 93).

As scholars, both indigenous and non-indigenous, unravel those prejudices, indigenous peoples can begin to see that within their own traditions, within their own knowledge bases, there is a store of knowledge from which they can rebuild, heal, recover, and restore healthy and connective relationships. They must acknowledge the colonial shadow through a thorough awareness of the sociohistoric reality that has created the current context and a great collective soul wound that has damaged their nations as a whole and many individuals (Duran & Duran, 1995). Once accepting this fact, we can move beyond the personal dimension of blaming ourselves and seek to heal the nation with each significant step we take.

What is becoming clear to educators is that any attempt to decolonize education and actively resist colonial paradigms is a complex and daunting task. We cannot continue to allow indigenous students to be given a fragmented existence in a curriculum that offers them only a distorted or shattered mirror; nor should they be denied an understanding of the historical context that has created that fragmentation. A postcolonial framework cannot be constructed without indigenous peoples' renewing and reconstructing the principles underlying their own world view, environment, languages, and communication forms and understanding how these construct their humanity. Finally, the fragmenting tendencies and universalizing pretensions of current technologies need to be effectively countered by renewed investment in holistic and sustainable ways of thinking, communicating, and acting together.

Notes

1. For a comprehensive examination of literacy traditions among the Mi'kmaq, see Marie Battiste (1984).
2. The Mi'kmaw Ethics Watch is comprised of several persons appointed by the Grand Council of Mi'kmaq in cooperation with the local, educational, and political institutions.
3. The Mi'kmaq College Institute address is PO Box 5300, Sydney, NS. B1P 6L2 902-563-1827.

References

Apple, M. W. (1982). *Education and power.* London: Routledge and Kegan Paul.

Apple, M. W. (1993). *Official knowledge.* New York: Routledge.

Apple, M. W. (1996). *Cultural politics and education.* New York: Teachers College Press.

Avison, D. (2004). A challenge worth meeting: Opportunities for improving Aboriginal education outcomes. Report of the Council of Ministers in Education, Ontario, Canada. Unpublished document.

Battiste, M. (1984). An historical investigation of the social and cultural consequences of Micmac literacy. Unpublished Ph.D. dissertation, Department of Education, Stanford University, Stanford, CA.

Battiste, M. (1986). Micmac literacy and cognitive assimilation. In J. Barman, Y. Hébert, & D. McCaskill (Eds.), *Indian education in Canada: The legacy* (pp. 23–45). Vancouver: University of British Columbia Press.

Battiste, M., & McConaghy, C. (Eds.). (2005). *Thinking place: The indigenous humanities and education.* Special issue of *The Australian Journal of Indigenous Education, 34,* 1–151.

Battiste, M., & Henderson, J. (Sa'ke'j) Youngblood. (2000). *Protecting indigenous knowledge and heritage: A global challenge.* Saskatoon, SK: Purich Press.

Cajete, G. (1995). *Look to the mountain: An ecology of indigenous education.* Durango, CO: Kivaki Press.

Canadian Council of Ministers of Education (CMEC). (2006). Ministers of Education reaffirm leadership role in pan Canadian education issues. Communiqué issued in St. John's, September 26. Available online at http://www.cmec.ca/releases/press.en.stm?id=47. Accessed October 21, 2006.

Corson, D. (1997). *Linking social justice and power.* Clevedon, UK: Multilingual Matters Ltd.

Daes, E. (1993). *Study on the protection of the cultural and intellectual property rights of indigenous peoples.* E/CN.4/Sub. 2/1993/28. Sub-Commission on Prevention of Discrimination and Protection of Minorities, Commission on Human Rights, United Nations Economic and Social Watch, Geneva.

Duran, E., & Duran, B. (1995). *Native American postcolonial psychology.* Albany: State University of New York Press.

International Labour Organization Convention on Indigenous and Tribal Peoples in Independent Countries (1989). No. 169, 28 I.L.M. 1382. Declaration of the United Nations High Commission for Human Rights. Text available online http://www.unhchr.ch/html/menu3/b/62.htm. Accessed November 28, 2006.

Mi'kmaw Ethics Watch (2000). *Principles, guidelines and protocols.* Sydney, NS: Mi'kmaq College Institute, University College of Cape Breton. Available online at http://mrc.uccb.ns.ca/prinpro.html. Accessed October 21, 2006.

Minnick, E. (1990). *Transforming knowledge.* Philadelphia: Temple University Press.

Royal Commission on Aboriginal Peoples (RCAP). (1996). *Final report.* 5 vols. Ottawa: Canada Communications.

Smith, L. (1999). *Decolonizing methodologies: indigenous peoples and research.* London: Zed Books.

Statistics Canada. (2001). Aboriginal peoples of Canada: A demographic profile. Available online at http://www12.statcan.ca/english/census01/ products/analytic/companion/abor/contents.cfm. Accessed October 21, 2006.

Chapter 6

Red Pedagogy
Indigenizing Inquiry or, the Un-methodology

Sandy Grande
Connecticut College

When Norman Denzin asked me to participate in this conference, my response was "Are you sure you have the right person?
I don't really do qualitative research." He graciously assured me
that, indeed, he did have the right person and if I talked about my
work on *Red Pedagogy* (2004) it would suffice. So, I accepted the
invitation but with doubt and trepidation as I'm still not sure how
my work fits into this conference. Consider, for example, the title
"International Congress of Qualitative Inquiry." The only word
that seems related to what I do is *inquiry*. As a Native person who
continuously struggles to define the relationship between indigenous peoples and the nation-state, I am even more uncertain of
our place in the inter-*nation*-al arena. Similarly, *congress* makes me
think of a lot of white guys sitting around making decisions that
inevitably contradict, negate, or diminish indigenous sovereignty.
And, other than the fact that I know *qualitative* stands in distinction to quantitative, I can't say I know much about qualitative
research.

So, ever since I received that invitation (and I was truly hon-
ored to be there) I've been thinking about (read: obsessing over)
qualitative research and methodology, asking everyone I know
how they define it, and trying to determine whether I do it or not.
It turns out that I don't. But that's okay because although I don't
collect data, engage human subjects, or encounter institutional
review boards, the specter of the congress has forced me to think
in new and interesting ways about what I do. What I figured out is
that my work/research is about *ideas*, especially as they come alive

within and through people(s), communities, events, texts, practices, policies, institutions, artistic expression, ceremonies, and rituals. I engage ideas in these contexts through a process of active and close observation wherein I live with, try on, and wrestle with them in a manner akin to Geertz's notion of "deep hanging out" (1998) but without the distinction between participant/observer. Instead, the gaze is always shifting inward, outward, and throughout the spaces in between, with the idea itself holding ground as the independent variable. As I engage in this process, I survey viewpoints on the genealogy of ideas, their representation, and potential power to speak across boundaries, borders, and margins and filter the gathered data through an indigenous perspective. When I say "indigenous perspective," I mean my perspective as an indigenous scholar. When I say "my perspective," I mean from a consciousness shaped not only by my own experiences but also those of my peoples and ancestors. It is through this process that Red pedagogy—my indigenous methodology—emerged.

Although the intricacies of Red pedagogy have been articulated elsewhere (see Grande, 2004), the essential characteristics are worth repeating here. Broadly speaking, it is an indigenous pedagogy that operates at the crossroads of Western theory, specifically critical pedagogy and indigenous knowledge. By bridging these epistemological worlds, Red pedagogy abandons what Robert Allen Warrior (1995) refers to as "the death dance of dependence" (p. 12). That is, the "vacillation between the wholesale adoption of Anglo-Western theories and stance that indigenous scholars need nothing outside of themselves or their communities to understand the world or their place within it" (Warrior, 1995, p. 12). On the contrary, Red pedagogy asks that as we examine our own communities, policies, and practices, we take seriously the notion that to know ourselves as revolutionary agents is more than an act of understanding who we are. It is an act of reinventing ourselves, of validating our overlapping cultural identifications and relating them to the materiality of social life and power relations (McLaren, 1997).

To allow for the process of reinvention, it is important to understand that Red pedagogy is not a method or technique to be memorized, implemented, applied, or prescribed. Rather, it is a space of engagement. It is the liminal and intellectual borderlands where indigenous and non-indigenous scholars encounter one another, working to remember, redefine, and reverse the devastation of the original colonialist encounter. Therefore, Red pedagogy is not something one does, but rather a process to engage; it is based on the presumption that ideas are neither borne in isolation nor are they inert.

Because Red pedagogy is always in the making, this chapter is about sharing with you where the process—the conversation—is at the moment. What follows is a series of "snapshots"—episodes from "deep hanging out"—that have reshaped my thoughts and therefore my "methodology." I expect at some point they will find their way more formally into the discourse on Red pedagogy.

Snapshot #1

I recently was asked to speak at a forum at Harvard University on Education and Catastrophe: Communities of Color Responding and Moving Forward. Although the panel was explicitly about the notion of catastrophe broadly defined, it was also implicitly about education in the wake of Hurricane Katrina. As I prepared for this discussion, the first thing that came to mind was what I consider to be the defining catastrophe of this nation: the genocide of American Indians. The catastrophe, however, isn't limited to the loss of whole peoples and nations; rather, it is the ongoing dismissal of this reality and its relevance to our everyday lives. It's about the depths of our historical amnesia and the national psychosis that emanates from the denial of genocide and its sister project of colonization. I think somewhere in the catacombs of our collective consciousness lies the thought: so what if each year brings some tribes, cultures, and languages closer to the brink of extinction? Isn't that what museums are for?

Because we don't have to think about the current state of Native America, we also don't have to read about it, write about it, learn about it, or teach about it. Even in times of so-called crisis when we are forced to look at ourselves in the mirror, the Indian question rarely arises. I remember in the midst of Katrina I kept waiting for the analysis from the vantage point of indigenous peoples and the experience of colonization, but it never came. Yet, to me, the connection was both immediate and obvious. As a nation, we witnessed the indelible images of mostly black bodies being corralled and penned in the Louisiana Superdome in New Orleans and then subjected to the chaotic and violent process of relocation, where already fractured families were forced to disperse to unknown lands with no guarantee of return. It seemed like déjà vu all over again.

Though on an entirely different scale, the last time a whole class of people was rounded up and forced to migrate at the hands of the U.S. military at the order of the president was in 1838. Thousands of Cherokee men, women, and children were taken from their land, herded into makeshift forts with minimal provisions, and forced to march a thousand miles. In the end, nearly 4,000 Cherokee met their death on the journey known as the Trail of Tears or in Cherokee, *Nunna daul Tsuny* ("The Trail where They Cried"). Who could have predicted that over a century and a half later, so many people would cry again. The so-called evacuation (or was it *removal*?) of the peoples of the Ninth Ward in New Orleans signals to me that I need to rethink the notion of colonization and the scope of Red pedagogy. Specifically, I need to broaden the conception of colonized peoples to include those isolated and contained by poverty and exploitation, to build coalition among the nations dispossessed and disenfranchised.

Snapshot #2

I'm currently living in New York City and went to the Tribeca Film Festival with a friend from the Diné nation to see the premier of the film "The Canary Effect," a documentary about the history of Native peoples, genocide, and the current state of Native America. We sat inconspicuously in the back of the theater looking out at a vastly white audience. The film was a simple but interesting montage of the worst-of-the-worst in American Indian history and people in the audience were clearly moved. At the end of the film there was a Q & A session with the filmmakers—a young British fellow and even younger Native woman.

The discussion that followed was surreal. Despite watching a sixty-minute film recounting the atrocities committed by the (white, male) leaders of this nation—from Andrew Jackson's genocidal campaign to George W. Bush's public display of ignorance on the meaning of tribal sovereignty—no one had questions about the content or process of the film. Instead, the room reverberated with desperate pleas from the audience begging for answers. What can we do? How can we save them? Why can't they save themselves? Is there any hope for Indians? The questions came like rapid-fire and were fielded unintelligibly by the young and overwhelmed filmmakers. After the discussion took an even more unfortunate turn, with the filmmaker positing casinos as the saviors of Indians—my friend and I felt compelled to interject. We needed to disrupt the discourse, to throw ourselves in front of the moving train wreck, taking the leap as did Geronimo, thinking "today is a good die to die."

At the same time, we were hesitant to "out" ourselves from the safety of our relative anonymity. So we made a pact. We would both raise our hands, I would speak, but she would stand by my side in solidarity. We never got called on. We were, however, adamant about speaking, so as the filmmaker attempted to close the session, satisfied that he had solved the "Indian problem," we stood up and literally interrupted his speech. I said,

> Excuse me, but we felt we just had to say something before this ended. We wanted people to know that we are here—I am a professor and my friend is a computer engineer and contrary to your statistics—we are not a vanishing race. In fact, according to the last census there are more people identifying as Native American than ever before. We've been sitting back here listening to everyone talk about Indians as the problem and we are dumbfounded. How can you watch a film depicting unspeakable violence and heinous crimes committed by the nation's supposed best and brightest—its senators, presidents, and policymakers—and still define Indians as the problem? We are sitting back here wondering—is there hope for white people?

The room fell silent, people turned and stared, and then it was over.

Ever since I uttered the words, is there hope for white people, I've been thinking about the implications of my own question. Maybe Red pedagogy needs to speak more to the dehumanizing effects of colonization *for the colonizer*, to revisit Memmi's (1991) notion that "colonization can only disfigure the colonizer." I need to speak more about the hope of decolonization for *all* peoples. Kill the whiteness; save the man?

Snapshot #3

Soon after I moved to New York City, I learned that there are over 70,000 Native peoples living there. From that moment on, I have been preoccupied with knowing their history. I began with a casual search for Native professors and Native studies programs in all the major universities. When this search led to only dead ends, I launched a more concerted effort to find courses, books, researchers, anything. To my absolute amazement, I found nothing. No Native faculty, no Native Studies programs, no history books or research projects on Native New Yorkers. I can't seem to reconcile the invisibility with the reality. Everywhere you look in the city—from street names to layout, to city skyline—Indian people are everywhere yet nowhere, an experience that underscores the depths of the amnesia. The other day I was walking down Broadway with an Aleut woman, and it really hit home. There we were making our way down the oldest Indian trail in the country and I was thinking about ingenuity of it, the ways it cuts through all the important aspects of the city and ends up in the Long Island Sound; a perfect spatial location. All that wisdom, insight, and knowledge about the paradise of *Man-hat-tan* literally paved over; used but forgotten, vitally integral but erased. Somehow, I sense that part of our collective salvation lies in the unveiling of Broadway—in unpaving paradise, peeling off the layers, and recognizing that, indeed, we are because they were and they are because we were.

Closing Thoughts

When I think of reaching a state of being that is beyond survival, I think of the Native New Yorkers and the peoples of the Ninth Ward and for the need of a transgressive pedagogy that moves beyond struggles of "identity," toward an awareness of the broader structures of exploitation—capitalism, patriarchy, and white supremacy. At the Harvard conference (mentioned above), I was captivated by one of the other speaker's stories about the rebuilding and revitalization efforts in New Orleans. He spoke with great sadness about the devastation and the disbelief that citizens of this country could be so ill-treated, forgotten, and discarded. At the same time, he lamented the lack of leadership not only among the nation's leaders but also within the predominantly African American community of the Ninth Ward. In his experience of working with community relief agencies, he noticed a marked absence of solidarity; specifically, there is a division between old and new schools of thought. The "old school" leaders felt passionately about retaining strongly defined borders between "us" and "them" and in believing that the only peoples they could trust were themselves. They were concerned with questions such as "How do we move forward as African Americans and peoples of the Ninth Ward?" The "new school" leaders felt equally passionate about building political solidarities the reached across the ossified borders of race and class. They were concerned with questions such as, "How do we move forward as U.S. citizens and New Orleanians?"

It seems that in the age of global capitalism (i.e., colonialism) there needs to be a political project that operates at the crossroads of these questions. That is, we need to continue to develop pedagogies that not only support who we are distinct peoples, sustaining our sense of history and collective consciousness of what it means to be African American, Jewish, Quechua, Catholic etc., but also pedagogies of resistance and transgression that speak to our desperate need to build political solidarities and broad-based coalitions. Our central concern should be, "How do we move forward as colonized peoples against the dehumanizing effects of colonization and global capitalism?" Toward this end, the development of future leaders is paramount.

In this sense, I believe that the sister struggle of decolonization—sovereignty—must *precede* the more provincial "American" struggle for democracy. I am aware that in this moment of jihadist politics these are dangerous words. So, I want to be clear that I am not advocating any sort of separatist discourse. On the contrary, sovereignty needs to be understood as a restorative process. Indeed, Deloria implores indigenous peoples to learn to "withdraw without becoming separatists ... to reach out for the contradictions within our experience" and open ourselves to "the pain and joy of others" (Warrior 1995, p. 124). This sentiment renders the struggle for sovereignty a profoundly spiritual project, asking us to ponder who we are as a people. Although this process is necessarily deliberative, it is not (as in critical and postcolonial theories) limited to the processes of "conscientização." Rather, it is an inward- and outward-looking process of reenchantment and ensoulment, that is at once both deeply spiritual and sincerely mindful.

The guiding force in this process must be the tribe, the people, the community, their connections to land and place. As Lyons (2000) notes,

> rather than representing an enclave, sovereignty ... is the ability to assert oneself renewed—in the presence of others. It is a people's right to rebuild its demand to exist and present its gifts to the world ... an adamant refusal to dissociate culture, identity and power from the land. [p. 457]

In other words, the vision of tribal and community stability rests not only in the desire and ability of colonized peoples to listen to each other but also to the land. The wisdom of this is apparent whether one considers the peoples of the Cherokee Nation, *Man-hat-tan,* or the Ninth Ward of New Orleans.

The hope is that Red pedagogy will help us define a space of transgression and solidarity. It aims to assist in the reimagining of schools around a "*decolonial* imaginary," where indigenous and non-indigenous peoples build transcultural and transnational coalitions to construct a nation free of imperialist, colonialist, and capitalist exploitation. Within this context, Red pedagogy serves as an invitation for scholars, educators, and students to exercise critical consciousness at the same time they recognize that the world of knowledge far exceeds our ability to know. It is beckoning all of us to acknowledge that only the mountain commands reverence, the bird freedom of thought, and the land comprehension of time.

I believe that *the primary lesson in all of this is pedagogical*. In other words, as we are poised to raise yet another generation in a nation at war and at risk, we must consider how emerging conceptions of citizenship, sovereignty, and democracy will impact the (re)formation of our national identity, particularly among young people in schools. As Mitchell (2001, p. 5) notes, "the production of democracy, the practice of education, and the constitution of the nation-state" have always been interminably bound together. The imperative before us as citizens is to engage a process of unthinking our colonial roots and rethinking democracy. For teachers and students, this means that we must be willing to act as agents of transgression, posing critical questions and engaging dangerous discourse. Such is the basis of Red pedagogy. Based on the above imperatives, I've developed the following seven precepts of Red pedagogy, which will continue to be redefined over time:

1. Red pedagogy is primarily a pedagogical project wherein pedagogy is understood as being inherently political, spiritual, and intellectual.

2. Red pedagogy is fundamentally rooted in indigenous knowledge and praxis. In particular, it aims to mitigate, disrupt, and overturn the dilatory effects of colonization—for both the colonizer and colonized.

3. Red pedagogy is informed by critical theories of education, searching for ways it can both deepen and be deepened by engagement with critical theory and praxis.

4. Red pedagogy advocates education for decolonization, which makes no claim to political neutrality but rather engages a method of analysis and social inquiry that troubles the capitalist-imperialist aims of unfettered, competition, accumulation, and exploitation.

5. Red pedagogy is a project that interrogates the constructs

of democracy and indigenous sovereignty. In this context, sovereignty is broadly defined as "a peoples right to rebuild its demand to exist and present its gifts to the world ... an adamant refusal to dissociate culture, identity, and power from the land" (Lyons, 2000, p. 449).

6. Red pedagogy actively cultivates a praxis of collective agency. It aims to build transcultural and transnational solidarities among indigenous peoples and others committed to reimagining a social, political, and educational space free of exploitation.

7. Red pedagogy is grounded in hope. That is, not the future-centered hope of the Western imagination, but rather a hope that lives in contingency with the past—one that trusts the beliefs and understandings of our ancestors, the power of traditional knowledge, and the possibilities of new understandings.

In the end, a Red pedagogy is about engaging the development of community-based power and Vizenor's notion of *survivance*—that is, a state of being beyond "survival, endurance, or a mere response to colonization," toward "an active presence ... and active repudiation of dominance, tragedy and victimry" (Vizenor, 1993, p. 5). The notion of survivance is particularly relevant to indigenous peoples; long perceived as the vanishing race, they not only persist but also "actively repudiate" their evisceration. Perhaps nowhere is this more evident than on the island of *Man-hat-tan*, tucked among the glistening skyscrapers, the burgeoning masses, and the constant din of people in motion is a vibrant indigenous presence. Indian artists, musicians, engineers, stockbrokers, teachers, doctors, lawyers, counselors, and activists, among others, assert through their very being-ness that "Indian country" spans beyond the isolated borders of reservation land. Their collective survivance affirms that this is a Red nation, first and foremost build on the lifeblood of indigenous peoples. Still intrepid, still proud, still Red.

References

Geertz, C. A. (1998). Deep hanging out. *The New York Review of Books*, *45*(16), 16. Available online at http://www.nybooks.com/articles/article-preview?article_id=703. Accessed November 28, 2006.

Grande, S. (2004). *Red pedagogy: Native American social and political thought.* Lanham, MD: Rowman and Littlefield.

Lyons, S. R. (2000). Rhetorical sovereignty: What do American Indians want from writing? *College, Composition and Communication*, *51*(3), 447–468.

McLaren, P. (1997). *Revolutionary multiculturalism: Pedagogies of dissent for the new millennium.* Boulder, CO: Westview.

Memmi, R. ([1957] 1991). *The colonizer and the colonized.* Boston: Beacon Press.

Mitchell, K. (2001). Education for democratic citizenship: Transnationalism, multiculturalism, and the limits of liberalism. *Harvard Educational Review*, *71*(1), 51–78.

Vizenor, G. (1993). The ruins of representation. *American Indian Quarterly*, *17*(3), 1–7.

Warrior, R.A. (1995). *Tribal secrets: Recovering American Indian intellectual traditions.* Minneapolis: University of Minnesota.

Chapter 7

Inner Angles

A Range of Ethical Responses to/with Indigenous and Decolonizing Theories

Eve Tuck
The Graduate Center, CUNY
In conversation with
Michelle Fine
The Graduate Center, CUNY

It all started in Urbana–Champaign, 2006, or maybe hundreds of years ago.

For years, Eve Tuck and I have been working together, talking through our shared work on school drop-outs, how youth of color have been shredded by public education, converted into disposables by the economy, and criminalized even as they are denied access to meaningful public spaces. In the spring of 2006, Eve and I shared the keynote platform at the 2nd Congress of Qualitative Inquiry. Speaking together, and separately, from the stage, we addressed questions of participatory methodology with youth, ethics, politics, and sovereignty.

The next day, Eve was pulled aside by a woman who wanted her to know that Eve's remarks on the implications of indigenous sovereignty on the praxes of participatory action research (PAR) were appreciated; however, clamping her hand onto Eve's arm she said, "I went home last night and looked up the word sovereignty after your talk. I didn't really find anything in the definition that I could apply to me, so I am going to instead carry with me the word autonomy." Eve says she let herself think for a moment and responded, "Sovereignty resonates with me in a way that autonomy doesn't; a dictionary might not be the best place to get at that resonance." The woman told her that she had looked in several different dictionaries. "Sovereignty feels different to me than autonomy," Eve repeated. "Of course it would, *for you*," the woman said, and then offered another thanks and hurried away. Eve says of the rest of the story, "A few minutes later she touched my arm again, 'I didn't mean anything by that you know.' I let her know that I did."

Eve and I have talked then, and since, with friends and colleagues, about this incident and what it embodied. We've tried to think through critical and indigenous theory and ethics, trying to surface, analyze, and reimagine what happens politically, intellectually, emotionally, and in the body when indigenous knowledge, history, theory, and methods are tossed into the room. The naming of and calling for sovereignty, from the podium at a major conference *on* indigenous thought and qualitative methods, is enough to induce a linguistic "correction." We tried to understand this woman and this moment of "contact" as iconic; her desire to connect, and in so doing, to erase. We know that indigenous history and knowledge are not news; that intense social and psychic labors are at work, keeping the stories of blood, greed, and genocide silent, suppressed, or gated in the bodies of some. But we know, too, that these stories float through all of us, just beneath that unstable but ever-hegemonic story about U.S. history, prosperity, and progress, civilizing institutions, and democracy. An already disciplined and petrified conversation systematically annihilates the story(ies) that yearn/deserve to be told.

Eve has written this chapter to engage an analysis of the social dynamics unleashed when the official national amnesia is pierced by indigenous memory and knowledge. These dynamics are aged, living in the bodies of those who have survived and those who have been sacrificed; these dynamics also careen through the bodies of those who believe themselves unaffected. In the academy, social policy, and community life these dynamics obstruct most of us from knowing, seeing, researching, and speaking, and they keep some of us gated actively at the margins of social thought. These dynamics may perform what David Eng calls racial melancholia for white people, but/and they function as an ideological/intellectual stranglehold on the throats of those who dare to speak. That is, they have everything to do with social theory, method, and ethics.

This chapter is rooted in the deep particularities of history, colonized spaces, and minds, yet it also seeks to recognize a solidarity of structural violence in the United States and globally by the United States that cuts deep across time, place, and community. That is, the conversation opened (again) with this chapter begins with the recognition that some groups, some communities, and some institutions have long suffered from the same sword of state-sponsored exclusion and violence launched by the U.S. government in the name of democracy, accountability, citizenship, and nation building.

—Michelle Fine

◊ ◊ ◊ ◊ ◊

This chapter is organized around four corners. Not the four opposing corners of a square, but a circle in quadrants, and in the center, an inner circle made by the corners of the perpendicular lines. Let's not mistake these angles as opposite angles of a square, but read them as the intimately bound corners of a circle—not too much travel between them, like standing on the four corners of the U.S. states of Utah, Colorado, New Mexico, and Arizona that meet on the lands of Navajo and Ute nations.

Rather than a series of sequential recommendations, this chapter seeks to move—no, grapple—through the four corners, not as a progression, but as an assemblage, an accumulation of offerings. These inner angles are in balance, linked, not linear, and this chapter pauses in each of their territories: (1) the hegemonic voice-over of colonization; (2) that which is obscured by colonizers' guilt; (3) how indigenous and decolonizing theories might/already inform an epistemological shift; and (4) PAR praxes participatory action research praxes as praxes of self-determination. These inner angles represent a range of ethical responses to/with indigenous and decolonizing theories. They are not in a fixed order as it is only a single footstep, or a shift in weight between New Mexico and Arizona or New Mexico and Utah, all afforded by the hospitality of Ute and Dine people.

Much can be learned about popular ideology and commitments by looking at how the U.S. government has treated/treatied indigenous people. Sorting and resorting tribal nations onto parcels of land reservations reveals a fetishizing of the notion of private property. The 1971 Alaska Native Claims Settlement Act that broke Alaskan Natives into thirteen regional and approximately 220 village corporations reveals a worship of the corporate model and belief in the balancing power of the market.

In a chapter I wrote with Michelle Fine and Sarah Zeller-Berkman, "Do You Believe in Geneva? Methods and Ethics at the Global Local Nexus" (Fine, Tuck, & Zeller-Berkman, forthcoming), we wondered aloud how an overemphasis on a global audience (that is, the Human Rights Convention in Geneva) might undermine the desires, needs, and demands of the local and were moved by the comments of Aliou, a researcher from Cameroon in the project Global Rights: Partners for Justice-Sponsored Amplifying Youth Voices, "I don't know that I believe in Geneva" (Fine, Tuck, & Zeller-Berkman, forthcoming). This chapter, in many ways a coda on that chapter, a coda on our disbelief, tries to take up the challenge to "detach and dethink the notion of sovereignty from its connection to western understandings of power and relationships and base it on indigenous notions of power" (Grande, 2004, p. 53) by articulating the methodological and ethical dynamics of what happens when indigenous epistemologies are at the center of praxes of qualitative inquiry.

This chapter takes up theories and theorists who emphasize decolonization as a central project, not only for indigenous communities but also non-indigenous communities: for indigenous sovereignty to be taken seriously as a prerequisite to democracy, decolonization must be a common project on multiple social justice agendas. The rights of indigenous and disenfranchised people to claim a right to self-determination, complex personhood, and sovereignty have been erroneously cast as property rights, "even though notions of sovereignty and equality are personal rights" (G. H. Smith, 2000, p. 219).

Because decolonization is political and disruptive (L. T. Smith, 1999), those of us who are engaging in decolonizing theories often find ourselves, as Marker suggests of the indigenous perspective, "up against the wall" (2006, p. 6). However, as Alfred reminds us, "the time has come for people who are from someplace

Indian to take back the discourse on Indians" (1999, p. 143), and I add that it is time to take back the discourse on knowing. The inner angles of each of the corners that follow sort through the range of ethical responses that make up a disbelief in dominant beliefs of entitlement, power, research, and knowing.

Corner One

This corner critiques the hegemonic voice-over from the false perspectives of a colonization that is over, as distraction buffered by patriotism and blind nationalism, and as ignorant of an already ongoing conversation across indigenous spaces.

The hegemonic voice-over of indigenous experiences of colonization worships artificial timeness of social/cultural development. "(I)t presumes the cultural neutrality of science and technology, indigenous ecological understandings are dismissed as exotic, but irrelevant, distraction" (Marker, 2006, p. 2). All of this as if colonization could ever be over. Reducing the violences of first contacts to the birth pangs of a nation or new order contains them to a delineated time and place. Indeed, it justifies these violences by that very fixed moment in history: colonization that is over can popularly be forgiven as the sins of our fathers; colonization that is ongoing and under constant renovation and normalized as everyday practice is in no position to be forgiven but warred on. It is strikingly similar to the predicament of Mrs. Winchester, the widow of the inventor of the Winchester rifle, who, to keep the souls of those killed by her husband's invention from tormenting her, kept her mansion in San Jose, California, under 24/7 construction for thirty-eight years until her death. Her home, steeped in superstition, a maze of stairs and doors to nowhere, and windows without purpose, stands much like the contraptions of dominant infrastructure and rhetoric that distract and postpone full admission and reparation of colonization and occupation.

"Science," at the will of scientists who as Vine Deloria 1994 writes, "hold in great disdain all traditions except the one in which they have grown up and received rewards" (quoted in Marker, 2006, p. 8), has systematically worked similarly to bookend indigenous colonization: pathologizing and criminalizing those who haven't assimilated or who ask questions. Artificially bookending indigenous experiences falsely distills colonization as an event relegating contemporary Native poverty, illness, and depression as an "Indian problem." Actually, "the 'Indian problem' is not a problem of children and families but rather, first and foremost, a problem that has been consciously and historically produced by and through the systems of colonization: a multidimensional force underwritten by Western Christianity, defined by white supremacy, and fueled by global capitalism" (Grande, 2004, p. 19). The question at heart: what could have ever been expected to happen from this except for this?

Further, the hegemonic voice overlubricates the distractive engines of patriotism and blind nationalism away from the U.S. export of globalized oppression.

> Culture, underpinned as usual by faith, law, and revisionary history, has proven only too capable of doing what main force could not, which is to make the colonizer capable of sleeping at night or reaching across the dinner or communion table without recoiling from the sense of the blood of the "Other" on his hands. [Findlay, 2000, p. x]

This same hegemonic voice was at work when George W. Bush declared the war in Iraq over in the spring of 2003: to bookend something when it is so painfully untrue, a strong-arm-induced tipping point itself an act of aggression.

A critique of the hegemonic voice-over is threatening in the United States; as Sandy Grande notes, it is only recognized by the "whitestream" as an

> inherent threat to the nation, poised to expose the great lies of U.S. democracy: that we are a nation of laws and not random power; that we are guided by reason and not faith; that we are governed by representation and not executive order; and finally, that we stand as a self-determined citizenry and not a kingdom of blood or aristocracy. [Grande, 2004, p. 32]

What exactly is voiced over? The question is, why not acknowledge indigenous sovereignty? What does indigenous sovereignty have to do with current unilateral decisions to occupy?

What keeps superpower nations from recognizing the sovereignty of other nations? Is it fear of retribution? Scarlet letters that spell out unpatriotic? A map of an empire that shrinks rather than spreads over time? A disillusionment with global development?

I contrast this fear by turning to indigenous representations of sovereignty: In a recent National Indian Education Association conference presentation, Roberta Tayah-Yazzie (2006) used an image of a sixteenth-century beaded treaty belt that features two black lines on a background of white to describe sovereignty as paths that flow peacefully in the same direction, but do not intersect. Indigenous visions of sovereignty can be interpreted by the historical and contemporary high participation of Native people in the U.S. military; the high regard with which Native veterans are received in their communities; the display of the U.S. flag flying alongside tribal emblems carried by color guards into opening circles, songs, and ceremony dances; anthems sung side by side; stars and stripes incorporated into the skins and cloths of traditional Native regalia—all of this to designate the discourse of sovereignty not as a separatist discourse, but a discourse of acknowledgment, a "restorative process" (Grande, 2004, p. 54). It is not unpatriotic to demand a reorienting of history and acknowledgment of sovereignty. But this, too, yields too much power to a discourse that seeks to silence dissent.

In a crowded session on schooling and dropping out that the First Alaskans' Institute is facilitating during their Elders and Youth Conference, Alaska Native young people and Elders are talking about what school feels like. Several presentations by young adult college students illustrate the pitfalls of being a young person in rural Alaska and how they were admirably able to overcome them. Stories of neglect, abuse, self-hatred, and loss, both in and out of school are swapped and the room feels full with the stories that number too many to be just a fluke. In this fullness, an Elder stands, telling us that he remembers to this day the hatred that his last teacher had for him—he speaks as though the teacher still hates him, though he left school before graduating over sixty years ago. He addresses the young people there, "Maybe this is what it feels like for you? Can you tell me if you feel this hate?" We are in a contemplative quiet, breathing before one of the youth responds, willing to go wherever this question will take us, knowing that we had come to hear this question, to ask this question, to let this question ring in our ears, and to listen to what this question stirs up in the youth.

Like a party that has accidentally opened on a place of healing, a new white teacher in the bush takes up the pause: "But what am I supposed to do when I can't even get them to pick up their pencils?"

◊ ◊ ◊ ◊ ◊

And this is a violence, too. A violence, but also evidence of an important attempt at contact; no more violent than those in the room who gawk but do not contribute, those who take but do not replenish, those who deny their solidarity.

The element of the hegemonic voice-over that affords both this discussion and the ignorance toward already ongoing conversations is entitlement, the felt impetus to ask about the pencils. The hegemonic voice-over blankets but cannot undermine the discourses, the blankets that we are building. I don't mean to dismiss or demonize the teacher who worries about the pencils. I don't mean to discourage her from bringing her whole self to her students in rural Alaska. But I would ask her to ask herself where her ears were—to ask herself what was happening in that room, our room, that compelled her to speak at that moment. How did it feel like the appropriate moment to assert that we were a they to her?

There is a legacy of polyvocal conversation about how indigenous people would like to be read and listened to, how we would like to be recognized, how we would like to research ourselves, educate our children, and maintain and rebuild our subsistence lifestyles. Indigenous people are already self-determined, and yet at the same time live the reality of the ditch that Fannie Lou Hamer spoke of, "What you don't understand is that as long as you stand with your feet on my neck, you got to stand in a ditch, too. But if you move, I'm coming out. I want to get us both out of the ditch" (as quoted by Fine, 2006, p. 12). The hegemonic voice-over that claims "You got the casinos, what more do you want?" "They can't be raised in their homes" "Kill the native, save the man" "Maybe you were Native, but you're not anymore!" "You're on the verge of extinction" "I'm just a dumb Native," is keeping us all in the ditch (Grande, 2004; Marker, 2006).

Corner Two

In this section, I discuss that which is cloaked, overshadowed by colonizer's guilt—the acknowledgment of oppression and the simultaneous retreat from responsibility for change.

◊ ◊ ◊ ◊ ◊

And then a well-meaning member of the mostly white[1] audience asks, "What can I possibly do?"

This is the windexed window that discussions hosted by indigenous theorists for academic audiences at national and local conferences, brown bag lunches, community forums, and other presentations around decolonizing projects often career into. It has happened to me and has happened in almost every Q & A discussion with other indigenous scholars I can recall. There is a moment and a string of moments when members of the audience begin to feel implicated, personally responsible for the ongoing colonization of indigenous peoples. And so one person stands and says, "What can I possibly do?" And that response, although frustrating (because it echoes of asking about the pencils, because it is so quick to get that big guilt off its back, to shift from being under the eye of scrutiny) is understandable only if because it is so typical. Understandable if the audience misunderstands/takes the indigenous project as swapping one agenda for another, as if merely sliding a new checklist beneath the academy's waiting pen: "A new site to be eyed/I-ed" (Fine, 2006, personal communication).

Recently, while preparing for a conference presentation, two young women of color who work with me as researchers, worried aloud how to respond to questions during the Q & A session that might be ageist, racist, and misogynist. Already having had a taste of others' patronizing surprise that they might be able to discuss their own work with sophistication and credibility, and in an academic tongue at that, my coresearchers anticipated that folks' first remarks often are dressed up as heralds, but betray the questioner's assumptions about what young women of color are and are not capable of. Not wanting to betray their own disgust with eye rolling and an undignified reply, we devised a simple phrase to disengage and refocus the discussion, "That's not what we're talking about here."

I'm locating that same courage to say, "That's not what I'm talking about," when confronted by the question, "What can I possibly do?" because this question, steeped in the privilege of white ideology, reeking of false generosity, asks me to do the work of the question poser. An element of white privilege is to reduce someone's theoretical work to a honey-do list for white people. Or perhaps a more effective response would be, "This is not the time for that discussion," because the time would be when we are both prepared to speak to one another in ways that are mutually beneficial, where I am not expected to reveal more of myself than you for your learning, where I will not take on more of the residue of the conversation than you will when we part, when we speak with equal thoughtfulness, and we both feel that enough is at stake to let our talking together have resonance and meaning in our work and lives.

Gloria Anzaldúa wrote a letter to Third World women writers in the spring of 1980, a letter that has been very important and educational to me. Because it continues to be so personally resonant, I have shared it in many different circles and circumstances to disrupt the silence that secures white privilege:

> The Third World woman revolts: *We revoke, we erase your white male imprint. When you come knocking on our doors with your rubber stamps to brand our faces with DUMB, HYSTERICAL, PASSIVE PUTA, PERVERT, when come with your branding irons to burn MY*

PROPERTY on our buttocks, we will vomit the guilt, self-denial and race-hatred you have force fed into us right back into your mouth. We are done being cushions for your projected fears. We are tired of becoming your sacrificial lambs and scapegoats. [Anzaldúa, 2002, 167; italics in the original]

This letter, in my experiences, evokes responses of alarm, indignation, and distress in white women and white men. "I didn't know." "I didn't mean it." "I don't know how to stop it." "What can I possibly do?" These questions freeze, petrify. These responses of white guilt and colonizers' guilt distract from what a real/an ethical conversation about ongoing colonization and ongoing decolonization requires: preparedness, listening, reflection, and reparation.

Preparedness involves an intimate epistemological shift, thoughtfulness, and anticipation; listening; humility; and respect. Reflection, an attention that circles back and forward. Reparation requires coming clean, coming out, investing in infrastructure, honoring sovereignty, *un*forgetting. *Un*forgetting can happen within an epistemological frame that rejects individualism, and so doing, occupation.

This epistemological shift might be described as one in which, as scholar Graham Smith (2000) writes of Maori culture, "Individuals do not hold knowledge for themselves they hold it for the benefit of the whole group" (p. 218). The Aleut/Unangax̂ approach to knowing is an approach of *praxis*: learn and do, think and be, respect and be, all are comprised in knowing our family, our history, our land, sea, nature, our subsistence-sustenance, our language-definition. It is a praxis of Txin achigalix anĝaĝigumin anuxtanatxin ax̂saasaduukux̂tin²/always learning and maintaining a balance (Unangam tunuu, eastern dialect).

There is an ugly underbelly to what I am suggesting, an epistemological shift in the footsteps of indigenous theory. It is very important to consider these matters with a complex and critical eye and voice. I intentionally write of footsteps, both to attend to and reprove that romanticized vision of the Indian guide, that noble savage leading the white folks to the clearing, the earth and brook that will make real again the sterility of modernity (V. Deloria, 1970). This is a new old kind of footsteps, footsteps that are kadaliiĝin maqax̂takan txichin aguqangin/the way of our beginning, our ancestors (Unangam tunuu, eastern dialect).

The appropriation of indigenous knowledge, images, and meanings has been long accepted among the "whitestream" of the United States—from colonial protests against England such as the Boston Tea Party; to the literary misrepresentations for an audience that cares little about such minor matters as cultural and historical accuracy, the relationships of the authors to the tribes they do or do not represent, or sacred materials; to the outright invention of the Indian and his symbols of the New Age movement—that which is indigenous in the United States is up for grabs to be stretched and strangled, divvied up and burned, decentered, and possessed (P. Deloria, 1998).

Sherman Alexie has written, "In the Great American Indian novel, when it is finally written, all of the white people will be Indians and all of the Indians will be ghosts" (1996, p. 95). Indeed, indigenous materials "become fair game to anyone seeking to pilfer, copy, and re-create such goods and practices, reaping considerable profits in a capitalist marketplace that craves the exotic and authentic" (Grande, 2004, p. 111). This tradition of pilfering is combined with what Daes (2000) calls "a fundamental weapon used by most colonizers against colonized peoples," which serves "to isolate the colonized from all outside sources of information and knowledge and then to bombard them with propaganda carefully aimed at convincing them that they are backward, ignorant, weak, insignificant, and very very fortunate to have been colonized!" (p. 7). Marie Battiste (2000) has called this *cognitive imperialism*.

Without careful treading while drawing comparisons across indigenous and non-indigenous spaces, we can inadvertently smooth over the tangled relationships of exploitation and pain that indigenous peoples and nations have with colonizing peoples and nations and their collaborators.

> Being Indigenous, the Indigena are not metaphors. Those of us who are Indigenous have experienced the everyday realities of continued colonization which has shaped the ways in which we think of ourselves, one another and the 'whitestream' and the ways in which we write, speak, and come to research. Those of us who are

not Indigenous have been profoundly shaped by our witnessing of colonization, by our roles as accomplices, abettors, exploiters, romanticizers, pacifiers, assimilators, includers, forgetters, and democratizers. [Fine, Tuck, & Zeller-Berkman, forthcoming]

Still, without making connections between indigenous experiences and the experiences of politically disenfranchised non-indigenous experiences in the United States, we quite simply let the power elite get away with far too much. Further, without lifting up and connecting the instances and legacies of domination that take place *across* indigenous and non-indigenous spaces, we run the risk of undermining or submerging crucial structural analyses without which individuals and communities are often pathologized as lazy, ignorant, soulless, savage, pathetic, uninspired, unmotivated, and destined for failure.

Corner Three

With all of this as a context, the question I am going to address in corner three is "How might indigenous and decolonizing theories inform a crucial epistemological shift?" I begin with three calls toward revisioning made by indigenous theorists for qualitative researchers. The first is a call to both forge new spaces of inquiry and to interrupt/intervene on existing theory (Battiste, 2000; V. Deloria, 1988; Grande, 2004; G. Smith, 2000; L. T. Smith, 1999; Tuck, forthcoming). The second is a call to reframe democracy, to resist the prevailing undefined version of democracy that has historically and even now been employed in the United States as a cover for domination, occupation, and assimilation (Grande, 2004; L. T. Smith, 1999; Tuck, forthcoming). This is a challenge for critical theorists, critical pedagogues, and participatory action researchers: there can not be democracy without indigenous sovereignty.

Finally, indigenous theorists encourage us to reclaim spaces and narratives that have been used against us. Linda Tuhiwai Smith's (2005) work teaches us that, "Research, like schooling, once the tool for colonization and oppression is very gradually coming to be seen as a potential means to reclaim languages, histories and knowledge, to find solutions to the negative impacts of colonialism and to give voice to an alternative way of knowing and of being" (p. 10). What Smith has called "researching back"—a decolonizing project of recovery, knowing, analysis, and struggle—can also be practiced as what I have called *theorizing back*—a practice of close description and analysis of education and social policy through theory with urban, Native, and disenfranchised youth (L. Smith, 1999; Tuck, forthcoming; Tuck and the Collective of Researchers on Educational Disappointment and Desire, forthcoming).

◊ ◊ ◊ ◊ ◊

I am Navajo. But I am a researcher. What has happened to me?

—Tim Begaye, 2006

In the remainder of this section, I will discuss the ongoingness of a conversation, that conversation that has been voiced over, obscured by colonizers' guilt, but is always already ongoing. As long as there has been colonization, there has been decolonization, territorialization, deterritorialization (Deleuze and Guattari, 1987). Further, I will describe how indigenous experiences as the research subject have crafted indigenous research methodologies and a decolonizing ethic(s).

My grandmother, Masura, had a beautiful home, no matter where. Clean and bright and clean. One part of the clean was that her home was filled with lovely things from her travels all over the world—her house was always filled with guests, who enjoyed her good food and laughter, and they were invited to take up space there, to admire her collections with both their eyes and hands, and there was no dust, no cobwebs, every possible path and route cleared and welcoming to her guests. The other part of the clean, the part I understand better now, was that her childhood home on St. Paul of the Pribilof Islands on the Aleutian Chain could be split open at the whim of the white government officials that "kept order" on the island for a white-glove inspection. A trace of dirt brought punishment. These are only two of the many parts of the clean.

Research has been waged on indigenous communities in the

United States, much of it not dissimilar from white-glove inspection. Stories of teeth counting, rib counting, head measuring, blood drawn, bones dug up, medical treatment withheld, erroneous or fabricated ethnography, unsanctioned camera lenses, out-and-out lies, empty promises, cover ups, betrayals; these are the stories of our kitchen tables. Graham Smith (2000) writes, "The distrust of academics, research, and institutions by indigenous peoples is well founded and relates to a history of hurt, humiliation, and exploitation that has been perpetrated by some institutions and academics, with disastrous outcomes for some people" (p. 213).

Decolonizing theory and research methodologies offer analyses. Better yet, they offer a framework of ethical responses to forced removal, dispossession, invisibility, and dual status nature of disenfranchised people within systems of domination, especially useful in the United States as in other governments in which colonization has been the primary relationship to its people.

As indigenous researchers, the very nexus spun by our experiences and the experiences of our relatives and ancestors as the object/subject of the outside researcher and our own coming to a counterhegemonic approach to research necessitates a departured ethic. "This, I think, is one of the ironies of indigenous struggle: it is the actual process of struggle that makes us strong and committed and that helps us to consolidate why we are struggling. That is, struggle constantly forces us to identify and review what we stand for and what we stand against" (G. Smith, 2000, p. 210). It is through this struggled ethic that indigenous people have long engaged in rehistoricizing the future. Thus,

> Decolonizing research is not simply then about challenging or making refinements to qualitative research. It is much a broader but still purposeful agenda for transforming the institutions of research, the deep underlying structures and taken for granted ways of organizing, conducting and disseminating research and knowledge. [L. T. Smith, 2005, p. 6]

There/here is an explicit need to construct a critique of colonizing, imperialist, racist, classist social structures across indigenous and non-indigenous spaces without zero-summing indigenous and non-indigenous experiences. Across the waters of the Bering Sea or the waters that broke the levees in New Orleans, across the sands of the Southwest or Iraq, across the snows, across the winds, across the blood and bones, this linked analysis is central to any work toward systematic social justice, sovereignty, and freedom.

I offer here four ongoing analyses—of forced removal, dispossession, invisibility, and dual status—cultivated in the work of indigenous scholars. I do so by offering an example/engagement with an element of my own research that details the patterns of domination that have encroached on indigenous communities and urban youth of color and urban poor youth, focusing on those who have been implicitly and explicitly pushed out from school. These groups, of course, are not mutually exclusive. Across the globe and across the Unites States, from New York to, and especially in, urban Alaska, Native youth are pushed out from schools at alarming rates, denied access to the primary route to individual and community sustainability and self-reliance.

The data I use here have come from my work with CREDD, the Collective of Researchers on Educational Disappointment and Desire, a PAR collective I cofounded with a group of New York City youth aged sixteen–twenty-two. In 2006, my coresearchers and I mounted a comprehensive study, The Gateways and Getaways Project, that interrogates the abuse of the GED as a cover for removing unwanted students in New York City public high schools .

In urban cities across the United States, indigenous youth, youth of color, working-class and poor youth, queer youth, homeless youth, and other disenfranchised youth know implicitly and explicitly that their schools have not been intended for them and that they are not welcome. Often, this is translated to us in the field of education but also popular audiences as a "drop-out problem." In New York City, for instance, figures of those who do not graduate in four years range between 30 and 70%, a range so huge it's almost not useful, except to say that 30% is too high anyway, and this percentage disproportionately includes indigenous youth, youth of color, and poor youth. CREDD's work aligns itself with a newer legacy of describing these "drop-out" youth rather as those pushed out of schools, shifting the gaze from youth's bodies onto the school policies and practices that implicitly and explicitly push students out.

The first critique is a critique against forced removal: implicit and explicit push-out practices are bound to notions of forced removal. Further, New York City youth of color and poor youth are often forced to attend schools outside of their communities, and, being at the whim of ever-changing school policies, might attend a different school each school year. Some youth in our research have reported changing schools more than six times before being pushed out. Having to travel for up to two hours to attend schools in wealthier communities that see them as infiltrators discourages these youth from ever taking root in these schools.

A second critique aims itself against the dispossession of youth of color and poor youth and their families and communities in regard to the curriculum and instruction they receive. Out of local hands, government-mandated testing–based curricula are most severely imposed on poor schools, reducing learning and teaching to test preparation, disgruntling both students and educators. Part of a nationwide trend toward mandatory state exit exams, in New York State, as of 2001, all students are required to pass five state Regents' exams in addition to their coursework to graduate.

These exams, which in most years are subject to scandals because of racist and misogynist questions, dominate the classroom experience, and youth are encouraged by teachers, administrators, and guidance counselors to pursue a GED if these power players determine that they will not pass these exams. This is compounded by young people's perceptions that by pursuing a GED they are swapping one series of tests for another, without all the hassle of sitting in a classroom where the teacher has little hope for them and resents their being there to drag down test scores, and where there aren't enough seats for them anyway. Some of the youth who have participated in our study report that they first had a sense that they were not cut out for school as early as the fifth grade, and that a teacher or administrator had suggested that they attain a GED rather than a high school diploma as early as the seventh grade, two years before they ever set foot in a high school. This is a serious violation of students' rights to attend public high school until the age of twenty-one in New York State.

A third critique interrogates the invisibility of pushed-out youth. As I have described earlier, the ambiguity with which student completion rates are reported, along with the fact that many students report being pushed out between ninth and tenth grade with the anticipation that they would not pass the tests three years later and that this issue has been constructed as a drop-out problem, has made this population of students invisible, uncounted, and pathologized as lazy, crazy, unteachable troublemakers.

A quality of this invisibility is that youth take the blame, both in the media and in their own imaginations of themselves, for what, by uncloaking this silence and invisibility, would be better described as a systematic problem. This silence guarantees those who benefit by denying youth of color and poor youth their rightly access to free quality schooling freedom from worrying that these youth will ever appreciate their critical mass and demand reparation.

Finally, a fourth critique offers insight into the dual status nature of pushed-out youth: both bound up in schooling but ousted, self-blaming yet powerful, these youth have a wealth of wisdom on the institutions that have shut them out. Michelle Fine writes, "Critical perspectives on social institutions are often best obtained from exiles, that is, persons who leave those institutions. This is perhaps why exiles' views are frequently disparaged as deviant and in some cases, conspicuously silenced" (Fine & Rosenberg, 1983, p. 257). Taking up this claim, I have elsewhere theorized the experiences of pushed-out urban youth as the experiences of *present exiles*—those who are both not there but there, rejected but resisting, choked but speaking (Tuck, forthcoming).

There is no other body of theory that can better address the experiences of forced removal, dispossession, invisibility, and the dual status of present exiles than indigenous and decolonizing theory.

Corner Four

In this fourth corner, I will discuss PAR as a praxis of self-determination, a key ingredient toward praxes of (indigenous) sovereignty. This corner, the seedling of the four, has hopes for continued and increased mutually beneficial, ethical collaboration between indigenous and non-indigenous researchers, and a deeper acknowledgment of what might be learned and achieved within the footsteps of indigenous theory. Further, I offer to and from my indigenous colleagues, the radical possibilities of PAR spaces as spaces in which sovereignty can be recognized, practiced, theorized, and cultivated. The following list, adapted from a prior list (Fine, Tuck, & Zeller-Berkman, forthcoming), pulls material from across conversations of indigenous theorists to describe what sovereignty within praxes of inquiry might look like, not only for indigenous participants but also, without zero summing, other disenfranchised participants.

Sovereignty as a prerequisite to democracy involves the cease and desist of Eurocentric, colonizing power formations. This includes the rights to:

- resist or reject Eurocentric theory (Battiste, 2000)
- resist or reject versions of ourselves that are fantasies of the power elite (Mihesuah, 1998)
- resist or reject cognitive imperialism (Battiste, 2000)
- explore epistemological differences (Marker, 2006)
- reclaim that which has been stolen from us (Marker, 2006)
- question democratic models of one person, one vote, and majority rule, or the Westminster model of democracy, which reifies the goals of dominant groups and squashes the rights of those in numeric minority (G. Smith, 2000)

Sovereignty as a prerequisite to democracy also calls for us to mind what is sacred. This includes the rights to:

- keep what is sacred sacred, and to make/mark new spaces and knowledges as sacred
- choose what is and what is not on the table for documentation
- seek the blessings or permission of our own communities of peers and elders to reveal significant information

Finally, sovereignty as a prerequisite to democracy involves what Avery Gordon (1997) has called the right to complex personhood, including the rights to:

- work and learn and exist in wholeness and to thrive in our relations with other peoples (Grande, 2004, p. 171)
- be the sources of our own healing and renewal (Daes, 2000, p. 5)
- work, learn, and exist in ways that are proactive, not only reactive
- resist or reject propaganda carefully aimed at convincing us that we are backward, ignorant, weak, insignificant (Daes, 2000, p. 7)
- make together a research community that "provides stable institutions and policies, fair and effective processes of dispute resolution, effective separation of politics from business management, a competent bureaucracy, and cultural match (Grande, 2004, p. 54)

Contrasting what might be understood as a methodology and ethic of assimilation to a methodology and ethic that honors indigenous sovereignty, Linda Tuhuwai Smith (2005) writes,

> The desires for "pure" uncontaminated and simple definitions of the native by the settler is often a desire to continue to know and define the Other whereas the desires by the native to be self defining and self naming can be read as desires to be free, to escape definition, to be complicated, to develop and changes and be regarded as fully human. In between such desires however are multiple and shifting identities and hybridities with much more nuanced positions about what constitutes native identities, native communities and native knowledge in the anti/post colonial times. [p. 3]

In my experiences with the Collective of Researchers on Educational Disappointment and Desire and other participatory research spaces, the approach afforded through PAR can initiate/ encourage sites of self-definition and self-determination, nuanced and multipled, and like the image of the treaty belt, made of many paths that do not choke one another.

Rather than a fixed methodology, PAR is a politic, an epistemology (Fine & Torre, 2004, 2006; Torre & Fine, 2003, 2006; Tuck, forthcoming; Tuck and the Collective of Researchers on Educational Disappointment and Desire, forthcoming). Elsewhere, my coresearchers and I have written about PAR as including the following characteristics which differentiate it from other methodologies and approaches: the design is collaboratively negotiated and co-constructed; research questions are co-constructed ; there is transparency on all matters of the research, from administrative details like institutional review board approval to the budget to the theory and reasoning behind practice; analysis is co-constructed; research products are collaboratively crafted (Tuck, forthcoming; Tuck and the Collective of Researchers on Educational Disappointment and Desire, forthcoming).

Concerning these elements, PAR spaces are definitionally and intentionally self-determined spaces. PAR demands that researchers untangle otherwise jumbled ethics, make transparent otherwise inaccessible practice, and speak what is otherwise silenced. Further, for these reasons, I contend that PAR collectives are prime sites to explore what it might mean to praxis sovereignty. The experience of struggle and possibility that is inherent to working out how to create within a working space that which has been systematically denied to us, the power of arrival of it, and the long-lasting body and spirit memory that is taken away from a PAR collective can be revisioned and rearticulated as part of an otherwise unacknowledged legacy of indigenous struggles for sovereignty worldwide.

I close this corner with an invitation to indigenous researchers working across many sites to consider how participatory action research that takes sovereignty as a prerequisite to democracy seriously might open up new possibilities for our theoretical work and for our sovereign approaches to education, subsistence, wellness, and knowledge in our communities, both for our ancestors and Aniqdun ngiin aqaaĝan aĝnangin qulingiin akux̂ gumalgaku/ for the coming generations that we don't see yet, for their time here (Unangam tunuu, eastern dialect).

Intimately Bound Corners of a Circle

The inner angles of our praxes as researchers, writers, and fighters for social justice take up space and negotiate each of the four corners I have described here—the hegemonic voice-over; that which is blanketed by colonizers' guilt; that necessary episte-mological shift and ever reshift; possibilities for sovereignty and self-determination—and beyond those territories to corners forgotten and corners now forming. The make and magnetism of these arriving corners will depend on our ongoing ethical responses to colonization and occupation and to the signifi-cance we attribute to preparedness, listening, reflection, and reparation in our work and everyday lives.

Notes

1. A note on whiteness: I contend that it is most useful to talk about whiteness as those experiences that are fixed to a white ideology; it is an ideology that is self-serving, self-supremacist, self-norming, but not self-reflective. When I speak and write of whiteness, this is what I think I mean. Ideology is malleable, it can be informed and reformed, and there is much possibility in this quality. But it is not only about ideology, it *is* about skin, too: as a white-skinned Aleut woman, I benefit by and negotiate white privilege daily, although I operate within a different ideology.

2. All Unanagam tunuu translations by Moses L. Dirks and Illidor Philemonoff in "The Right Way to Live as an Unangax̂," by Ada Michael Lestenkoff, distributed by the Unangan Elders Academy, the Association of Unangan Educations, and the Aleutian Pribilof Island Association, Inc.

Acknowledgments

Thanks to Michelle Fine, Sarah Zeller-Berkman, The Aleut Foundation and Tara Bourdukofsky, Jovanne Allen, Alexis Morales, Maria Bacha, Jodi-Ann Gayle, Sarah Quinter, Jamila Thompson, Melody Tuck, Caitlin Cahill, Brett Stoudt, Maria Torre, and Algie Frisbey.

References

Alexie, S. (1996). How to write the great American Indian novel. In *The summer of black widows* (pp. 94–95). Brooklyn, NY: Hanging Loose Press.

Alfred, T. (1999). *Peace, power, righteousness: An indigenous manifesto.* Oxford: Oxford University Press.

Anzaldúa, G. (2002). Speaking in tongues: A letter to 3rd World women writers. In C. Moraga & G. Anzaldúa (Eds.), *This bridge called my back: Writings by radical women of color* (pp. 165–180). Berkeley, CA: Third Woman Press.

Battiste, M. (2000). Introduction: Unfolding the lessons of colonization. In M. Battiste (Ed.), *Reclaiming indigenous voices and vision* (pp. xvi–xxx). Vancouver: University of British Colombia Press.

Begaye, T. (2006). Complicating decolonizing research, a grounding conversation. Paper presented at the 2nd Congress of Qualitative Inquiry, Urbana, Illinois, May 3–5.

Daes, E. I. (2000). Prologue: *The experience of colonization around the world.* In M. Battiste (Ed.), *Reclaiming indigenous voices and vision* (pp. 3–8). Vancouver: University of British Colombia Press.

Deleuze, G., & Guattari, F. (1987). *A thousand plateaus: Capitalism and schizophrenia.* Minneapolis: University of Minnesota Press.

Deloria, P. J. (1998). *Playing Indian.* New Haven, CT: Yale University Press.

Deloria, V., Jr. (1970). *We talk, you listen: New tribes, new turf.* New York: Macmillan.

Deloria, V., Jr. (1988). *Custer died for your sins: An Indian manifesto.* Norman: University of Oklahoma Press.

Deloria, V., Jr. (1994). *God is red: A native view of religion.* Golden, CO: North American Press.

Findlay, L. M. (2000). Foreword. In M. Battiste (Ed.), *Reclaiming indigenous voices and vision* (pp. 1–2). Vancouver: University of British Colombia Press.

Fine, M. (2006). Repertoires of privatization: Critically theorizing the gating of public education. Paper presented at the 105th American Anthropological Association Conference, San Jose, California, November 15–19.

Fine, M., & Rosenberg, P. (1983). Dropping out of high school: The ideology of school and work, *Journal of Education, 165*(3), 257.

Fine, M., & Torre, M. E. (2004). Re-membering exclusions: Participatory action research in public institutions. *Qualitative Research in Psychology, 1*(1), 15–37.

Fine, M., & Torre, M. E. (2006). Intimate details: Participatory action research in prison. *Action Research, 4*(3), 253–269.

Fine, M., Tuck, E., & Zeller-Berkman, S. (Forthcoming). Do you believe in Geneva? Methods and ethics and the global local nexus. In N. Denzin, Y. S. Lincoln, & L. T. Smith (Ed.), *Handbook on critical and indigenous methodologies*. Thousand Oaks, CA: Sage.

Gordon, A. (1997). *Ghostly matters: Haunting and the sociological imagination.* Minneapolis: University of Minnesota Press.

Grande, S. (2004). *Red pedagogy: Native American social and political thought.* Lanham, MD: Rowman and Littlefield.

Marker, M. (2006). After the Makah whalehunt: Indigenous knowledge and limits to multicultural discourse. *Urban Education, 41*(5), 482–505.

Mihesuah, D. (1998). Introduction to *Natives and academics: Researching and writing about American Indians.* Lincoln: University of Nebraska Press.

Smith, G. H. (2000). Protecting and respecting indigenous knowledge. In M. Battiste (Ed.), *Reclaiming indigenous voices and vision* (pp. 209–224) Vancouver: University of British Colombia Press.

Smith, L.T. (1999). *Decolonizing methodologies: Research and indigenous peoples.* London: Zed Books.

Smith, L. T. (2005). *On tricky grounds: Researching the native in an age of uncertainty.* In N. Denzin & Y. Lincoln (Ed.), *Handbook of qualitative research*, 3rd ed. (pp. 85–107). Beverly Hills, CA: Sage.

Tayah-Yazzie, R. (2006). Using historical information to create contemporary understanding of the Navajo Nation sovereignty in the Education Act of 2005. Paper presented at the 37th annual National Indian Education Association Conference, Anchorage, Alaska, October 19–22.

Torre, M. E., & Fine, M. (2003). Youth researchers critically reframe questions of educational justice. *Evaluation Exchange, 9*(2), 6, 22.

Torre, M. E., & Fine, M. (2006). Researching and resisting: Democratic policy research by and for youth. In S. Ginwright, J. Cammarota, & P. Noguera (Eds.), *Beyond resistance! Youth activism and community change: New democratic possibilities for policy and practice for America's youth* (pp. 269–285). New York: Routlege.

Tuck, E. (Forthcoming). Trajectories for theory in the rhizome of researching back. In J. Anyon (Ed.), *Critical social theory and research in urban education* (in preparation).

Tuck, E., and the Collective of Researchers on Educational Disappointment and Desire (Forthcoming). PAR praxes for now and future change. In J. Cammarota & M. Fine (Eds.), *Revolutionizing education: Youth participatory action research in motion.* New York: Routledge.

Chapter 8 | Research as Solidarity

Corrine Glesne
Independent Scholar

Solidarity is horizontal. It respects the other person and learns from the other. I have a lot to learn from other people.

—Galeano, 1999

Oaxaca, Mexico, 2006

I was told to hold the candle with both hands at eye level. Nine more candles flickered on the altar. The *curandera*, the healer, was behind me, an unembodied voice that said, "The flames are moving, the soul is here. Whom have you called?"

"My brother," I answered.

"He is here. What do you want to tell him?" she continued.

"Tell him that…"

She interrupted, "You tell him. I am leaving the room so you can talk."

Tears streamed down my face as I held a conversation of sorts with my brother who had died over twenty years ago. At the point when I felt peace, the *curandera* returned and filled my hands with smoke from incense of copal and motioned for me to wash it over my head, neck, and shoulders, pushing what remained toward my feet.

"This life," she said, "is but a dream. When we grow up, we know this. We know we dream the dream."

Question: How Do We Know What We Know?

"How" seems to affect "what" we know, what we think we know, what we dream to know. Let's begin with considering how we've gone about knowing. Less than fifteen years ago, qualitative research was seen as the "alternative paradigm" (Guba, 1990). Historically rooted in anthropology, qualitative inquiry became more widespread through the context of civil rights and feminist movements. Although many of us were embracing this alternative paradigm that sought to reveal the range of experiences rather than a norm, technology and capital were working to homogenize the world in the image of the West.[1] Increasingly, however, Western ideologies are met with resistance as other cultures seek to maintain or regenerate their own perspectives of the "good life" (Esteva and Prakash, 1998). Western science is questioned as well, including the qualitative paradigm (Smith, 1999, Vidich & Lyman, 2000).

Here, I touch on four ways qualitative inquiry is resisted and suggest some alternative ethics to guide us in our research. My perspective has been shaped by interactions with Gustavo Esteva and people of southern Mexico, in particular, and with indigenous groups in India and New Zealand as well as by various scholarly works (i.e., Escobar, 1997; Esteva, 1987; Esteva & Prakash, 1998; Harding, 1998; Sachs, 1992; Smith, 1999). The generic "we" throughout the chapter refers primarily to Western social scientists, generally white, whose perspectives have dominated research acts.

First Resistance: Research Purpose

We tend to believe that a purpose of qualitative inquiry is to help us understand a social phenomenon. The more I experience, the more I wonder if I can ever fully understand anything. Presumption and arrogance often accompany our claims to understanding, which are partial at best (Lincoln & Denzin, 2000; Richardson, 2000). Perhaps we and those we do research with would be better served if a purpose were one of "solidarity."

Esteva (personal communication) paraphrases Zapatista Subcomadante Marcos[2] and tells international volunteers, "If you have come to help us, you can go home. If you have come to accompany us, please come. We can talk." Many of us are dismayed by economic, political, gendered, or racial inequities we perceive in different parts of the world and we want to do something. A primary motivator seems to be the need to make a difference and a belief that we can help. This belief tends to be grounded erroneously, however, on an assumption that others want to be and should be just like us, to live as we live in the United States (Illich, 1968). The desire to help co-occurs with the privilege of having the means and time to become involved in lives half way around the world. And it feeds on the addicting sensations of novelty and learning that, for many, are part of interacting in different cultures. Cross-cultural research involves similar motivations and sensations.

I think we can rephrase the advice of Esteva and the Zapatistas and caution, "If you want to research us, you can go home. If you have come to accompany us, if you think our struggle is also your struggle, we have plenty of things to talk." As researchers, we need to examine the sense of entitlement that often comes along with us into spaces not our own. A research purpose of "solidarity" helps make us do so. Solidarity implies working with others in a research endeavor determined by others' needs and perceptions in conjunction with our own.

Second Resistance: Data Collection through Participant Observation

To those who are observed, the process of an outsider noting actions and words is objectifying and often offensive. A group of young people with whom I was working in Mexico found troubling the actions of a young woman who came to "research" them. They granted permission, thinking she was coming to learn from them, but were upset when she mostly wanted to sit in their compound and note what she heard and saw. The way in which the woman set herself apart is not the only way to be a participant observer, but her actions demonstrated how alienating it is to be the recipient of another's gaze. The term "participant observation" is, itself, sometimes resisted because it suggests the "fly on the wall" approach. Tedlock (2000, p. 465) notes that the term is, after all, an oxymoron that urges engagement and distance, involvement and detachment. The decision to accompany, rather than to be a participant observer, works better in the solidarity model. Field notes are kept, generally written at the end of the day, but these notes become group documents, subject to discussion and mutual comment and learning.

Third Resistance: Data Collection through Individual Prestructured Interviews

In *Becoming Qualitative Researchers* (Glesne, 2006), I tell the story of staying in an indigenous village in India with a group of students with whom I was traveling as part of a year-long program in five different countries. Our first evening there, villagers met with our group: women with the women and men with the men. As usual, we—the outsiders—began the interaction with a series of questions. One student was doing a comparative research project focused on reproductive health and asked, "What kinds of problems do women have during childbearing?" Our interpreter suggested that instead, she ask each woman there to state how many children she had born and, of those, how many were living. One by one, the women answered, "I have borne seven children, three are living." "Five, two are alive." "Nine, four are still with me." Suddenly, the students had many more questions—Why had their children died? What happens when a child dies? Finally, a student asked the women if they had any questions for us.

The villagers turned our question around and asked us, at least twenty women of childbearing age, how many children we had had and how many had died. None of us had children. They wanted to know how many of us were married, because we were all beyond the age at which they marry. None of us were married.

They asked questions we hadn't considered asking of them—what songs we sang in the evenings, what dances we danced together. The only dance we could come up with that we all knew was the hokey-pokey.

Their questions of us helped us learn as much about the women and their lives as their answers to our questions. We also saw our own lives differently. The one-on-one interview used in many qualitative inquiries is a fairly recent construction that generally depends on the individualization of the self, rather than a "collective" self. We need to consider this when doing cross-cultural work and also ask how we can co-construct interviews and, in the process, co-construct knowledge.

Fourth Resistance: Data Interpretation through Preset Lenses

We may learn the language, hang out a year, talk with many people, and expand our horizons of knowing. Yet, it is difficult to break out of our Western categories of interpretation. For example, a focus of my work in Oaxaca became that of young peoples' interactions with the environment. At some point, after many discussions with different groups of youth, I'm told, "We don't really talk about the environment but about harmony." Previously, I had read about the importance of harmony in Oaxaca (Cohen, 1999; Nader, 1990). I had heard people talk about it just as I had also heard about *susto* or fright and its effects on health, about the *nagual* or animal allies, and about nature spirits of many kinds. Nonetheless, unconsciously, I kept assigning what I was reading and hearing and experiencing to my Western categories of people, animals, environment, religion or spirituality, etc. Hearing that phrase, "We don't really talk about the environment, but about harmony," I could suddenly see my categories and how, in Oaxaca, something else was going on, something quite different, something that did not segregate humans, nature, and spirits the way I was doing.

Our framework for understanding the world, our categories

for segmenting the world, are culturally determined mythologies (Panikkar, 1979) and difficult to see. In a solidarity research model, we would work to listen to and respect many different perspectives for understanding the world. This involves more than member checking or requesting the input of a confidant.

Question: What Ethics Practiced in non-Western Cultures Could Guide Us to Undertake Our Inquiries Differently?[3]

An Ethic of Community

A group of students and I were in Teotitlan de Valle in the central valley of Oaxaca. We spent a day with a group of women who card, spin, and dye wool that they weave into rugs, the mainstay of the village's economy. When it was lunchtime, the women led us into an adobe room in which tables had been set. At one end was an altar where the Virgin del Guadalupe joined photos of ancestors. As we were served beans and hand-made tortillas, one of the students asked about the room. "It was built before the Spanish came," a woman answered. "Our family has always lived here."

We, the wanderers, see lots of places with old histories. What we cannot completely fathom, however, is how being a part of those long histories would make us value things differently. I don't have a sense of allegiance to a place as Teotitlan villagers have, as many indigenous people throughout the world have. I don't have an allegiance to a community other than a widespread one of friends and family connected by the filaments of modern communication and travel. I don't have a vast extended family around me from which both rights and obligations flow. People in many parts of the world say that we from the United States are the homeless ones, those in need of pity.

Research as solidarity implies communal decision making rather than negotiating individual to individual. It implies being willing to take the time required for consensus if consensus is a practice there. It implies a willingness to become as much a part of a community as possible, with all the obligations and time that entails. And it implies that as researchers, we consider our academic communities and how our connections, constraints, and obligations there have implications for the people with whom we work.

An Ethic of Hospitality[4]

In New Zealand, each Maori community we visited hosted us on their *marae* or communal land and meeting house. Once welcomed officially through a call and response ceremony, we were fed amazing amounts of food and treated to songs and dances and stories of the *marae*, its history and current struggles—often involving access to land and rivers or combating effects of dams and other products of so-called development. They taught us how to harvest flax and weave simple baskets. They fed us more, sang to us more, and told us more stories long into the night. People gave freely of themselves and what they had.

This was a pattern that we became accustomed to in our travels. I try to find equivalents in the United States in which a community bestows such hospitality to invited strangers. Many U.S. communities are large and unconnected. Often, we don't know who lives next door. It is more likely to be an organization such as a church or school that would host a group. These organizations arrange for food (often catered) and set up tours of local sites, but do members spend unorganized time with the visiting group as well, sharing of themselves and what they possess? Some do, I'm sure, but in general, our society is more grounded in economic exchange than in hospitality.

What would an ethic of hospitality look like in our research acts? We are often met with hospitality, and we need to ask how we are hospitable in return. If our research is "in solidarity" with others, then we can give freely of ourselves in the research process. We can share what it is that we can do, not as an imposition, but as service determined in conjunction with others. We also have an obligation to be hospitable in our home communities, in our scientific disciplines, to many different voices and ways of coming to know.

First Concluding Question: What Are the Homographic Equivalents to Research?

A "homograph" is a word that is spelled the same way as one or more other words but is different in meaning, origin, and sometimes pronunciation as in "bow," to bend, and "bow," a decorative knot. I'm wondering what concepts get translated as "research" or are seen as synonyms for research, but are not procedural equivalents.

All communities learn and integrate new technologies. Sandra Harding (1998) discusses how "sciences (plural) and their cultures co-evolve" (p. 3). She states, "The distinctive ways that cultures gain knowledge contribute to their being the kinds of cultures they are; and the distinctiveness of cultures contributes to the distinctively 'local' patterns of their systematic knowledge and systematic ignorance" (Harding, 1998, p. 3). I want to know about these different patterns of systematic knowledge practiced in countries throughout the world and think about how they might inform us as qualitative researchers.

Second Concluding Question: What Happened in That Hour and a Half with the *Curandera* in Oaxaca?

I went for a *limpia*, a cleansing. I did not know she would call in spirits. She had not done so with a friend who had gone to her, and it had never happened before in other cleansings that I have experienced. Was my brother's spirit there? The whole time I was talking to him, part of my head was saying, "This is ridiculous, this is a finely produced psychological/emotional catharsis." Yet, simultaneously, I was noticing something else. When the *curandera* returned, I said, "I felt my grandmother here, too."

How do we know what we know?

Notes

1. The term "West" is problematic, as is the use of "North." Probably a better term would be the "One-Third World" (Esteva & Prakash, 1998, pp. 16–17), referring to the economically and politically dominant groups that make up a minority of the world's population, no matter the geographical location. I use "West/Western," however, because it has come to connote European and European American dominant thought and practices.

2. Esteva (personal communication) quotes Subcomadante Marcos as saying, "If you have come to help a group of poor Indians in struggles against a bad government, thanks, but no thanks. If you think that our struggle is also your struggle, please come. We have plenty of things to talk."

3. For further discussion on this topic, see Martin and Glesne (2002).

4. See Esteva and Prakash (1998) for their discussion of hospitality and its role in the dynamics of radical pluralism.

References

Cohen, J. (1999). *Cooperation and community: Economy and society in Oaxaca.* Austin: University of Texas Press.

Escobar, A. (1997). The making and unmaking of the Third World through development. In M. Rahnema & V. Bawtree (Eds.), *The post-development reader* (pp. 85–93). New York: Zed Books.

Esteva, G. (1987). Regenerating people's space. In S. Mendlovitz & R. Walker (Eds.), *Towards a just world peace* (pp. 271–298). London: Butterworths.

Esteva, G., & Prakash, M. S. (1998). *Grassroots post-modernism: Remaking the soil of cultures.* New York: Zed Books.

Galeano, E. 1999. Interview by David Barsamian. *The Progressive.* Available online at http:www.progressive.org. Accessed March 12, 2006.

Glesne, C. (2006). *Becoming qualitative researchers*, 3rd ed. Boston: Pearson Allyn & Bacon.

Guba, E. (Ed.). (1990). *The paradigm dialog.* Newbury Park, CA: Sage.

Harding, S. (1998). *Is science multi-cultural? Postcolonialisms, feminisms, and epistemologies.* Bloomington: Indiana University Press.

Illich, I. (1968). To hell with good intentions. Address given at the Conference on InterAmerican Student Projects, Cuernavaca, Mexico, April.

Lincoln, Y. S., & Denzin, N. K. (2000). The seventh moment: Out of the past. In N. K. Denzin & Y. S. Lincoln (Eds.), *Handbook of qualitative research*, 2nd ed. (pp. 1047–1065). Thousand Oaks, CA: Sage.

Martin, P., & Glesne, C. (2002). From the global village to the pluriverse? "Other" ethics for crosscultural qualitative research. *Ethics, Place and Environment*, 5(3), 205–221.

Nader, L. (1990). *Harmony ideology: Justice and control in a Zapotec mountain village*. Palo Alto, CA: Stanford University Press.

Panikkar, R. (1979). *Myth, faith and hermeneutics: Cross-cultural studies*. New York: Paulist Press.

Richardson, L. (2000). Writing: A method of inquiry. In N. K. Denzin & Y. S. Lincoln (Eds.), *Handbook of qualitative research*, 2nd ed. (pp. 923–946). Thousand Oaks, CA: Sage.

Sachs, W. (1992). One world. In W. Sachs (Ed.), *The development dictionary: A guide to knowledge as power* (pp. 102–115). New York: Zed Books.

Smith, L. T. (1999). *Decolonizing methodologies: Research and indigenous peoples*. New York: Zed Books.

Tedlock, B. (2000). Ethnography and ethnographic representation. In N. K. Denzin & Y. S. Lincoln (Eds.), *Handbook of qualitative research*, 2nd ed. (pp. 455–486). Thousand Oaks, CA: Sage.

Vidich, A., & Lyman, S. (2000). Qualitative methods: Their history in sociology and anthropology. In N. K. Denzin & Y. S. Lincoln (Eds.), *Handbook of qualitative research*, 2nd ed. (pp. 37–84). Thousand Oaks, CA: Sage.

Part III
Performing Ethics

Chapter 9 | Performative Writing

The Ethics of Representation in Form and Body

Ronald J. Pelias
Southern Illinois University, Carbondale

Performative writing, like other modes of qualitative inquiry, makes a bid as an alternative form of scholarly research. Such a bid often works by definitional opposition to positivist, objectivist logics that, as the argument goes, remain trapped in the Cartesian mind/body split. Work that is not qualitative is often called out as being cold and heartless, unreflective, unreadable and unread (boring), misguided, elitist, unethical, or simply wrong headed. Such name calling may seem a caricature when one remembers that objectivists operate from a desire to minimize, but not deny, the influence of researchers on those they study, to privilege others at the expense of themselves, and to predict so that they might take reasoned actions in the world. The "devil," dressed in such clothing, may not be as frightening a figure as qualitative researchers often suggest. Qualitative scholars feel that what is driving the uneasiness most likely comes from the devil's rejection of their claims to legitimacy. Earning legitimacy, however, does not have to come by constituting a devil and then calling for its demise. I would rather not make the case for qualitative inquiry in oppositional terms, although I have done so in the past (Pelias, 1999, 2004). Suffice it to say that I believe qualitative scholars proceed in a different way, a way that offers insights into human behavior and works on behalf of social justice. If I am correct, I am happy to be engaged in this line of scholarship. In particular, I have found performative writing a most appealing and productive research strategy.

This chapter, however, is not a celebration of performative

writing, although I remain ready to toss the confetti at the performative writing dance. Instead of tossing confetti, I take this opportunity to tell a cautionary tale in the back corner of the performative writing festivities. My design is not to spoil the performative writing party, but to enhance its ethical practice. This cautionary tale, then, is an inquiry into the ethics of performative writing but without any desire to stop the celebration. It locates performative writing by outlining its definitional complexities before identifying a number of ethical issues about performative writing as a representational form. I end the chapter with a performative writing oath. I see it as a personal guide and as an invitational call for ethical practice. Much of what I have to offer can be applied equally well to a number of other associated forms. As I make my case, I quote researchers who speak directly to performative writing, those who would encompass performative writing under their own labeling, and those who may feel uncomfortable with my application of their ideas. To the last group, I apologize and hope that my borrowing is seen as a tribute to the productivity of their offerings.

Locating Performative Writing

Performative writing is a slippery term, in part because it resists its own containment. It is always writing and performing its way against satisfied representations. At its core, performative writing is an intervention in the crisis of representation. The intervention may stake its claim as a better, but never complete, form of representation, as an ongoing critique of representation's seduction, or as a continual, but never attainable, effort to escape language's hegemonic force. Despite this commonality, scholars, who have wed these two close, but at times squabbling, writing, and performing cousins, remain unsure of their own enunciation. "Performative" emerges as the contested cousin, even though "writing" carries its own troublesome history. Two differing, but not incompatible, conceptions of "performative" are prevalent, one that privileges "performative" as an adjective and the other that underlines it as a noun.

As an adjective, "performative" qualifies writing, telling

what kind of writing is operative. In this usage, the page becomes a place where a performance can happen, where a writer can present for consideration a self speaking from the body, evocatively. The performance on the page parallels a performance on stage. It offers a bodily staging of a speaker—conceived variously—who engages personal, relational, cultural, historical, and political phenomena. Through monologue or dialogue, it makes present its topic, notes its investment, and is reflective and reflexive about its own workings. This ludic enterprise lives in the subjunctive, the "as if" (Turner, 1982, pp. 82–84), always holding itself up as a possibility. It "stands in" (Wilshire, 1982) for those who audience, offering language they may or may not claim as resonant. As it calls on the sensuous, the figurative, and the expressive, it is simultaneously confidant in and skeptical of language's abilities. Its speakers command, order, and trust in their linguistic constructions as well as mock, reject, and wrestle with their own efforts.

As a noun, "performative" is a speech act that accomplishes what it says (Austin, 1980). In this sense, language is a constitutive action, a productive mechanism that can reify and dismantle ongoing normative logics. Language, always repetitive and reiterative, is an obstinate discursive system, but it allows space for alternative possibilities, for disrupting the conventional and taken-for-granted, and for substantive change. As an utterance participating within or against performativity, a performative, then, is always partial and material. Its partiality speaks to its inadequacy; its materiality recognizes its force. When working to disturb and alter the normative, the performative labors in excess, engages in an ongoing play between presence and absence, and, in the doing, becomes a material intervention.

Thinking of "performative" as an adjective and a noun implies an emerging set of procedural precedents or stylistic conventions associated with performative writing. In this chapter, I rely on four organizing features of performative writing to begin the discussion of the ethical issues related to the form. I deploy the labels embodied, evocative, partial, and material as defining characteristics. Such a generic move may permit some organizational tidiness, but it obscures performative writing's power to perform against its own established boundaries. This reminder is in keeping with Pollock's (1998) caution before giving her own list (evocative, metonymic, subjective, nervous, citational, and consequential) of the "descriptive/prescriptive, practical/theoretical" characteristics of performative writing. She notes her intent is "to map directions/directives for performative writing without foreclosing on the possibility that performance may—at any moment—unhinge or override its claims" (Pollock, 1998, pp. 80–81). I use embodied, evocative, material, and partial in the same spirit, recognizing that the ethical issues discussed below are both prevalent and provisional.

The Ethics of Performative Writing's Form

Embodied

Performative writing's call for embodied speech is a bid to make the body relevant, a recovery gesture designed to intervene in the mind/body split. It asks the body to stand in for a number of perceived absences in traditional research practices. In general, the body is solicited to bring forth the researcher's presence. As Spry (2001) notes, "Performative writing composes the body into being. Such a praxis requires that I believe in language's representational abilities, thus putting my body at (the) stake" (p. viii). This interpellated presence takes four primary, and at times, combined forms, each carrying ethical pitfalls.

First, the body becomes a *troubling presence* by acknowledging that all claims are filtered, positioned, subjective, located in interaction, historical, cultural, and so on. The troubling presence is a nervous one, always questioning its own assertive rights, always reminding listeners to be leery of its claims, always turning back on itself to inquire: What, if anything, do I really know? What, if anything, can I claim without doing harm? The troubling presence emerges as humble, self-conscious, and self-effacing. In its reflexive move, however, it may take more space than it ethically requires or deserves. Those who encounter such accounts may wish researchers would simply get on with the claims they wish to make.

Second, the body is rendered as an *affective presence*. It is a container of our sensate and emotional beings. This affective presence speaks from and to the senses; it speaks of passions and feelings; it speaks from the heart. It offers a vulnerable self, exposed, presented bare for its personal and social curative value, for its articulation of a site for identification, and for its power as political intervention. The affective presence insists on its right to speak in its own register knowing that it may ridiculed, sacrificed, and dismissed. It finds comfort in Behar's (1996) claim that research "that doesn't break your heart isn't worth doing anymore" (p. 177). Such comfort, however, begs the ethical question of what should be told, of whose interests are privileged in the telling. It opens the door for those who would claim that the affective leads to self-indulgence, narcissism, and public therapy (Parks, 1998; Shields, 2000), to privileging self over others (Buzard, 2003; Hantzis, 1998; Madison, 2006), and to situating listeners into problematic stances (Terry, 2006). Such concerns, I believe, are misplaced. A more productive ethical question is what work is accomplished by an affective self.

Third, the body is brought forth as an *authentic presence*. As an authentic presence, it strives for an honest unfolding of self, a genuine display of the real, hidden self. The "true self" is there to be uncovered, probed, revealed. The authentic is what one deeply feels, what one seldom says. This construction carries the questionable assumptions that the authentic is found most fully in the hidden rather than in the typically shared, that the authentic is stable and unchanging, storied into coherence rather than always in flux and contingent, and that the authentic is something one possesses rather than something constituted in interaction. Regardless of how an authentic presence might be conceived, the ethical task reaches toward both self and other. As Guignon (2004) explains, "Authenticity is a personal undertaking insofar as it entails personal integrity and responsibility for self. But it also has a social dimension insofar as it brings with it a sense of belongingness and indebtedness to the wider social context that makes it possible" (p. 163). Embodied authenticity carries its greatest ethical force when it invites individual introspection as well as social deliberation and connection.

Fourth, the body emerges as a *political presence*. In doing so, it brings forward bodies that are marked differently, have been historically denied speech, and have been unrecognized and unacknowledged. The politically present body demands its rights in behalf of social justice, often placing itself at risk, often becoming a location where others can rally. It asserts its identity, claims its voice, refuses to back away. It also brings forward bodies that are familiar, normative, and privileged, in control of the legislative and material apparatus that makes their presence of little surprise. Such voices, if speaking on behalf of themselves, may seem selfish, unaware, calculating; if speaking on behalf of others, they may seem presumptuous, pedantic, and self-righteous. Making the body present is always a political act, raising the ethical questions of who gets to speak, who gets to speak for whom, and who should remain silent. Speaking for those who have been denied access can become an ethically silencing gesture. Failing to do so carries its own, more troubling, ethical risks.

These four presences articulate the body as a sensuous, originating center that situates speech in the felt, muscular, and somatic; as an identity marker, perhaps estranged, that requires personal and cultural negotiation; and as an authentic and truthful representation of self that can be deployed on behalf of oneself and others. When the body speaks as an originating center, it may assume that perception is direct, uncontaminated, untouched by historical and cultural circumstances. It may miss how the senses censor and contain. When it speaks as an identity marker, it stands in for others who may identify, but it places itself in danger. The self becomes vulnerable, subject to others' mercy and judgmental predilections, open to others' control and policing capabilities. The self emerges as "the person who …," a labeling that reduces the self into its identity claim. In some cases, the self is stigmatized, marked with suspect value and exposed to psychological and physical violence. As Ellis (2006) succinctly puts it, "You become the stories you write" (p. 20). Caught between the demand to tell and to be silent, the ethical choices weigh heavy on the body that performs its positionality. When the body speaks as an authentic representation of self, it reifies the mind/body spilt, exchanging the body for the mind. It forgets Gingrich-

Philbrook's (2001) reminder that "cast[ing] 'the body' as performative writing's champion and 'language' as logic's, pitting them against one another … we jeopardize the mutuality of language and the body" (p. 1). It forgets, as Gingrich-Philbrook says, "My body makes language. It makes language like hair" (p. 3). When the body speaks as a political agent, its advocacy always comes at personal, cultural, and perhaps legislative cost. It is engaged in an exchange of power.

Evocative

Performative writing resides in the evocative, housed as an expressive and provocative form. As an expressive form, it summons the creative, the imaginative. It claims literary status. Its bid for the literary comes not only by reference to the various critical norms of poetry, prose, drama, and creative nonfiction, but also insists that the evocative be coupled with the embodied, partial, and material for its critical criteria. In other words, performative writing is its own form. To the extent, however, that it reaches for the literary it may be productive to ask if creative practices lead performative writers to compose with an affinity for, to use Lockford's (1998) distinction, "true *to* experience" rather than "true *in* experience" (p. 217; emphasis in the original). If so, performative writing confronts the same charges that fabricated memoirs such as James Frey's *A Million Little Pieces* and Binjamin Wilkomirski's *Fragments* face. To knowingly misrepresent when under the contract of truth telling is unethical. This principle carries significant weight for performative writing, a form of scholarly writing. To lie intentionally is the equivalent of falsifying data.

The notion of truth and lies, however, may become the target of performative writing, particularly when truth and lies are linked to power. The expressive task is to call into suspicion easy comfort in any narrative. Such work often takes away what it gives through an ongoing process of constant deferral and proliferating excess. Afraid of exchanging one system of power with another, performative writers may offer what Gunn (2006) calls a "shit-text," a text that stands as an endless generation of possibilities, but none sufficient, except, I would argue, its own implicit assumption of its own value. Although such writing celebrates the possible in its often witty and playful uncovering, it is hard to know where ethically to land, to decide what ethical action should be taken. Even so, such expressive displays are often provocative.

As a provocation, it is critical and rhetorical, challenging the status quo and calling for action. It is a speech act, a performative with the potential to stir, dismantle, and proliferate discursive systems. Prodding, always trying to change the direction of the herd, it persuades by bringing forward alternative pastures for our consumptive needs. Its efficacy depends on the evocative power of language to present imaginative visions against performativity's ongoing reiterations. The ethical burden, particularly given its playful textuality in constituting possibilities, is to become a counter-force, an animating center for social intervention. It runs the risk of never pointing beyond itself.

Partial

Performative writing recognizes that regardless of the number of possibilities one might generate, all accounts are partial, incomplete. There will always be slippages, gaps, and hauntings in any claim one might wish to make. Performative writing attempts to speak to those slippages, gaps, and hauntings by offering selves who, following a concentrated consideration of who they story themselves to be, are willing to stand by and question their commitments in the social world. As they do so, they write themselves and others.

Writing themselves, they construct speakers who, in their best renderings, are open, inquisitive, empathic, cautious, dialogic, and committed to social justice. In their worst articulations, they may appear disgruntled (nothing is right with the world), arrogant (my position is the only correct position), and saintly (see the good I do in the world). Equally problematic, a speaker will seldom appear who is unlikable, insincere, or unsympathetic, even when the speaker tells about his or her own social or moral inadequacies. Such limiting representations miss the potential, as Hoagland (2003) suggests, that "there is truth-telling, and more, in meanness" (p. 13). Hoagland desires a space where "the decency of the speaker" (p. 13) is not a predetermined or mandatory compositional strategy.

Writing others, like writing oneself, is always an exercise in partiality and always ethically inflected. Doty (2005), in discussing the memoir, offers an instructive summary of what is at stake:

> My picturing will distort its subject. ... This particular form of distortion—the inevitable rewriting of those we love we do in the mere act of describing them—is the betrayal build into memoir, into the telling of memories. ...The lives of other people are unknowable. Period. I wouldn't go so far as a poet colleague of mine who says that "representation is murder," but I would acknowledge that to represent is to maim. [p. 17]

He then adds, "But the alternative, of course, is worse: are we willing to lose the past, to allow it to be erased, because it can only be partially known?" (p. 17). Performative writing is caught in the same negotiation: how does one negotiate the rights of others with the rights of the individual to formulate his or her story, particularly when the self is understood, not as autonomous, but as a relational being? The writer, possessing the power of the pen, may be at less ethical risk than others but should not be neglected in our ethical considerations. We might ask: with what rights do writers write? Having raised that question, I want to turn to four ethical issues in the representation of others.

First, informed consent, the standard requirement of institutional review boards, is an essential but insufficient step. As Denzin (2003) rightly remarks, "Obtaining a person's signature on an informed consent form is not the same as demonstrating true respect" (p. 252). Participants, after giving their initial approval, may have recognize that they have agreed to more than they bargained for, may feel trapped by the emergent interpersonal relationship that at times develops between participants and researchers, or may decide that their participation requires disclosures they are uncomfortable making. Whatever the reason, following Ellis's (2006) counsel to engage in ongoing participant checks or even to consider co-constructed narratives is ethically sound. But even when researchers operate with such careful consideration, participants are unlikely to be aware of how they might feel once a piece receives response from an external audience. Anticipating the consequences of being rendered a particular way is at best difficult. Such was the case, for example, for the South Carolina students who appeared in the mock-documentary film, *Borat: Cultural Learnings of America for Make Benefit Glorious Nation of Kazakhstan*. Initially, they gave their consent and accepted payment for their participation, but after seeing how they were perceived, they filed a lawsuit. The lawsuit reads that the film "made plaintiffs the object of ridicule, humiliation, mental anguish and emotional and physical distress, loss of reputation, goodwill and standing in the community" (CNN.com, 2006). Such responses typically come, not in negotiation with researchers, but from viewing reception. Helping participants understand how their renderings might be seen becomes a researcher's obligation.

Second, negotiating facts when representing others is tricky business. As Eakin (2004) notes, criticism comes to writers "for not telling the truth" as well as "for telling too much truth" (p. 3). "Not telling the truth" and "telling too much" have a number of permutations. Intentional deception, as noted above, is a problematic stance for researchers. But the principle is not always easy to follow. Sometimes, researchers fail to tell the truth by omission. Such lies are often motivated by good reason—denied consent, fear of harming others, ideological sensitivity. Such reasons are no small matters but do not escape the problem of representing others in less than full light. Noting what cannot be told may at least make the light a bit brighter. Other times, researchers hide behind the production of truth (i.e., since "X" really happened, I am not responsible for the consequences of sharing it). Because a tale may be true, however, does not mean it serves a productive purpose in the world. It begs the question of how researchers should write with or against, partial though it may be, the discursive systems they confront.

Third, representations invite identification. This invitation may allow others to find their own voice and to take political action, but it may also permit false associations and lessened obligations. Constructing texts that essentialize attributes may encourage false associations by suggesting that the target audience shares the same position as the speaker. Duped into believing that the speaker is one of them, they allow the speaker to do their work, to become their surrogate, to shoulder their responsibilities. Their identification is too easily claimed. Just as easily, identification may be too quickly dismissed. The reluctance or refusal to associate, to claim alliances, diminishes membership in the human community and weakens political will. Given such potential responses, performative writers should both establish commonality and demonstrate individuality. This charge is not only ethical but also fosters good writing. Representations also invite "disidentification" (Muñoz, 1999). Such is the case when writers offer a portrayal that audiences see enough similarities to recognize themselves but reject the depiction as fully resonant. Again, the ethical burden is to write toward marking commonality and specifying individuality.

Fourth, the failure to portray and the frequency of representation of others also lead performative writers to additional ethical considerations. People who are not rendered in a given account may feel slighted, surprised, or suspicious that the writer did not see their presence as essential to the tale. Some may wonder why a writer has not considered their relationship worthy of written commentary, particularly in situations in which they understand their relationship as close. Others may believe that they are occupying more space in a writer's work than they desire or merit. In extreme cases, they may feel that they are being stalked by the pen. Who to include and to what degree and who to omit in a given account requires relational and ethical consideration.

Do no harm, the common ethical adage offered to those who represent others, is not an easy task and begs the question of how harm might emerge. Partial renderings cannot be escaped but solipsism is not the corrective. Representation demands, more than anything else, an empathic sensibility, a move toward others that is relationally figured and practiced with compassion. As Doty (2005) suggests, writing "becomes, unexpectedly, an empathic adventure, a quest for trying to see into the lives of others. Even if such a 'seeing into' is by nature partial, an interpretive fiction, it's what we have" (p. 20). The simple but insufficient advice—don't share anything about a person you wouldn't share if that person were present—assumes an ethical desire and insists that empathy is the first mandate for ethical responsibility.

Material

Performative writing has consequences. It is taken in, processed, used. It carries a material force. Calling on the performative to pull against performativity's weight, it is both a material substance that locates its presence and an action in the world that articulates the unsaid, unnoticed, and unquestioned. It languages potential, by promising alternatives and propagating prospects. In this way, it is a "mobilizing praxis" that intervenes in language's endless deferral by "materializing possibility" (Pollock, 1998, p. 96). It pushes the unseen into the real, offering utopian visions and pedagogical exemplars. As a pedagogical practice, it turns "the performative into the political … allow[ing] us to dream our way into a militant democratic utopian space" (Denzin, 2003, p. xiii). Such a critical performative pedagogy is, as Alexander (2005) explains, "radical and risky—radical in the sense that they [performative methods] strip away notions of a given human condition, and risky in that our sense of comfort in knowing the world is made bare" (p. 425). Performative writing embraces this risk in the name of social justice.

The desire for social justice, however, may require more than articulating possibilities. Opening possibilities may allow for action but may not be of much help to the transvestite who walks down the wrong street, the person of color who wants a quality school for his or her children, or the Sudanese people who daily confront genocide. Possibilities, in such situations, are a weak helping hand; they are necessary and productive but, in many cases, insufficient to alter material circumstances. Short of fostering legislative change, writing, no matter how provocative, may seem empty. Writer D. W. Fenza (2006) offers a chilling reminder:

> While intellectuals of the right engineered the conservative control of the House, Senate, White House, federal budget, tax codes, state courts, federal courts, news media, public opinion, and a few foreign nations, intellectuals of the left seized control of the Norton anthologies. Never before in the history of liberalism have so many words been spilled to accomplish so little. [p. 32]

Perhaps performative writers have settled for their own

righteousness, finding too much comfort in the utopian language of social justice, care, and hope. Such abstractions, unless made concrete, may be good rallying calls but transform little.

I complete this discussion of the ethical issues surrounding performative writing without explicitly describing the ethical principles guiding my concerns. These concerns take their roots in Denzin's (2003), Alexander's (2005), Conquergood's (1991), Madison's (2005), Ellis's (2006), and others' calls for ethical practice. Based on their foundations, my desire has been to write in their spirit. I end this chapter with a performative writing exercise designed to make evident my ethical convictions implied throughout by my questioning and demanding claims.

A Performative Writing Oath for Ethical Performative Writing

I must write.

I must write naming and unnaming and, then, name again. Language is my most telling friend, my most fierce foe. I must write knowing that categories collapse without details and details contaminate containment. I must write with promises I cannot keep. I must write with hope in my failure.

I must accept that with every utterance I am guilty. Power lurks, will grab me at every turn. I must stare it down, write it down.

I must write a body, mine. I must write from my bruises and scars, from my skin that once was touched, from my demanding mouth.

I must trouble my body until its language tells more than it should.

I must identify myself so that I might turn on myself. I am implicated, always under suspicion, accused. The privilege of position offers no protection—neither a majority nor minority posture pulls a free pass. I must remember others deserve their turn.

I must let my body speak with its heart exposed. I must be raw, raucous, rabid. I must rage, razor sharp. I must cry out, cry in. Then, I must ask the reason. I must be sure I can deal with the mess after I spill my guts.

I must body myself next to others so that we move together, muscle together. I must feel the ache, the joy. I must speak while holding another's hand. I must let others tell me if I am sincere.

I must put my body where it needs to be, must know when it should be removed, ridiculed, revoked.

I must demand literature's presence; cheer and fear its seductions. I must figure the fictive for what it is. There is no telling the truth. There is only knowing the lie.

I must allow myself to enter, to see the possible. I must imagine what is not there, what seems to haunt, what needs a creative tug on language's sleeve.

I must provoke by pointing to power and must stand with authority. Then, I must question my power by pointing. I must consider defending my territory by inviting my enemies in, by offering what I can.

I must display myself, pants up or down, without arrogance. Even if I am right today, tomorrow I will be wrong. I must display myself without doing damage to myself, to others. I must display myself without delicacy, disguise, or delusion. I must disrobe the personal.

I must protect those I write as I protect the truth of my writing. If anyone must be sacrificed, I must sacrifice myself. I must do no harm, unless I must, and I must as I manage my motives, maneuver my methods, and market my ideas.

I must invite identification, empathy. I must call for the utopian us. I must beware of its dangers—slippery alliances sliding by substance, imposition of dominant positions, a tear substituting for social action. I must not let its dangers stifle me. It is my only chance for connection.

I must be responsible for my words—they break bones. I must sentence my way until my words might heal.

I must perform to accomplish what I believe, even if my belief is momentary, even if belief is all I have. I must perform feeling, for the sake of the felt. I must perform for the heart's reasons. I must perform to make a difference.

I must act. I must act without delay. Each word declares my death. I must act as if this were my last chance. I must build my legacy in sweat, in the street. I must make haste. I am falling away.

    I must be suspicious of this oath.

References

Alexander, B. K. (2005). Performance ethnography: The reenacting and inciting of culture. In N. K. Denzin & Y. S. Lincoln, (Eds.), *Handbook of qualitative research*, 3rd ed. (pp. 411–442). Thousand Oaks, CA: Sage.

Austin. J. L. (1980). *How to do things with words*. New York: Oxford University Press.

Behar, R. (1996). *The vulnerable observer: Anthropology that breaks your heart.* Boston: Beacon Press.

Buzard, J. (2003). On auto-ethnographic authority. *The Yale Journal of Criticism, 16*(1), 61–91.

CNN.com. (2006). Humiliated frat boys sue over "Borat" portrayal. Available online at http://www.cnn.com/2006/SHOWBIZ/Movies/11/10/film. boratlawsuit.ap/index.html. Accessed November 25, 2006.

Conquergood, D. (1991). Rethinking ethnography. *Communication Monographs, 52*(1), 179–194.

Denzin, N. K. (2003). *Performance ethnography: Critical pedagogy and the politics of culture.* Thousand Oaks, CA: Sage.

Doty, M. (2005). Return to sender: memory, betrayal, and memoir. *The Writer's Chronicle, 38*(October/November), 15–21.

Eakin, P. J. (Ed.). (2004). *The ethics of life writing.* Ithaca, NY: Cornell University Press.

Ellis, C. (2006). Telling secrets, revealing lives: Relational ethics in research with intimate others. *Qualitative Inquiry, 12*(1), 1–27.

Fenza, D. W. (2006). Advice for graduating MFA students in writing: The words and the bees. *The Writer's Chronicle, 38*(May/Summer), 30–35.

Gingrich-Philbrook, C. (2001). Bite your tongue: Four songs of body and language. In L. C. Miller &. R. J. Pelias (Eds.), *The green window: Proceeding of the Giant City Conference on Performative Writing* (pp. 1–7). Carbondale: Southern Illinois University.

Guignon, C. (2004). *On being authentic.* New York: Routledge.

Gunn, J. (2006). Shittext: Toward a new coprophilic style. *Text and Performance Quarterly, 26*(1), 79–97.

Hantzis, D. (1998). Reflecting on "a dialogue with friends": Performing the "other/self" OJA 1995. In S. Dailey (Ed.), *The future of performance studies: Visions and revisions* (pp. 203–206). Annadale, VA: National Communication Association.

Hoagland, T. (2003). Negative capability: How to talk mean and influence people. *American Poetry Review, 32*(March/April), 13–15.

Lockford, L. (1998). Emergent issues in the performance of a border-transgressive narrative. In S. Dailey (Ed.), *The future of performance studies: Visions and revisions* (pp. 214–220). Annadale, VA: National Communication Association.

Madison, D. S. (2005). *Critical ethnography: method, ethics, and performance.* Thousand Oaks, CA: Sage.

Madison, D. S. (2006). The dialogic performative in critical ethnography. *Text and Performance Quarterly, 26*(4), 320–324.

Muñoz, J. E. (1999). *Disidentifications: Queers of color and the performance of politics.* Minneapolis: University of Minnesota Press.

Parks, M. (1998). Where does scholarship begin? *American Communication Journal, 1.* Available online at http://acjournal.org/holdings/vol1/Iss2/special/parks.htm. Accessed October 1, 2002.

Pelias, R. J. (1999). *Writing performance: Poeticizing the researcher's body.* Carbondale: Southern Illinois University Press.

Pelias, R. J. (2004). *A methodology of the heart: Evoking academic and daily life.* Walnut Creek, CA: AltaMira.

Pollock, D. (1998). Performative writing. In P. Phelan & J. Lane (Eds.), *The ends of performance* (pp. 73–103). New York: New York University Press.

Shields, D. C. (2000). Symbolic convergence and speech communication theories: Sensing and examining dis/enchantment with theoretical robustness of critical autoethnography. *Communication Monographs, 67*(4), 392–421.

Spry, T. (2001). Preface. In L. C. Miller &. R. J. Pelias (Eds.), *The green window: Proceeding of the Giant City Conference on Performative Writing.* Carbondale: Southern Illinois University.

Terry, D. P. (2006). Once blind, now seeing: Problematics of confessional performance. *Text and Performance Quarterly, 26*(3), 209–228.

Turner, V. (1982). *From ritual to theatre: The human seriousness of play.* New York: Performing Arts Journal Publications.

Wilshire, B. (1982). *Role playing and identity: The limits of theatre as metaphor.* Bloomington: Indiana University Press.

Chapter 10 | Notes toward an Ethics of Memory in Autoethnographic Inquiry

Arthur P. Bochner
University of South Florida, Tampa

Language brings us together; it pulls us apart; it makes possible our fictions of the past, and our imaginings of the future.

—Annette Kuhn, 1995

I am forced to admit that memory is not a warehouse of finished stories, not a gallery of framed pictures. I must admit that I invented. But why?

—Patricia Hampl, 1999

Ernest Hemingway once remarked, "There is nothing to writing. All you do is sit down at the typewriter and bleed." This feeling of opening our veins is familiar to those of us who write personal narratives or autoethnography. To do our work, and do it well, we must dwell in the dialectical space of agony and pleasure. Some of that agony is born of the inadequacies of language. When we attempt to fit language to experience, we learn that there is always a cleavage between experience and words, between living through and narrating about, between the chaos and fragmentation of living a life and the smoothing orderliness we bring to it when we write, between what we remember *now* and what we can say took place *then*, between how we mourn and work through the past and what shape our grieving gives to our future. As if the suffering we felt in living through the experiences we want to write about were not enough, we bleed again as we try to put life and truth on the page. We bleed not so much because we have to relive, at least in our minds (and often in our bodies), the painful events of which we write, but because of the obligation we feel to produce a truthful account of the past.

The activity of remembering is an essential quality of autoethnography. I cannot write about events in my past if I don't remember them. Remembering something important, perhaps traumatic, I use my memory to arrive at some truth. The scars of past wounds linger and give me pause to ask what sort of truth is memory's truth and to what extent am I obliged to remember and use my memory in the service of healing.

Memory is presumed to be a kind of knowledge, like perception or understanding and, as Ricoeur (2004) observed, what really happened must continually concern me. Of course, my gravest obligation is not to lie. But the space between lying and telling the truth can be vast. If telling the truth is merely saying what I remember, then I have set the bar of obligation extremely low. Once the past was there, now it is gone. I want to be faithful to the past, but what I remember of my history is anchored by what summons me *now* to remember, and my memory is, in part, a response to what inspires my recollections.

Consider a brief example. My father dies suddenly of a heart attack and I am drawn back to memories of my childhood, my interactions with my father, my disappointments, and our misunderstandings (Bochner, 1997). My memory is contextualized by current circumstances. Looking back on my childhood—remembering—is a response to my father's death, and it is tied to the responsibility I feel to better understand the relationship we had when I was a child. My memory is punctuated by present events, and what I remember is addressed not only to my present desires but to the Other writ large—to my father—whose shadow hovers over my recollections. Am I remembering for him, or me, or for us? What purpose does my memory work serve?

These questions point to a pragmatist account of memory, which emphasizes how memory is used in the here and now and the personal and relational functions it can serve as well as a phenomenology of memory that emphasizes remembering as an activity that is always under the influence of the present. The present perspective or frame from which I look at the past *now* is something I must always contend with when I am engaged in the activity of remembering (Kerby, 1991).

In autoethnography and personal narrative, we must worry not only about the connection between the present *in which* we remember and the past *of which* we remember, but also the relation between what we remember happening in the past and the stories we tell about what happened—how we retell or recount the past. Our work as autoethnographers entails making stories, and this means we must find language that fits or coheres with the experiences we are recounting. Thus, autoethnography involves two kinds of interrelated work: (1) memory work and (2) story-making work. Both of these oblige us to fulfill certain responsibilities and thus draw us into the realm of what the Jewish philosopher Avishai Margalit (2002) calls an "ethics of memory."

For Margalit (2002, p. 7), an ethics of memory begins with the questions, "Are we obliged to remember people and events from the past?" and "If we are, what is the nature of the obligation?" According to Margalit (2002), memory is saturated with ethical issues but has very little to do with moral questions. I believe this distinction is particularly useful for the practice of autoethnography, which normally centers on intimate relationships, what Margalit (2002, p. 7) calls "thick relations." Our parents, friends, and lovers belong to the category of thick relations. Our connection to them is anchored in a shared past and tied to shared memories. Thin relations, on the other hand, are marked by distance and typifications, such as gender, race, and ethnicity. The two categories, thick and thin, draw attention to differences between those who are near and dear and those who are remote and largely unacquainted or unfamiliar to us.

The distinction between thin and thick relations can be helpful in clearing some of the confusion between ethics and morality. Margalit's (2002) view is that our thick relations, those near and dear to us, must be guided by ethics, whereas morality is left to regulate our thin relations. Thus, when we ask how much license we should have to tell stories that implicate others with whom we are or have been intimate, we enter the dominion of ethics, where questions of loyalty and betrayal cannot be avoided. It is one thing to write about such lofty topics as the human condition, the human community, or humanity; it is quite another to write about my father, my brother, or my lover. When it comes to intimate relations, memory is the glue that bonds us together; any consideration of ethics in personal narrative, memoir, or autoethnography must eventually come around to interrogating the workings of memory.

◊ ◊ ◊ ◊ ◊

Our personal narratives and autoethnographies are works of memory, stories about the past, and all such stories are made, not found. The work of memory begins with the activity of remembering, a working through and toward the past, making what has been absent come into presence. Kerby (1991) points out that the material of recollection, the content of what we remember, is like the product of an archaeological dig, a trace of the past always in need of interpretation. Terms such as "remembering" and "recollecting" remind us that the result of memory work always involves some transformation; it is not the past, only a form or representative of the past. Thus, we are engaged in the active remaking of the past, transforming *then* to *now*. Freud saw that the truth of the past could not be reached directly, but required a long and painstaking excavation of the traces, tokens, and images of the past (Brill, 1938) expressed through the activities of remembering and narrating. When we talk about memory as work, we recognize and signify that remembering is active and continual; it is personal, political, emotional, and relational. Memory is also a destination, a place we inhabit or revisit to question and reflect on the meaning of the past. Thus, memory is inquiry.

Even if we bracket the difficult challenge of grasping the truth in our memories, we still come up against the narrative challenge of finding language that is adequate to represent the past. Every survivor's story returns the survivor to the past, and every such story can be viewed as retroactive redescription and reexperiencing of human actions and behavior. The problem is not what we remember people doing; the problem is knowing what they actually did (Hacking, 1995). Usually, our narratives produce descriptions that attribute agency and intentionality to other peoples' actions. One critical issue, then, for an ethics of memory, is the attribution of intentionality and its connection to language. As Hacking (1995) observes, new ways of talking and new descriptions and terminologies are constantly evolving, and when they move into circulation in the culture they become available to you and to me; that is, new intentions become available and you and I come to live in a world of new opportunities.

The trouble is that we are constantly inventing new ways to be culturally sanctioned unhappy persons (Hacking, 1995). As Kenneth Gergen (1994) notes, Western culture is rife with vocabularies of psychological and social failure and these deficit discourses "add exponentially to the sense of human misery" (p. 143). The rub is whether we should be content to apply such new terms retrospectively and retroactively to actions and events that took place when these new ways of talking and describing were not part of the vocabulary or conceptual space of the day. Hacking (1995) refers to this as "semantic contagion," drawing attention to the cleavage between action and language that can result when we apply present modes of description to actions that took place a long time ago. The action I am describing may have taken place, but not the action under this description (Hacking, 1995). Here is where resistance and inquiry come into play. Even if we put aside the vexing question of the accuracy of our descriptions, shouldn't we at least be obliged to question or look into the desirability or utility of the terms we use to depict the intentions of the characters we depict in our stories and the consequences of their actions on our own lives?

This is an issue that I agonized over when I wrote "Narrative and the Divided Self," a story that told of my struggle in the aftermath of my father's death to understand the meaning of his volatile temper and violent behavior. In the story, I wrote a scene, vivid in my memory, that recounted one of dozens of episodes of violence. Here is a short excerpt from that scene:

> "Mike, stop. You'll hurt him," my mother shouts, grabbing at him, but he pulls away and she moves back. Doubled over from the force of his punch, I can't escape. He's too large; I'm too weak. The room is too small and too cluttered. I'm his prey, cornered

in his territory, and the fierce, frenzied look on his face shows he won't be denied. Now he moves in for the kill. Unbuckling his belt, he grabs me by the collar with one strong, meaty hand, and holds me tightly. Over and over and over again, he belts me with his strap. "I work like a slave, while you play! I'll teach you. You no good little liar. You'll learn." [Bochner, 1997, p. 426]

It didn't take much to provoke my father's rage and, looking back, I sometimes feel it's a miracle that I survived the beatings. After my father died, I needed to better understand his uncontrollable anger. I could have started by asking, "What turned my father into a child abuser?" But Hacking cautions against the impulse to place old actions under new descriptions He points out that "there is no canonical way to think of our own past. In the endless quest for order and structure, we grasp at whatever picture is floating by and put our past into its frame" (Hacking, 1995, p. 89). To say I was abused by my father would be to apply a term that was totally outside the interpretive structure of the community in which I was raised. If the men and women in my community were asked to account for such beatings, I could just hear them saying, "Abuse? Who knew abuse? We didn't know from abuse, we knew from discipline." Situating my father's violence within the cultural narrative of child abuse would be an act of semantic contagion, endowing my father's actions with meanings and intentions that weren't available at the time these events were lived.

The pertinent ethical question we must ask is, "Where do we draw the line between the terms we use to describe our ways of thinking about the meaning of one's actions *now*, and the intentions that motivated those actions *then*?" If I ask, "Did my father intend to abuse me" when I know that the idea and vocabulary of child abuse did not exist *then* in the ways in which we understand it *now*, then I am forced to consider that the meanings and intentions of his actions may be considerably less determinate, less certain than I may want to make them out to be. In the community in which I was raised, which included many Eastern European immigrants, parenting operated under the moral code that it was a father's responsibility to prepare his son for a harsh, cruel, unforgiving world.

Had my father known that one day his actions would be

called child abuse would he have acted the way he did? Not having the idea of child abuse was he deprived of choices, important choices, about how to behave toward his children? Did he lack the opportunity to decide not to behave in violent and enraged ways because the vocabulary that might have provided that choice did not exist at that time? And what about me; can I be a reliable and truthful narrator if I don't take into account that the actions that took place *then* are actions that did not take place under the terms I am inspired to apply to them *now* (largely because they are part of the vernacular, the prevailing deficit vocabulary of my time)?

My memory of events is my memory *now*; it is what I know and remember *now*, not what I knew *then* in the past; From an epistemic point of view, the most I can say is it is knowledge *from* the past and not necessarily knowledge *about* the past (Hacking, 1995). The point is not to question whether the events took place but rather to question whether the events under the descriptions we apply to them took place. We should not underestimate the complexity of this question. As time passes we rethink, redescribe, even refeel the past as part of our ongoing sense-making endeavors. When we make our stories, we have arrived at a conclusion about the past, some small truth that we want to establish about past events.

But making stories from one's lived history is a process by which ordinarily we revise the past retroactively, and when we do we are engaged in processes of languaging and describing that modify the past. What we see as true today may not have been true at the time the actions we are describing were performed. Thus, we need to resist the temptation to attribute intentions and meanings to events that they did not have at the time they were experienced.

I did not sit in my room after an episode of my father's rage and agonize over his abusive behavior; at the time, I did not think of myself as abused or of my father as an abuser. So, how accurate would it be for me to apply that vocabulary to his actions now? The point is that we need to think of actions in the past as being to a certain extent indeterminate. The rub is the impulse we may feel to make a good story, one that situates past actions in coherent narrative accounts, explanations, or interpretations that achieve a certain sort of narrative tightness by implying intentions and causal structures that give meaning to actions in the past. In our quest for self-understanding and desire to heal the wounds of the past, we may be faithful to our memories but at the same time unfaithful to our pasts (Hacking, 1995).

◊ ◊ ◊ ◊ ◊

As the work of autoethnography and personal narrative progresses, I expect we will focus increasingly on the ethics of memory and the connections between memory, experience, and language. We can benefit greatly, I think, from circumspect attention to memory work, taking an inquiring attitude toward how the past is constructed, reconstructed, and modified by, in, and through memory and language. Flaubert remarked that his use of language seemed "like a cracked kettle" on which he could hardly manage "to beat out tunes for bears to dance when all the time we are longing to move the stars to pity" (Zaner, 2004, p. xi). Those who have taken up the call to autoethnographic storytelling usually recognize how difficult it is to write or talk honestly about issues such as abuse, violence, sexuality, discrimination, harassment, pain, hurt, or anger, especially when the experiences being described are one's own, when the person in question is oneself. Tolstoy's Ivan Illych (Tolstoy, 1960) comes to mind, a character who Robert Blythe (1991) said, "had a coldly adequate language for dealing with another's death, but remained incoherent when it came to his own" (p. 10).

Skeptics might ask, "Does it really matter if what I say I remember really happened the way I say? Isn't it enough that it was more or less as I remember it?" If I'm supposed to pick up my wife at 4:00 and I thought she said 5:00, or to take my neighbor's son to soccer practice at 6:00 and it turned out to be 5:00, I'm going to anticipate certain consequences for getting it wrong. Of course, there is a scale of damage or hurt. If a woman cuts off all contact with her family because she wrongly remembered that her father abused her and her mother was complicit—she knew but remained silent—then certainly the family suffers grievous harm.

Some memories do more harm than others, and it is often difficult to untangle the false, deceptive, or protective memories from
those we might on further reflection or evidence call authentic.

Memory is not a video or DVD recording of the past and
even if it were, as recent legal history has shown, it would still
be vulnerable to multiple interpretations and sense-making processes. Like it or not, if we're honest we have to admit that our
memories shade, reconcile, and piece together; they delete, select,
and edit. Memory is not an archive or a repository. In many
respects, it is better to think of memory as a perspective or point
of view. In this respect, there is little difference between memory
and narrative. Like the tales we tell about the past, our memories
are not a recording of events and feelings. Memories are useful
to us, they have a pragmatic sense-making function, and acts of
remembering labor under the demand for coherence to the rest of
our lives, with the canonical stories in which we are enmeshed,
and with the creative process in which we use them to fashion
ourselves as characters who possess or gain self-understanding,
deem our life as good or worthy, and view our life story as the tale
of a person who has come to know him- or herself. This is to say
that remembering is akin to narrating (Ryle, 1949). Not unlike
narrative, memory is full of invention and rife with omission.
Both memory and narrative are, in part, workings of the imagination and works of fiction. This may seem a threat to the project of autoethnography, but I don't think so, especially if we see
our stories as inquiring into the meaning of the past. As Ricouer
(2004) observed, fictions can come closer to what really happened
(than historical narratives) because they go directly to the meaning beneath or beyond the facts. Besides, as Alice Walker (1998)
wrote, "The crucial distinction is not the difference between fact
and fiction, but the distinction between fact and truth. Because
facts can exist without human intelligence, but truth cannot" (p.
193). Or as Richard Rorty (1989) put it, "Where there are no sentences, there is no truth" (p. 5).

◊ ◊ ◊ ◊ ◊

I am not trying to undercut memory as a means of getting at some kind of truth of the past, but rather to caution that an ethics of memory obliges us to understand that the sort of truth to which we aspire in our memory work can never be unvarnished. When we write stories from our past, we necessarily engage in narrative smoothing, polishing and moralizing and we risk, as Hacking (1995, p. 254) warns, that "the colors with which we paint (may not have existed) when the episodes occurring in the scenes actually occurred."

Our memories should not be treated as transparent or authentic truths but as a certain sort of evidence that can be appreciated and interrogated, mined for meanings and feelings and opportunities to better understand the performances of memory as an expression of an indeterminate past. I would like to see autoethnography viewed as a genre of the performance of memory, a kind of staging of memory that invites further inquiry into the meaning of the past and its reconstruction through the inextricably integrated processes of languaging and remembering. To the extent we think of ourselves as interpretive ethnographers, we should view what is remembered and described about the past not as transparent accounts of events but as material for interpretation, inquiry, and engagement. Memory never provides unmediated access to the past as it was; indeed, memory work is itself a form of mediation, of rewriting, revising, remembering, and recounting. There is no fixed truth of the past to which we can gain access; everything we say and mean and make of the past is a form of revision.

But the idea of an indeterminate past should not be taken as a blight, criticism, or indictment of our work as narrative scholars or autoethnographers writing about intimate others. As Robert Coles (1989) remarked, "The beauty of a good story is its openness—the way you or I or anyone reading it can take it in and use it for ourselves" (p. 47). This view of storytelling should apply to the performance of memory in autoethnography—our memories produce traces of our past that we adoringly or not so adoringly preserve, defend, and protect. Our work is not about holding a mirror to the past through memory work, or about the authenticity of our memories. An ethics of memory calls us to the question of what we do with our memories, how we use traces to make stories that give meaning to our lives now and change who we can be in the future. The best and most ethical autoethnography invites and opens us to rethink the possibilities and meanings of human experience because it provides an open and malleable frame in which a person struggles to come to terms with an ever-changing, ever-reconstructed, and reconstituted reality, an indeterminate past marked by pain and suffering, and the struggle toward self-understanding.

There can never be a uniquely true, correct, or completely faithful autoethnography because the process of producing and constructing autoethnographic work is not to arrive at propositional truths of this sort. As Mark Freeman (1997) argues so persuasively in his development of the idea and ideal of narrative integrity, we are simply stuck with the reality that there is no life apart from the stories told about it, and there are no stories apart from the ethical realm. Narrative integrity and narrative truth thus rest in the conceptual space where autoethnographic identity converges with the ethical question of what it means to live a good and meaningful life. Desiring a healthy and ethical relationship to the past, the autoethnographer hikes down the trail of her memories, "not so much a survivor with a harrowing tale to tell as that older sort of traveler, the pilgrim, seeking, wondering" (Hampl, 1999, p. 37).

References

Blythe, R. (1991). Introduction. In L. Tolstoy, *The death of Ivan Ilyich* (p. 10). New York: Bantam Books.

Bochner, A. P. (1997). It's about time: Narrative and the divided self. *Qualitative Inquiry, 3*(4), 418–438.

Brill, A. (Trans.) (1938). *The basic writings of Sigmund Freud.* New York: Random House.

Coles, R. (1989). *The call of stories: Teaching and the moral imagination.* Boston: Houghton Mifflin.

Freeman, M. (1997). Death, narrative integrity, and the radical challenge of self-understanding: A reading of Tolstoy's *Death of Ivan Ilych*. *Ageing and Society*, *17*(4), 373–397.

Gergen, K. (1994). *Realities and relationships: Soundings in social construction.* Cambridge, MA: Harvard University Press.

Hacking, I. (1995). *Rewriting the soul: Multiple personality and the sciences of memory.* Princeton, NJ: Princeton University Press.

Hampl, P. (1999). *I could tell you stories: Sojourns in the land of memory.* New York: W.W. Norton.

Kerby, A. (1991). *Narrative and the self.* Bloomington: University of Indiana Press.

Kuhn, A. (1995). *Family secrets: Acts of memory and imagination.* London: Verso.

Margalit, A. (2002). *The ethics of memory.* Cambridge, MA: Harvard University Press.

Ricoeur, P. (2004). *Memory, history, forgetting.* Chicago: University of Chicago Press.

Rorty, R. (1989). *Contingency, irony, and solidarity.* Cambridge, UK: Cambridge University Press.

Ryle, G. (1949). *The concept of mind.* London: Hutchinson.

Tolstoy, L. (1960). *The death of Ivan Ilyich and other stories.* London: Penguin Books.

Walker, A. (1998). The site of memory. In W. Zinsser (Ed.), *Inventing the truth: The art and craft of memoir* (pp. 183–204). Boston: Houghton Mifflin.

Zaner, R. M. (2004). *Conversations on the edge: Narratives of ethics and illness.* Washington, DC: Georgetown University Press.

Chapter 11 | "I Just Want to Tell My Story"

Mentoring Students about Relational Ethics in Writing about Intimate Others[1]

Carolyn Ellis
University of South Florida, Tampa

"I just want to tell my story about taking care of mom and dad during their last days. Why do I have to get consent from others to do that?" a new student Jackie[2] asks, near tears. "My parents are dead, so they can't respond. My siblings can tell their own stories, if they want. We hardly talk about what happened. They're mad at me for taking control and I'm mad at them for not helping enough."

"When you write your story, by definition you also will be writing others' stories, including those of your siblings," I say.

"You didn't act in isolation. One of the main tensions you experienced as your parents were dying was your disagreement with your sister over whether or not to consent to certain medical procedures. It's not possible to leave others out of the story. When we write autoethnographic stories about our lives, by definition we also write about intimate others with whom we are in relationships. Don't we have responsibilities toward them?"

"How do I decide to whom I have responsibilities and what all they entail?" the student inquires. "And what if those I ask don't like the way I've written the story? Does that mean I can't publish it? That doesn't seem fair. What should I do?"

This vignette brings to the forefront some of the ethical issues that arise when we include our lives in our research and writing. Most of these issues are not acknowledged by institutional review boards (IRBs), which ground their guidelines on the premise that research is being done on strangers with whom we have no prior relationships and plan no future interaction. This is not the case in autoethnography (where we include others who already are in our lives), and usually not the case in ethnography (where we often have prior connections with participants or develop relationships with them in the course of our research). In these instances, the question of how to honor and respect our relationships with intimate others while being true to what we perceive to be the truth of our story is a difficult ethical issue with which researchers must grapple.

These ethical issues are complex and no simple mandate or universal principle applies to all cases. Authors' stories about how they made ethical decisions about relational others demonstrate that many researchers thoughtfully consider their options when confronted with issues of relational ethics (see, for example, Adams, 2006; Carter, 2002; Ellingson, 2005; Ellis, 1995b, 2001, 2004, 2007; Ellis et al. 2007 (this volume); Etherington, 2005, in press; Foster, 2007; Goodall, 2006; Jago, 2002; Kiesinger, 2002; Marzano, in press; Perry, 2001; Poulos, 2005; Rambo, 2005). Responses to these concerns include: not publishing the story, delaying publication until after the death of a person, publishing under a pseudonym, fictionalizing the story, using pseudonyms or no names for participants, deciding to publish without seeking approval from participants, seeking approval after the fact, working out with participants the story to be told and sometimes omitting or changing identifying details and problematic passages, adding multiple voices and interpretations, and seeking and successfully obtaining consent from those involved.

The ethical decisions are difficult and the choices many. Yet, similar to the speaker in my opening vignette, students who write personal narrative want to know, "How do I decide? What should I do?" In this chapter, I seek to address these questions by examining the discussions I have with students in mentoring sessions and classes when we talk about researching and writing about intimate others.

Relational Ethics

Relational ethics requires us as researchers to act from our hearts and minds, to acknowledge our interpersonal bonds to others, and initiate and maintain conversations (Bergum, 1998; Slattery and Rapp, 2003). The concept of relational ethics is closely related to an ethics of care (Gilligan, 1982; Noddings, 1984), communication ethics (Arnett, 2002), and feminist and feminist communitarian ethics (see Christians, 2000; Denzin, 1997, 2003; Dougherty and Atkinson, 2006; Olesen, 2000; Punch, 1994).

Slattery and Rapp (2003), after Martin Buber, describe relational ethics as doing what is necessary to be "true to one's character and responsible for one's actions and their consequences on others" (p. 55). Relational ethics recognizes and values mutual respect, dignity, and connectedness between researcher and researched, and between researchers and the communities in which they live and work (Lincoln, 1995, p. 287; see also Brooks, 2006; Reason, 1993; Tierney, 1993). Central to relational ethics is the question "What should I do now?" rather than the statement "This is what you should do now" (Bergum, 1998).

Relational ethics draws attention to how our relationships with our research participants can change over time. If our participants become our friends, what are our ethical responsibilities toward them? What are our ethical responsibilities toward intimate others who are implicated in the stories we write about ourselves? How can we act in a humane, nonexploitative way, while being mindful of our role as researchers? (Guillemin & Gillam, 2004, p. 264).

Howard Brody (1987) contrasts relational ethics to decisional ethics in patient care. Ethical decision making in an intensive care unit, he says, falls under the purview of decisional ethics, because it occurs between people without a prior history, who must carry out "discrete and generally predictable actions" over a limited time and who most likely will have no future interactions. In contrast, in a primary care physician's office, the parties involved plan to engage in a long-term relationship, their future actions and relationship are somewhat vague, and the maintenance of that relationship might be more important than particular behaviors (Brody, 1987, p. 172). Thus, in the decisional situation, the question addressed is likely to be: "Should I disclose this particular piece of information to this patient at this time?" The relational situation produces a series of relational questions, such as: "What

can I assume this patient already knows, judging from past discussions? On the basis of those same past discussions, what can
I assume he wants to know? What should I say now? How will I
judge how what I have said has affected the patient? What will be
my next opportunity to add to or modify what I will say, in light
of that reaction?" (Brody, 1987, pp. 172–173).

A similar set of issues emerges in research situations when
our participants are people we already know or people with whom
we develop close relationships. What can I assume is appropriate
for me to tell about my relationship with the participant in my
study and/or the person in my story? How will this person feel
about what I have said? Must I get this person's consent to write
my story? What if this person doesn't like or agree with the way
I portray what happened? Given our relationship, what are my
responsibilities to my participants? How will what I write affect
our relationship? Our success as researchers often depends on how
deeply we think about and how well we address these questions.

Even after many years of field research, autoethnographic
writing, teaching, and directing student research, these kinds of
ethical questions continue to swirl around me like a sand storm.
Just when I think I have a handle on a guiding principle about
research with intimate others, a student presents a new project and
my understanding unfurls into the intricacies, yes-ands, uniqueness, and ethical quandaries of the particular case under question.
Each choice has consequences, but choose we must. What, then,
do I tell students to help them move on and avoid sinking into the
quicksand of indecision?

What Do I Tell My Students?

First, I tell students that my experiences writing ethnography and
autoethnography have taught me that I have to live the experience
of doing research with intimate others, think it through, impro-
vise, write and rewrite, anticipate and feel its consequences. There
is no one set of rules to follow. As Arthur Frank (2004) says,

> We do not act on principles that hold for all times. We act as best
> we can at a particular time, guided by certain stories that speak to

that time, and other people's dialogical affirmation that we have chosen the right stories. ... The best any of us can do is to tell one another our stories of how we have made choices and set priorities. By remaining open to other people's responses to our moral maturity and emotional honesty ... we engage in the unfinalized dialogue of seeking the good. [pp. 191–192]

I tell my students to seek the good.

I tell them that "[t]he wisest know that the best they can do ... is not good enough. The not so wise, in their accustomed manner, choose to believe there is no problem and that they have solved it" (Malcolm, 1990, p. 162). I tell them to be wise and self-critical but not cynical.

I tell them to pay attention to IRB guidelines, then warn that their ethical work is not done with the granting of IRB approval. I tell them no matter how strictly they follow procedural guide lines, relational situations will come up in the field and in interviews that will make their heads spin and their hearts ache. I tell them they should make ethical decisions in research the way they make them in their personal lives. Then I caution them to question more and engage in more role taking than they normally do because of the authorial and privileged role that being a researcher gives them.

I tell them to ask questions and talk about their research with others, constantly reflecting critically on ethical practices at every step (Guillemin & Gillam, 2004; see also Canella & Lincoln, 2004; Mason, 1996). I tell them relationships may change in the course of research—that they may become friends with those in their studies—and to be aware that ethical considerations may change as well. Ethnographic and autoethnographic research are emergent.

I tell them that often relationships grow deeper over time, but sometimes they don't, and even when they get consent from those in their study, they should be prepared for new complexities along the way. I tell them to practice "process consent," checking at each stage to make sure participants still want to be part of their projects (Etherington, 2005; Grafanaki, 1996). I tell them that people change their minds, back out, don't want to talk to you or participate in your studies anymore. I tell them that sometimes along the way their research projects will change in character and that what they have told participants may no longer apply.

"Then what?" they ask.

"Then you have to make sure your participants still want to be in your research," I say.

"But what if they don't? What happens then?"

"You need to have back up plans," I tell them. "If you can't make what you're doing makes sense to those in your studies, maybe you ought to reconsider what you're doing." The students doodle on the blank pages in front of them. This is all too complicated.

"Perhaps including multiple voices and multiple interpretations in your studies will help," I tell them, offering a ray of hope.

My strategy works; their faces brighten. Then I caution them not to ask too much of participants who may get little out of being part of their study.

I tell them to think of the greater good of their research—does it justify the potential risk to others? Then I warn that they should be cautious that their definition of "greater good" isn't one created exclusively for their own good.

I tell them to think about ethical considerations before writing, but not to censure anything in the first draft to get the story as nuanced and truthful as possible. "Write for yourself," I say. Then, I warn, "Later, you must deal with the ethics of what to tell. Don't worry. We'll figure out how to write ethically. There are strategies to try. You might omit things, use pseudonyms or composite characters, alter the plot or scene, position your story within the stories of others, occasionally decide to write fiction."

I tell my students they should inform people they write about and get their consent. "People in our lives deserve their privacy," I say. "Because of their relationships to us, they often are identifiable in our stories."

"My brother abused me," says one student. "I wouldn't be comfortable asking for his consent. But I still want to write this story."

"Isn't your brother's side of the story relevant?"

"I'm sure it is, but not for my purposes," she says. "I need to write this story for me so that I can move on in my life, not work out with him what happened. That's another project."

Situations like these make me modify what I think. I don't think a focus on consent should stand in the way of a student doing a project that might help her heal and get on with life. I tell her we'll consider how to handle the ethics later, if she decides to publish this story.

I tell them that, whenever possible, they should take their work back to participants. "Write as if your participants will be in your audience," I say. "Don't hide behind our esoteric journals, thinking 'Oh, they'll never see it there.'" I tell them how a former professor took my book about the fisher folk into the community and read passages I wrote about how the people smelled like fish, had promiscuous sex, and couldn't read (Ellis, 1986). "Because many were illiterate, I had thought they would never see what I had written," I admit.

Then I tell the students that a similar thing occurred when I wrote about racism in my home town (Ellis, 1995c). "What happened?" they ask.

I tell them how a colleague in Tampa, an African American woman, moved to my home town, a thousand miles away, and shared the story I had written with the parents of my best friend from high school. "I never thought anybody there would find out about the story."

"Oh my," their raised eyebrows and tense postures convey. "Don't you know publications are public? Why would you ever think that way?"

Why indeed? I contemplate, hoping that my mistakes prod students to think more deeply about their research. "It's not that in hindsight I wouldn't have said any of these things or written these pieces," I tell them. "But I would have looked deeper and considered more fully what needed to be said, who needed to hear it, who might want to speak back, how I was implicated, and how best to explain others' lives given the cultural context in which the events occurred" (Ellis, 1995b).

These experiences guide my response to a student studying mental health teams that care for at-risk children and their parents (Davis, 2005). Cris writes in an e-mail,

I plan to publish my dissertation, and while I can pretty well presume that the mother won't be reading academic texts, what if she does? I offered to everyone on the team that they could read it, and she was the only one who didn't express an interest. What if she had? Should I have given her an edited version? How ethical is that? When I interviewed her, I never let on that I thought she and her home were "dirty," so how surprised would she be to find out what I really thought? Should I have been more candid? Would that have been more or less ethical? [Christine Davis, personal e-mail correspondence]

To Cris, I respond:

People never get over being called dirty. Rewrite the offending passages—try to show the dust and clutter without saying they're dirty. Concentrate on what in your life makes you so bothered by her living conditions and leads you to construct her as dirty. That will take away a little of the sting if she ever reads your dissertation. Assume everyone in your story will read it.

"We have to take responsibility for our own perceptions," I tell students, when I relay this experience.

"What does it mean to inform anyway?" I suddenly ask. The students stare at me blankly, as though the answer is obvious. Before they can respond, I tell them about omitting some of the passages that I thought might be hurtful when I read a story to my mother that I had written about her. They say nothing, but their eyes are wide with surprise. "Haven't you learned anything?" the expressions of some of the more critical students seem to ask.

"What was more important?" I ask. "That I could tell my colleagues I read every word to my mother, or that I protect the loving relationship she and I had and try to ensure my words caused her no pain?" When I put it that way, an entirely different answer seems obvious. They nod in understanding.

"What if those we write about give us their consent but don't fully comprehend what it means to be written about?" I ask then. "Though my mother gave me consent to publish the story I had written about her and I let her read the text before I published it, I'm not certain that she understood everything in the story, especially the details that indicated she was working class with little education."

"So was it right to publish this story then?" one asks.

I tell them:

> With each story I read her, each caregiving experience we had, my relationship with my mother grew deeper, more open, and more caring. As our feelings grew in the context of caregiving, we openly shared more of our selves with each other and this enabled me to feel more confident in my decisions about what was appropriate to tell. In this context, it felt right to reveal our life together even though my mother was not aware of every word I wrote nor every nuance in what it meant to be a main character in my tale. [see Ellis, 2001, p. 615]

The students smile.

(At this moment, my decisive declarative sentences signal me to question if I'm really so sure. I resist the impulse to raise further questions out loud. It feels good to have a resolution and to feel I did the right thing.)

"What if those we write about give us their consent, but then are uncomfortable with what we write?" Robin asks, complicating ethical considerations even further. Robin is writing her dissertation, "Southern Black Women: Their Lived Realities" (Boylorn, 2006) about her home town, a small black and rural community in North Carolina, and the everyday lives of women there, including family members. In the middle of writing her first draft, she sends me an e-mail about how she feels unable to write:

> Something has paralyzed me. Is it fear? This story scares me at the same time that it excites me. I am not afraid of the story, but rather I am afraid about how the story will impact the participants, my family. I plan to share drafts with them, but what if they are hurt? Will they tell me? I read the first lines of the story to my mother over the phone and she listened, quietly. When an extended pause marked the end, I asked for her reaction. "Well ... that was how it was," was all she said. I didn't know if that was a positive or negative reaction, but it paralyzed me. [Robin Boylorn, personal e-mail communication]

"Another time my mother said that my writing made her 'look so bad,'" Robin tell me when we discuss this in my office. I tell Robin, "No wonder you are paralyzed."

Robin tells me she wants to show her grandmother, another

primary character in her text, what she is writing. I tell her that it might be too early in the process. "Wait until you have edited and revised, and are sure that this is material you want to include and the way you want to tell it."

"But I don't want to organize the whole manuscript around these scenes and then find out that my grandmother is hurt by them and doesn't want them included."

I tell her that I see her point. Robin and I have numerous meetings about these issues. I tell her that I think that for now she has to write her stories before we can figure it out. "Anything can be changed; the story can be replotted later."

"But wait a minute," a student objects, on hearing what we have decided. "That's a lot of work to throw down the drain. What about your mother? Can't you just ask her?"

"I did," Robin says, "and she said I overreacted to what she said. That I should write whatever I need to write."

"Then it's okay," the students say.

"She wants her daughter to get her Ph.D.," I say. "That's what matters most to Robin's mother. Given that, perhaps she feels she has little choice about approving what Robin writes."

"I think you're trying too hard to psychoanalyze Robin's mother," a student accuses. "You can't know what she really thinks. People don't always say what they really feel. We can't be responsible for that. She approved it. That's all that matters."

"Is it?" I ask. "We try to make sure that strangers can refuse to be in our studies. Isn't that important for our loved ones as well?"

"Much more important," says Robin.

> But if they feel obligations to us, if they feel they have to do these things so that we can succeed, then how should we respond? It's especially difficult if they don't tell you they're feeling that way. I've tried to convey my project to my family as honestly as I can. But it's not in my best interest to try to convince them not to give consent. I will struggle with this dilemma until this project is done, and likely years after it is published. [Robin Boylorn, personal e-mail communication]

"Even if we assume that Robin's mother approves, doesn't Robin owe something to the larger community of southern black women?" I ask them. "Shouldn't she think about whether what she says might reify negative stereotypes and hurt the very people she's trying to give voice? Shouldn't relational ethics be informed by a social justice agenda?" (Buzzanell, 2004; Dougherty & Atkinson, 2006).

"It depends on who we write for and for what purpose," a student responds. The rest sit quietly.

Situations like these make me modify what I say. Now I tell students that taking our projects back to those we write about is a complex undertaking and has to be handled with care. The student who tells the story about being abused by her brother writes a publishable paper at the end of the semester, but she feels that publishing this story will unravel a family system that is, after many long years, finally intact. (A few years later, she and her brother will become even closer and he will offer financial assistance so that she has more free time to pursue her Ph.D. I am glad now she never showed him what she wrote or that she published it.)

"If you decide not to inform, get consent, or take your work back to those you write about and you want to publish it, you should be able to defend your reasons for not seeking responses of those in your study." I tell the students that sometimes giving our work to participants could damage the very people and relationships we're intent on helping (see also Kiesinger, 2002). In rare cases, taking projects back to those we write about might even be irresponsible. Sometimes getting consent and informing intimate others would put students in harm's way, such as from an abusive partner or parent (Carter, 2002; Geist & Miller, 1998; Rambo, 2005).

"Then shouldn't we wait to write about people until after they die? Then they won't see it or be hurt. And then they can't hurt us," says one student.

I tell them that writing about people who have died will not solve their ethical dilemmas about what to tell, and sometimes the dilemmas become more poignant. I tell them that dead people can't give them permission, approve what they say, or offer their accounts, and that they will feel a tension between their implicit trust provisions (Freadman, 2004, p. 143) with those who have died and telling what is necessary for their own healing, construction of self, and offers of comfort to readers. "Besides, others in your life will still care and you'll have to deal with them," I warn.

They ask how I feel about having written about both the good and bad times in my relationship with my former partner Gene. I tell them that in writing *Final Negotiations* (Ellis, 1995a), I tried to balance my portrayal of Gene between what I needed to tell for my own healing and growth and my attachment to the narratively truthful account I felt I owed my readers (see Ellis, 2007).

"But wasn't that really your story to tell?" a student asks, growing tired of the ethical complexities. "We just want to write our own stories," she tells me, defiantly, speaking now for the class. I repeat that self-revelations always involve revelations about others (Freadman, 2004, p. 128). I tell the students they don't own their stories. That their story is also other people's stories. I tell them they don't have an inalienable right to tell the stories of others. Intimate, identifiable others deserve at least as much consideration as strangers and probably more. "Doing research with them will confront you with the most complicated ethical issues of your research lives."

This issue hits home when I write about my own childhood, a topic I have not written about before. The vivid and detailed experiences that come to mind involve family secrets. I write them and then put the pages in a drawer. At the end of a year, I get them out and decide not to publish them. I question whether they represent my childhood, whether this is the picture I want others to have of my family, whether it is right to freeze my parents in this frame, whether I need to tell these stories, whether these events compose the story I want to remember. Then I ask myself: "On the one hand, do I owe it to myself to tell this story so that I might learn as much about my life as possible? Do I owe it to students who I have encouraged to write what is hard for them? Do I owe it to the advancement of autoethnography itself? On the other hand, hasn't the writing itself—without publication—done its work?"

"Won't sharing with others do more, for you and readers?" the first hand argues back. "How can you ask others to write these stories if you don't?"

Instead of publishing these stories, I write an article about why I am not publishing them. At the end, I claim the right to change my mind about this at a later time (Ellis, 2006).

"Sometimes we might need to write but not publish the stories of our lives," I tell my students, who then want to know how they will ever get academic positions if they don't have publications.

I tell my students they have to live in the world of those they write about, just as I have to live in the world of my siblings who might be upset about my revealing family secrets. I tell my students they have to live in the world of those they write for and to. I tell them they must be careful how they present themselves. "If you write about eating disorders, then also write about other less sensational topics," I tell students seeking academic positions. "If you write autoethnography, also write something more traditional. Make good decisions for yourself. Keep your options open."

I suggest to Barbara, a former student, that she might not want to write about her depression and suicide attempt while taking sick leave and trying to earn tenure. She does, saying that she has to write herself out of her depression (Jago, 2002). She gets a teaching award the next year, publishes more autoethnography, and earns tenure.

> Maybe I'm too cautious sometimes. But I feel I owe it to my students to be cautious for them; at the same time, I try to take on the risks myself. I understand the damage that can be done to careers in the name of fearing autoethnography. I want to protect students until they are settled in careers; then I hope they will share the risks for those following behind them.

I tell students that our studies should lead to positive change and make the world a better place. "Strive to leave the communities, participants, and yourselves better off at the end of the research than they were at the beginning," I say. "In the best of all worlds, all of those involved in our studies will feel better. But sometimes they won't; you won't." I tell them that what is most important to me is that they not negatively affect their lives and relationships, hurt themselves, or others in their world. I tell them to hold relational concerns as high as research. "When possible, research from an ethic of care. That's the best we can do."

"But what about those who kept secrets from me, who hurt me?" they ask, and I reply, "Write to understand how they put their worlds together, how you can be a survivor of the world they thrust upon you. How you can find meaning in the chaos." Sometimes I say, "I don't know."

Lately I've been wondering—but haven't dared say so—whether autoethnographers consider others too much as we write. Perhaps sometimes there might be value in throwing a temper tantrum and "writing mean" (Hoagland, 2003, p. 13),[3] at least during initial story drafts when we are trying to recreate ourselves as "survivors" of whatever happened to us. As autoethnographic writers, we tend to cleanse our stories. We want to be likable, sympathetic, and fair-minded narrators. But some topics—racism, incest, abuse—are not nice topics, and writing mean might reveal important truths that help us find meaning in our experience. As Anne Lamott says, "If my family didn't want me to write about them, they should've behaved better" (Douglas Flemons, personal communication). I have come to believe that the well-being of the researcher is not always less important than the well-being of the other, especially others who have behaved badly.

I worry that students will dredge up situations through writing that are too difficult for them to handle. I warn that they are not therapists, so they should seek assistance from professionals and mentors when they have problems. I tell them I am not a therapist, but that I will be there for them.

Sometimes I fear I—or worse, autoethnography—will be blamed if their lives go awry.

I seek to make my relationship with my students similar to what I want their relationship to be with those they study—one of raising difficult questions and then offering care and support when answers come from deep within. I tell them we will take each project on a case-by-case basis, and I promise to be available to discuss conflicts each step of the way. I tell them that every case has to be considered "in context and with respect to the rights, wishes, and feelings of those involved" (Freadman, 2004, p. 124).

I tell them that not only are there ethical questions about doing autoethnography, but that autoethnography itself is an ethical practice. In life, we often have to make choices in difficult, ambiguous, and uncertain circumstances. At these times, we feel the tug of obligation and responsibility. That's what we end up writing about. Autoethnographies show people in the process of figuring out what to do, how to live, and what their struggles mean (Bochner & Ellis, 2006, p. 111).

I tell them that there is a caregiving function to autoethnography (Bochner & Ellis, 2006). Listening to and engaging in others' stories is a gift and sometimes the best thing we can do for those in distress (see Greenspan, 1998). Telling our stories is a gift; our stories potentially offer readers companionship when they desperately need it (Mairs, 1993). Writing difficult stories is a gift to ourselves, a reflexive attempt to construct meaning in our lives and heal or grow from our pain.

I tell them I believe that most people want to do the right thing, the sensible thing. As human beings, we long to live meaningful lives that seek the good. As friends, we long to have trusting relationships that care for others. As researchers, we long to do ethical research that makes a difference. To come close to these goals, we constantly have to consider which questions to ask, which secrets to keep, and which truths are worth telling.

That's what I tell them. Then I listen carefully to what they say back about their ongoing experiences, feelings, and thoughts. Working from specific cases to guiding principles and then back again, over and over—that's the process we use for deciding what we should do.

Notes

1. This chapter expands a short section from another article (Ellis, 2007). I'd like to thank Arthur Bochner and Robin Boylorn for helpful comments on this chapter.

2. Jackie is a composite character. Other characters mentioned in this story represent actual students. All conversations come from remembered experiences, though they did not necessarily occur in the time, place, or order in which I present them here.

3. Thanks to Ron Pelias for discussing this idea with me and leading me to this reference.

References

Adams, T. (2006). Seeking father: Relationally reframing a troubled love story. *Qualitative Inquiry, 12*(4), 704–723.

Arnett, R. C. (2002). Paulo Freire's revolutionary pedagogy: From a story-centered to a narrative-centered communication ethic. *Qualitative Inquiry, 8*(4), 489–510.

Bergum, V. (1998). Relational ethics. What is it? *In Touch,* 1. Available online at http://www.phen.ab.ca/materials/intouch/vol1/intouch1-02.html. Accessed February 19, 2005.

Bochner, A. P., & Ellis, C. (2006). Communication as autoethnography. In G. Shepherd, J. St. John, & T. Striphas (Eds.), *Communication as...: Perspectives on theory* (pp. 110–122). Thousand Oaks, CA: Sage.

Boylorn, R. (2006). Southern Black women: Their lived realities. Unpublished Ph.D. dissertation, Department of Communication, University of South Florida, Tampa (in progress).

Brody, H. (1987). *Stories of sickness.* New Haven, CT: Yale University Press.

Brooks, M. (2006). Man-to-man: A body talk between male friends. *Qualitative Inquiry, 12*(2), 185–207.

Buzzanell, P. M. (2004). Revisiting sexual harassment in academe: Using feminist ethical and sensemaking approaches to analyze macrodiscourse and micropractices of sexual harassment. In P. M. Buzzanell, H. Sterk, & L. H. Turner (Eds.), *Gender in applied contexts* (pp. 25–46). Thousand Oaks, CA: Sage.

Cannella, G., & Lincoln, Y. S. (2004). Epilogue: Claiming a critical public social science—Reconceptualizing and redeploying research. *Qualitative Inquiry, 10*(2), 298–309.

Carter, S. (2002). How much subjectivity is needed to understand our lives objectively? *Qualitative Health Research, 12*(9), 1184–1201.

Christians, C. (2000). Ethics and politics in qualitative research. In N. K. Denzin & Y. S. Lincoln (Eds.), 2nd ed., *Handbook of qualitative research* (pp. 133–155). Thousand Oaks, CA: Sage.

Davis, C. S. (2005). A future with hope: The social construction of hope, help, and dialogic reconciliation in a community children's mental health system of care. Unpublished Ph.D. dissertation, Department of Communication, University of South Florida, Tampa.

Denzin, N. K. (1997). *Interpretive ethnography: Ethnographic practices for the 21ˢᵗ century.* Thousand Oaks, CA: Sage.

Denzin, N. K. (2003). *Performance ethnography: Critical pedagogy and the politics of culture.* Thousand Oaks, CA: Sage.

Dougherty, D., & Atkinson, J. (2006). Competing ethical communities and a researcher's dilemma: The case of a sexual harasser. *Qualitative Inquiry, 12*(2), 292–315.

Ellingson, L. (2006). *Communicating in the clinic: Negotiating frontstage and backstage teamwork.* Cresskill, NJ: Hampton Press.

Ellis, C. (1986). *Fisher folk. Two communities on Chesapeake Bay.* Lexington: University Press of Kentucky.

Ellis, C. (1995a). *Final negotiations: A story of love, loss, and chronic illness.* Philadelphia: Temple University Press.

Ellis, C. (1995b). Emotional and ethical quagmires in returning to the field. *Journal of Contemporary Ethnography, 24*(1), 68–98.

Ellis, C. (1995c). The other side of the fence: Seeing black and white in a small, southern town. *Qualitative Inquiry, 1*(2), 147–167.

Ellis, C. (2001). With mother/with child: A true story. *Qualitative Inquiry, 7*(5), 598–616.

Ellis, C. (2004). *The ethnographic I: A methodological novel about autoethnography.* Walnut Creek: AltaMira.

Ellis, C. (2006). On not telling family secrets. Unpublished manuscript, University of South Florida, Tampa.

Ellis, C. (2007). Telling secrets, revealing lives: Relational ethics in research with intimate others. *Qualitative Inquiry, 13*(1), 3–29.

Etherington K (2005) Writing trauma stories for research. *Lapidus Quarterly, 1*(2), 25–31.

Etherington, K. (In press). Ethical research in reflexive relationships. *Qualitative Inquiry*.

Foster, E. (2007). Communicating at the end of life: Finding magic in the mundane. Mahwah, NJ: Lawrence Erlbaum Associates.

Frank, A. (2004). Moral non-fiction: Life writing and children's disability. In P. J. Eakin (Ed.), *The ethics of life writing* (pp. 174–194). Ithaca, NY: Cornell University Press.

Freadman, R. (2004). Decent and indecent: Writing my father's life. In J. P. Eakin (Ed.), *The ethics of life writing* (pp. 121–146). Ithaca, NY: Cornell University Press.

Geist, P., & Miller, M. (1998). What's in a name? The ethics and politics of nom de plume. Paper presented at the National Communication Association, New York, November.

Gilligan, C. (1982). *In a different voice: Psychological theory and women's development*. Cambridge, MA: Harvard University Press.

Goodall, H. L. (2006). *A need to know: The clandestine history of a CIA family*. Walnut Creek, CA: Left Coast Press.

Grafanaki, S. (1996). How research can change the researcher: The need for sensitivity, flexibility and ethical boundaries in conducting qualitative research in counselling/psychotherapy. *British Journal of Guidance and Counselling*, *24*(3), 329–338.

Greenspan, H. (1998). *On listening to Holocaust survivors: Recounting and life history*. Westport, CT: Praeger.

Guillemin, M., & Gillam, L. (2004). Ethics, reflexivity, and "ethically important moments" in research. *Qualitative Inquiry*, *10*(2), 261–280.

Hoagland, T. (2003). Negative capability: How to talk mean and influence people. *American Poetry Review*, *32*(March/April), 13–15.

Jago, B. (2002). Chronicling an academic depression. *Journal of Contemporary Ethnography*, *31*(6), 729–757.

Kiesinger, C. (2002). My father's shoes: The therapeutic value of narrative reframing. In A. P. Bochner & C. Ellis (Eds.), *Ethnographically speaking: Autoethnography, literature, and aesthetics* (pp. 95–114). Walnut Creek, CA: AltaMira.

Lincoln, Y. S. (1995). Emerging criteria for quality in qualitative and interpretive research. *Qualitative Inquiry*, *1*(3), 275–289.

Mairs, N. (1993). When bad things happen to good writers. *New York Times Book Review*, February 21, pp. 1, 25–27.

Malcolm, J. (1990). *The journalist and the murderer*. New York: Knopf.

Marzano, M. (In press). Informed consent, deception and research freedom in qualitative research: A cross-cultural comparison. *Qualitative Inquiry*.

Mason, J. (1996). *Qualitative researching.* London: Sage.

Noddings, N. (1984). *Caring, a feminine approach to ethics & moral education.* Berkeley: University of California Press.

Olesen, V. (2000). Feminisms and qualitative research at and into the millennium. In N. K. Denzin & Y. S. Lincoln (Eds.), 2nd ed., *Handbook of qualitative research* (pp. 215–256). Thousand Oaks, CA: Sage.

Perry, J. (2001). Sibling relationships and care of parents: Deconstructing memoirs and personal narratives. Unpublished Ph.D. dissertation, Department of Communication, University of South Florida, Tampa.

Poulos, C. (2005). Out of the shadows: Telling family secrets as healing praxis. Paper presented at the National Communication Association Conference. Boston, November 17–20.

Punch, M. (1994). Politics and ethics in qualitative research. In N. K. Denzin & Y. S. Lincoln (Eds.), *Handbook of qualitative research* (pp. 83–97). Thousand Oaks, CA: Sage.

Rambo, C. (2005). Handing IRB an unloaded gun. Unpublished manuscript. University of Memphis.

Reason, P. (1993). Reflections on sacred experience and sacred science. *Journal of Management Inquiry, 2*(3), 273–283.

Slattery, P., & Rapp, D. (2003). *Ethics and the foundations of education: Teaching convictions in a postmodern world.* Boston: Allyn & Bacon.

Tierney, W. G (1993). Introduction: Developing archives of resistance. In D. McLaughlin & W. G. Tierney (Eds.), *Naming silenced lives: Personal narratives and the process of educational change* (pp. 1–19). New York: Routledge.

Chapter 12

CODA

Talking and Thinking about Qualitative Research[1]

Carolyn Ellis
University of South Florida, Tampa

Arthur P. Bochner
University of South Florida, Tampa

Norman K. Denzin
University of Illinois, Urbana-Champaign

Yvonna S. Lincoln
Texas A&M University, College Station

Janice M. Morse
University of Utah

Ronald J. Pelias
Southern Illinois University, Carbondale

Laurel Richardson
The Ohio State University, Columbus

Nonchalantly, Carolyn finds her way to room 314A on the top floor of the Illini Union on the campus of the University of Illinois, Urbana-Champaign. This is the last panel following three very full days of the Second International Congress of Qualitative Inquiry conference. She has given a pre-conference workshop, attended and participated in many interesting panels, and met with old and new friends. The energy and passion at the conference has been palpable, but now she, like everyone else, is tired, ready to wind down.

"Here it is," Carolyn says to Laurel and Art, who are walking behind her, kibitzing about a panel they've just experienced. The talk stops as they enter the room and are immediately caught up in the bustling activity surrounding them. People crowd around the several hundred, already occupied chairs lined behind rows of long narrow tables. Others seek out available space on the floor of this large room, the size of three regular meeting rooms joined together. The resourceful busily carry in chairs from other rooms and try to find openings for them.

Apparently, this panel has struck a cord. Attendees have come, no doubt, to be in the presence of well-known academics, Carolyn thinks. But more than that, she believes they've come to hear leaders in the field talk informally about themselves and share their personal views on qualitative research. That there are no paper titles in the program is no doubt an attraction. With all the methodological and creative innovations in the field, qualitative scholars, similar to other academics, still spend their time together at conferences listening to their colleagues read long papers that have been scrunched into twelve to fifteen minute time slots, making them nearly impossible to follow. It is clear from the attendance here and the buzz in the room that conference attendees are hungry for something different.

Carolyn pauses and feels a moment of stage fright as she thinks of meeting their expectations. Then she springs into action, hurrying to the front of the room to make sure the panelists are ready and that things are in order. Laurel and Art join the other panelists at the front, seated behind a large rectangular table facing the audience. A large podium sets off to one side. The only mike in view is attached to the podium. How are we going to have a discussion in this large room without mics for everyone, Carolyn wonders, wishing she had checked the room ahead of the session. She moves to handing out her IRB (institutional review board) consent forms to the panelists. Chaos ensues as the panelists try to understand the need for the forms and figure out where to sign. Without further thought, Carolyn moves to the podium and places her tape player on the podium. Then she checks the mike. She is happy to see Cris McRae, one of her graduate students, holding a tape player. Crammed among other young people on the floor in front of her, he sits with his shoulders and legs drawn into himself, unable to even shift his weight without bumping another person. She hopes at least one of their tape recorders picks up the voices.

◊ ◊ ◊ ◊ ◊

Carolyn Ellis: Welcome everyone; it's so nice to see all of you here. This is incredible. We didn't expect the room to be so large and full. I am sorry that we don't have chairs for everyone and that we don't have a mic to hand to the participants. I guess we'll have to talk loudly if we want to hold a discussion.

I'd like to start the session by thanking Norman Denzin for hosting the conference. Isn't this one of the best parties you've ever been to? It's been an incredible couple of days. The energy is fantastic. Now having all of you in the same room makes me think the whole building might take off.

Let me give you some background on how this session evolved. I am teaching a graduate class at University of South Florida (USF) in Advanced Qualitative Methods. You've probably seen the twelve students in the class, all running around with their IRB consent forms in one hand and their brand new digital tape recorders in the other. We've all fallen in love with our recorders. For our class, we decided that we would do an ethnography of this conference. So, for the last few days, the students have been conducting formal and informal interviews and doing participant observation. It's been a lot of work but also a lot of fun. We hope to get current information about what's going on in qualitative methods and publish some of our papers.

Before arriving here, we went through the IRB process, which seemed appropriate given that this is a conference on Ethics, Politics, and Human Subject Research in the New Millennium. The main problem we had with the IRB was that they didn't want us to identify the people who responded to us. "No, you don't understand," I told them. "These are academics; they like to be cited and see their names in print. If I don't name them, I'll be in trouble!" It took many interactions back and forth and rewriting of the document before we actually got approval to name the people who we interviewed and quoted.

This session grew out of our project. I thought it would be interesting to ask in a group context some of the questions we're addressing in our individual interviews. That way, you as the audience would have the advantage of hearing the replies and observing the interaction. My goal, then, is to ask these distinguished scholars six questions and give each of them two minutes to answer each one. Can you imagine a professor answering in two minutes?

The audience laughs loudly.

I gave each panelist the questions beforehand, but I don't believe anybody has prepared a twenty-minute speech. At the end of each question, I had hoped to spend a few minutes with the panelists responding to each other. But now given the logistics, I don't know if that will take place or not. Good thing I'm into emergent research. Let's just go with the flow and see what happens.

After introducing the panelists, Carolyn begins.

Round 1

Carolyn: First, I have asked panelists to summarize in one to two minutes their personal history with qualitative methods. I suggested topics for discussion such as: where and from whom they learned it; approaches and transitions in their approaches; and where they locate themselves now. Ron, would you start?

Ron begins talking from his seat, first facing the panelists, then the audience. Then he stands.

Ronald Pelias: Can you hear me at all?

Audience: No.

Carolyn: [from the podium] Do you want to speak from here?

Ron: [nods and moves to the podium, while Carolyn sits down at the table] My background is in performance studies, and performance studies, as many of you know, is primarily a research or disciplinary area that's interested in using performance as a way of knowing. Throughout my academic career, I've been interested in staging performance text to discover the kinds of insights that staging might bring to bear. But when I turned to writing up performance, trying to translate what was discovered on the stage to the page, I found that my arguments often turned to citational proof. I found myself, as our tradition taught, making a rational case. Now, there was something very unsatisfying about that for me. Just making a rational case over and over and over again dropped out so much. It dropped out the thing that attracted me to performance in the first place—a method that allows the affective to live. The rational case took away the experience. So I turned to autoethnography, and I turned to performative writing as a way of trying to write what I felt was most meaningful in theatrical presentations. I turned to a strategy of writing that lets the heart be present.

Carolyn: Thanks Ron. Norm?

Norman Denzin: Well, I'm going to take four minutes then I'll pass on the second time I'm asked to come up. I'll combine question one and two in a narrative.

My tortured history with qualitative methods has gone through three or four phases. I'll sort of move through those and present that to you.

I came into this field through sociology in the 1960s in a quantitative Sociology Department. The department also had a social psychology wing where they taught George Herbert Mead and Herbert Blumer and the Chicago School and symbolic interaction. But as students, our methodology requirements were all quantitative in terms of statistical courses and research design. There was no teaching of qualitative methodology whatsoever. In my doctoral program, we read Mead, Blumer, and Cooley, and I studied with Manford Kuhn. We read at that time Goffman's *The Presentation of Self in Everyday Life* (1959), a complete participant observation project that had just come out. Nobody had any idea how he wrote it. *Boys in White* (Becker et al., 1961) appeared at that time and we didn't realize it then, but it was a very quantitative approach to doing qualitative research. It was filled with tables and quasi-statistics. Even as they wrote the book, Becker and Geer were publishing articles on problems of validity in participant observation. So, we were funneled through a kind of validity framework into qualitative methods insofar as we used that as our model.

When I came to Illinois in 1966, I was asked to teach field methods and I had never had a course in field methods. It was at that time that I wrote *The Research Act* (Denzin, 1988), to teach myself how to do field methods. I saw an interactionist methodology based on my reading of the Chicago School at that time. But I was also influenced by the concepts of internal and external validity emerging from Campbell and Stanley (1966), Eugene Webb and colleagues' (1966) notion of triangulation, and Blumer's (1969) notion that research methods aren't theoretically neutral. So, *The Research Act* was convoluted: methods are theoretically informed, but they have to be methodologically sensitive to issues of internal and external validity. Therefore, we have to combine multiple methods in what's called triangulation. That's the short story of *The Research Act*.

We were writing this in the middle of the civil rights movement and the Vietnam War and nobody's acting like that's going on. I'll stop here and come back to my epiphany as a basis of that war.

Carolyn thanks Norman and nods in Yvonna's direction.

Yvonna Lincoln: I'd like to give the honorable Senator Denzin some of my time. I'm a very simple person. "My personal history with qualitative research" by Yvonna S. Lincoln, or "What I did in the summer." I had two degrees in history—in medieval history actually—and so I came to graduate work in education very familiar with working with departments and records. But I also knew something about interviewing because I worked as both an undergraduate and a graduate student with a sociologist named Allen Beagle up at Michigan State University on the Ontonagon County. The project is the Out-Migration Project, which studied why young people were leaving the Upper Peninsula of Michigan. I did a variety of different kinds of research and data gathering and worked with a bunch of fun graduate students, each of whom had a chunk of this project. I learned a tremendous amount about fieldwork from Allen Beagle and John Rieger, a visual sociologist who still studies rural settings and what's happening to rural land.

My second experience with qualitative research came when I worked on my doctorate, and the RITE [Research in Teacher Education] project we were working on was in the process of being redesigned by the principle investigators who said, "Oh, we're going about this all wrong." That was back in the days when you could go to a reasonable project officer and say, "We misdesigned this study. We want to redesign it." The project officer would respond, "What is it you want to do?" You'd tell them, and if it made sense, they would say, "Okay and we'll give you another year's work while you redesign it." In the middle of that project, an extremely brilliant woman from the University of Minnesota found out about it and wanted to do some fieldwork. Mary Corcoran came down to work with David Clark, who was the director of my dissertation. I traveled a lot with Mary Corcoran. She taught me so much about fieldwork and how to get ready for it. She was my mentor, and she was and is a stunning woman, a very smart lady. I don't think she had any training in field methods either. She just picked them up over the years. So, that's my introduction to qualitative research. I would locate myself as a postmodern constructivist … I think.

Janice Morse: I'm Jan Morse. I've got to be careful of what I say because I've made a lot of mistakes and, of course, I don't want them to be published! I was at Penn State, which is a very quantitative school, where I completed a very fine Master's thesis—except it should have been qualitative. From there, I went to University of Utah and enrolled in anthropology concurrently with nursing (both heavily qualitative schools), and did two dissertations in Fiji—both mixed-method design. One was quantitative with a little bit of qualitative (anthropology [Morse, 1984a, 1984b]), and one was qualitative with a little bit of quantitative (nursing [Morse, 1989]). My first academic appointment was at the University of Alberta and I was assigned to teach qualitative research. Not only was it the first class I ever taught, but half of the faculty signed up. So, I really had to get my act together.

Carolyn: Thank you. Laurel?

Laurel Richardson: Hi. I'm sitting here and deciding whether to start with my qualitative experience at my birth. I think the fact that I've been a marginal person with a foot in two different culture from my birth on did construct me as a sociologist and later as a qualitative researcher. It's a gift. I've been fortunate to be born into two different cultures. What moved me forward was the capstone course I took as an undergraduate at the University of Chicago. That course was called The Organization, Methods, and Principles of the Sciences. In that course, we dealt with intuitive work, deductive work, induction, reduction; and it wasn't like there was only one way to do science. Rather, there were multiple ways by which you might come to know something. It struck a responsive chord in me. I've always been engaged with how one "knows" and how one "tells" what one knows. So, I'm going to talk about "knowing" now and I'll talk about "telling" later.

The idea of knowing has always just intrigued me. What claims do I lay to knowledge? How do I know anything? How do I claim I know anything? And being born into two cultures, you never quite know what you do know because it's denied in the other one.

When I went to graduate school, I was fortunate to work with Edward Rose who was one of the cofounders of ethnomethodology, and although he wouldn't call it qualitative, nevertheless my cohort was engaged in qualitative research. We did "natural" experiments about social life—breaching norms, breaking rules, creating new languages. At that time, I happened to be married to a mathematician, so they had me teaching statistics because clearly knowledge of such comes in the semen or something. So, I was teaching the statistics and methods classes, although I had never had a statistics or methods class. At Chicago, we didn't take methods, we just read those nice theory books. I was teaching methods and teaching myself methods and teaching myself statistics at the same time. I was always a week ahead of the students and I loved it. My dissertation was "Pure Mathematics, Studies in the Sociology of Knowledge." It was a historical analysis and a statistical analysis of math abstracts. (I had also done participant-observation and interviews with mathematicians, but this material had no place in the dissertation.)

Very early in my career, I was into content analysis, and I presented my first paper at the ASA [American Sociological Association] using content analysis displayed in nice neat tables. The first paper I sent to *American Sociological Review* was an interpretative qualitative study of women in science. The name of the paper was, "Women in Science, Why so Few?" The paper was rejected with a one-line sentence from the editor: "A woman obviously wrote this because no one but a woman would be interested." I did quantitative work for a little while after that. I'll come back later for the rest of my qualitative history.

Carolyn: Okay. Art?

Arthur Bochner: Like Jan, I've made a lot of mistakes. Unlike Jan, I've made a career of publishing them! So, I think the whole world knows about my history.

Carolyn asked, "From whom did you learn qualitative methods?" I didn't learn qualitative methods from anybody in particular, that is, from any teacher in particular. I just read a lot. I did have the good fortune, during my last year as a doctoral student, of being assigned as a research assistant to a faculty member who really didn't know what to do with me. So, he sent me to the library and told me to go to the current journals and look at every one that appeared to have any connection to communication research. "Take down the name of the editor, what sorts of articles they publish, and the submission instructions and put each one on a separate note card," he told me. So, I took out a carrel in the library—in those days you actually had to go to the library, you couldn't go to the library via the Internet—and I started at A and went to Z. Along the way I discovered journals I'd never been introduced to in my graduate education, such as *Symbolic Interaction* and *Family Process*, and I would sit there and read the articles in these journals one after another.

I recall one in particular, written by a young sociologist named Norman Denzin—of course, I didn't know he was young at the time—on ethnomethodology. Ethnomethodology, to a large extent, was my first introduction to qualitative methods.

I later discovered in *Family Process* work by the Palo Alto group of systems theorists. Under the influence of Gregory Bateson (1972), they were examining video recordings of families with children who had been diagnosed as schizophrenic. They were doing nothing more than watching the films and taking notes, trying to interpret what was going on in these families. The whole history of the double-blind theory of schizophrenia evolved out of that work.

When I left with my Ph.D., I was hired to be the token quantitative researcher and methodology teacher in the Department of Speech at Temple University. I was the only empiricist in a department, which was completely comprised of humanists doing rhetorical analysis and rhetorical theory. I had to subject my papers to my colleagues in the humanities, really; they had a great influence in pushing me toward thinking more about history, culture, rhetoric, and language.

Then, in 1974, I picked up a little book by Jules Henry called *Pathways to Madness* (1965), which still stands to me as a turning point in my life and career. Henry was a psychoanalyst and an anthropologist who took a room inside the homes of five different families who had children diagnosed with some mental illness and had been institutionalized. He did fieldwork in these families. In his book, he wrote theoretical novelettes about each family. They were narratives—stories that did the work of theory. I said to myself, "That's what I want to do."

◊ ◊ ◊ ◊ ◊

As Carolyn listens to these stories, she can't help but think how she'd tell her story, if she were one of the panelists:

I think I've been a qualitative methodologist since early in my life. What else does one do in a small southern town to keep interested and engaged? At the College of William and Mary, I got a B.A. in sociology and became mesmerized by the work of Erving Goffman. I was fortunate to get involved in an honor's thesis where I did fieldwork with the "fisher folk" (Ellis, 1986), an isolated community in the Chesapeake Bay. From that moment on, I was sold on qualitative methods and wanted to combine it with my interests in social psychology. In graduate school, I continued with my fieldwork in isolated fishing communities, working some with Jerry Suttles and Rose Coser. But it was with Gene Weinstein that I developed my social psychological and ethnographic eye.

I've continued being interested in qualitative methods and in the last two decades have turned more to autoethnographic methods, though I still enjoy teaching and doing qualitative work of all kinds. I consider myself a narrative ethnographer.

> After Round 1, Carolyn tries to figure out how the panelists might engage in conversation and concludes that it won't work, given the physical set-up. Besides, because of the number of panelists and the limited time, it would be difficult to have significant conversation anyway. Disappointed, she decides to move on to Round 2. Maybe on another occasion, she muses.

Round 2

Carolyn: My second question is about epiphanies. Was there a moment of epiphany that got you into qualitative work, or once you were there changed your perspective within the general arena of qualitative work? Some of you already started to address this so you can pick up wherever you left off. Ron?

Ron: As I was suggesting before, I had been doing all of this qualitative work in performance studies on the stage and as I was trying to translate that work to the page, it always felt like there was a certain kind of disjoint for me. The moment that allowed me to move into performative writing, autoethnography, and other alternative qualitative methods was when I read Buddy Goodall's *Casing the Promised Land* (1989). For me, that was my moment of awakening, my epiphany. I had been staging literature and performing poetry and fiction in theatrical frames, but it had never occurred to me that I might be able to use what I was learning on the stage, learning from literature, as a scholarly writing strategy for the page. It was that book in particular that allowed me to see a way that could be done.

Norm: By the end of the 1970s, I had hit a brick wall and other walls as well. I had taken symbolic interaction about as far as I thought I could take it or as far as I thought it could take me. And I was profoundly dissatisfied with the wall the perspective had hit. That is, it had become closed off from all sorts of other discourses that I was being exposed to on this campus in criticism and interpretative theory, which was an interdisciplinary program in the humanities. So by the late '70s, we were reading European social theory that was just being translated. Lacan, Heidegger, Foucault, the feminisms, and we were moving into semiotics. It was a three-year project of being saturated with theory that sociology was excluding.

About this time, we formed a traveling minstrel show and some of the members are on this panel: Carolyn, Laurel, myself, and Patricia Clough. We would go to the symbolic interactionist annual meetings and do postmodern performances, and we would get booed and hissed. One of the more profound moments was when Laurel presented the life of Louisa May, the poetic representation of an interview transcript. She later published this as "The Skipped Line" (Richardson, 1993). The room was like this, packed, and Laurel had distributed her transcript of this interview, which she then proceeded to poetically perform for us. I think it was Harvey Farberman, a symbolic interactionist, who raised his hand and said, "You skipped a line, and therefore the validity of what you are doing is at question. You are not being true to her life and to her words." That skipped line provoked a give and take in the journals and opened this space that we were in, a space of skipped lines, and it was okay to be there. Even if our colleagues didn't like it, that was the space we were going to be in. So then for several years, we did this kind of traveling road show and confronted a fair amount of hostility. But as we did, I think the momentum started to build behind us. I'll pick that up the next time I come up here.

Yvonna: I'm not sure how to talk about epiphanies because I think I've had a lot of them. I want to talk about an epiphany and an ethical crisis at once. But before I do, you should know that I lived a sheltered childhood. I grew up in a very traditional family.

My brothers ran wild. I was locked in the house for thirty-two years. So I didn't have very much experience with a lot of stuff, and my epiphany came when I was out on an evaluation contract. I was very new. I had had my doctorate for about a year and I was doing this evaluation contract and trying to be a good qualitative naturalistic evaluator. I began to suspect that in this project, the middle school coach was molesting some of the boys on one of his teams. And I didn't know what to do about that. That was before we knew very much about laws that said you had to report stuff. I went to the superintendent and said, "I don't have any hard evidence, but there is a bunch of kids who are telling me things and I think you need to do something about it." Once the young boys were questioned, it turned out to be true. I thought all qualitative researchers were all good and that they encountered only other good people in the world.

My epiphany was finding out there really is evil in the world; there really are hideous things that happen to kids that never should. I have to tell you that that came as an epiphany to me because it was the first time I realized that. I know that really sounds stupid—see this is one of the things that doesn't go in, right?—but this was the first time in my life that I felt that I had come face to face with what I geminately would describe as evil rather than bad or rude or discourteous or un-Christian. It was evil, just evil. I was very young; I don't think I was but thirty-one years old. It was quite frightening, and that was an epiphany for me.

Jan: I haven't been lucky enough to have an epiphany. But what happened at the University of Alberta comes under the category of "what doesn't kill you makes you stronger." Every time I wanted to do research in the hospital I had to go to the IRB and to a medical committee for approval and funding, They would ask me questions about qualitative inquiry, then my application would be tabled and I would have to come back the next month for another round. But it was that that made me a good methodologist. It made me confident about what I was doing. It taught me the answers that were sometimes not in the book. And it gave me the skills to explain the nuances and assumptions of qualitative inquiry.

But they made things difficult for a green faculty member. For example, I wanted to do a project that took restraints off the elderly confused in the psychogeriatric ward. Now, it's not very nice to do research and to tie somebody up—this is the early to mid-'80s — but it's okay to take restraints off. So, my plan was to videotape four elderly restrained patients for a week, to remove the restraints, and to tape for another week to document any behavioral change. The difficult thing was to keep these people safe while they were unrestrained. I took the proposal to the psychogeriatric unit. Of twenty-four beds, twenty-two of those people were restrained. And, of course, my proposal was tabled, and I had to go and lobby each of the committee members and think of a good reason why they should give $80,000 to do this research. The following month they approved the proposal, and I danced over to the unit and said, "Hey guys I can do this research now!" And they said, "Jan, your proposal was such a good idea, we've taken all the restraints off." But they had four patients who were incorrigible and still restrained, and I got to select two of those "difficult" patients (Morse & McHutchion, 1991; McHutchion & Morse, 1989)—which was interesting itself. The bottom line is, if you want to make change, you do not have to *actually do* research—just threaten to do it.

Laurel: I'm going to take some minutes off my question four and use them here. I love the word epiphany. Every part of your mouth gets going: e-pi-pha-ny. Marvelous word. And I think Norm is the one who's introduced it into our living research vocabulary. I want to quickly talk about two of my epiphanies.

I've always been a qualitative/quantitative researcher—what is now call mixed methods. I find them kind of fun. Mixed-up methods. But I had a major car accident and was in a coma for some while and I when I came out of that coma, I was not able to do my fourth-grade mathematics. That was a life-changing epiphany. I lived through that, but my mind was pretty scrambled up. My first paper was a power analysis of *Paradise Lost* (Milton, [1667] 2003). I hadn't read *Paradise Lost* since college. I didn't even know I knew it, but I did. Things were scrambled up, but I wanted to continue being an academic. My department didn't want to tenure me because I might be brain damaged (little did they know what was yet to come). At that time, feminism was growing but there was no structured way of teaching students about gender issues. I was a feminist, so I decided to write a textbook, *The Dynamics of Sex and Gender* (Richardson, 1977). Some of you may have read it. Writing that book introduced a new field and helped establish it as one that did not require knowledge of statistics to make sense of the world. That is, it established gender studies, women's studies, and sociology of women as fields of knowledge accessible to everybody. People without advanced mathematics. And through the writing, I retaught myself the bases of sociological reasoning. Writing for my life, writing so I would have a life. That was the first epiphany.

The second epiphany was having a book contract on unwed mothers and finding myself unable to write. I was frozen. The crisis of representation had truly hit me. I didn't know how to write. For whom do I write? Whose life can I write? What do I say? At the same time, I was experiencing the tension between two sides of myself: the scientist and the poet. I wanted to feel more integrated. How was I going to put myself together?

I ended up writing a life-history interview of the unwed mother, "Louisa May," as a narrative poem and presenting it a sociology conference. This experience—along with talking with others who were also involved with writing themselves out of the crisis of representation—created the space in the discipline and in our world where we could be a community. People who were interested in altering qualitative methods, who recognized poststructural thinking, postpostmodernist critique, feminism, queer theory, and so on, could now have a space in which to create community. The experience of performing Louisa May at an ASA convention, where people swore at me and accused me of fabricating my research, led to my involvement with others who had their epiphanies in the same space.

I position myself now as a feminist poststructuralist who is very happy to be alive and very happy to be here.

Art: Before I read Norm Denzin's book (1989), which focused on epiphanies, I didn't know what an epiphany was. Now I see them everywhere. In 1988, my father died suddenly of a heart attack. I was at an academic conference, a National Communication Association convention in New Orleans. And my world was shaken by that experience. I wrote about that in a story I call "Narrative and the Divided Self" (Bochner, 1997). My father's death exposed to me the cleavage of my experience as a human being and as an academic. I had always struggled with this distance between the personal and the academic. I realized after my father's death that my days were numbered, and it was time to stand up and do what my heart said was important.

At the time, I was in the somewhat enviable position of being the chair of the USF Communication Department and I felt it my calling, I guess, to develop a new Ph.D. program that very much embodied what Laurel just said about a sociology without quantities. I never believed that communication was the stuff of quantities to begin with. At that time, in 1990, we had the opportunity of developing this program that everyone in my discipline and even many in my home university said would never work. But I was firm in my conviction that there were people out there, especially women, Third World people, and indigenous populations, who were yearning for such an opportunity.

I also had a serendipitous meeting with Carolyn Ellis in 1990. I attended a lecture she gave in, of all places, the business school, and as I heard her give a short narrative taken from her book, *Final Negotiations* (Ellis, 1995b), I said to myself, "She's giving my talk. There's someone else out there in another discipline who believes all the things I believe." That, as they say, was the beginning of a beautiful friendship and the start of our project on ethnographic alternatives.

◊ ◊ ◊ ◊ ◊

With the introduction of her relationship with Art, Carolyn muses about how she would tell her story of epiphanies, all closely tied to relationships she has had.

My first epiphany occurred when my brother Rex died in 1982 in an airplane crash on his way to visit me. My world was turned upside down, and I think this was the only time in my life I would define myself as depressed. Not only had my brother died but my partner, Gene Weinstein, was entering the final stages of a chronic disease. The survey study on jealousy I was doing seemed insignificant and I craved to explore and try to understand what I was feeling—to get myself out of the depths of despair. That was the beginning of my turn to autoethnography, to exploring and writing about myself and my situation to learn about human behavior. Finally, I was able to connect my love for social psychology with my love for engaged qualitative methods.

My second epiphany came with the death of my partner Gene Weinstein and the responses I got to my writing *Final Negotiations* about our relationship and his dying. I felt the narrative story I was writing was the best sociology I had ever done, and to get the varied responses I received was mind-opening and mind-boggling: "This isn't sociology or research," "This threatens the whole sociological enterprise," and so on. All of it made me more determined to make my case that this was sociology. Norman's response to a paper I did on introspection—that I was being schizophrenic—helped me move from trying to fit into a mainstream sociological model to finding my own place on the margins, one that connected humanities and social science and advocated for an emotional sociology that cared about people.

My third epiphany occurred when I met Art Bochner and found a like-minded colleague and partner. Together we created a synergistic relationship and ethnographic project, and we were able to do more together to advance an interpretive and humanistic social science than either of us could have done alone. I count that as one of my luckiest days!

Round 3

Carolyn: My third question is about ethics. Have you ever experienced an ethical crisis in your qualitative work? If so, describe and tell what you did about it. If you've already answered this question, you might want to pass or you may talk about anything you want.

Ron: I've found myself in ethical trouble most often when I've written about others without first doing a participant check. So first, I would recommend a participant check. But I should also say that doesn't always solve the problem. I did a little piece once about my father having cancer, and I checked with him, talked with him, and showed him what I had written before it went to publication. When it finally came out and he read it again, he said, "I can't believe you told everyone I had cancer. I never had cancer." "Dad," I said, "remember, I had you look at this a while back." "No, I didn't," he answered. "I would have never said I had cancer." He did have cancer and was successfully treated but he had chosen to deny that part of his life. Seeing this description in print, he had difficulty accepting he was being written in that way publicly. Sometimes people don't realize the materiality of an article or book until it lands on their lap.

I'll share another little anecdote with you. In another piece, I wrote a composite character. I was trying to juxtapose the New Orleans' frats with the New Orleans' "yats." The "yats" speak in that rich New Orleans accent that turns "where are you at?" into "Where y'at?"—a greeting that translates into "How are you?" I was describing a female "yat," a composite. My sister, who more closely aligned herself with the frats, read this particular passage, thought I was describing her, and was deeply upset. It took her two years before she approached me with her concern. And I had to say, "No, it isn't you." All this is simply to say, even after participant checks, whenever we are evoking others or simply creating characters, we have to be ready to deal with the interpersonal consequence of those evocations.

Norm: I reset the challenge ... to wrestle with this crisis of representation concept that Laurel talked about. I think we may not understand what it is today, what that means to us. And what it meant to me in the early '80s was a profound interruption in the whole project. Here we had taught ourselves how to do, in my case, Chicago School sociology. I had written a book on my daughters learning how to speak. *Childhood Socialization* (Denzin, 1977) was a series of essays in which I studied my daughters as they played games and used language. It was in the tradition of Cooley and Mead. I was proud of it.

Then we get this notion that there is no clear relationship between reality and these representations. That as a writer you are deeply implicated in what you are writing and it is an unstable position, and your methodology is not neutral, but rather it is constitutive of the very thing you are writing about. So this raises the issue of how do we rearticulate ourselves to the empirical world? And where do we go?

My first attempt to resolve that was really not very satisfactory. I did a long ethnography of *The Alcoholic Self* (Denzin, 1987a) and *The Recovering Alcoholic* (Denzin, 1987b), which was published in two volumes. These were essentially autoethnographic works disguised as traditional ethnography, and I was on almost every page in one way or another. But I wasn't acting like I was writing about myself; I was still struggling with how to write about myself in this space.

I couldn't do that project today. The IRBs had not come forward in the early '80s in the way they are today. Because then we were still hovering under the whole framework of what anthropologists had been doing for decades. Which was, you go out in the field and you study people and you lie and you disguise your intentions. And I wasn't lying or disguising my intentions, but I was taking notes in my mind about something I was going to write, which I later wrote. When that was all done, I experienced another crisis, which was that I had no right to do that. What gave me the license to write about those people? Because I had taken the license of my discipline as permission to write what I had written.

So I came to where I stopped doing fieldwork and I did a series of studies of what I call video ethnography. I turned to cinema and wrote critical books on cinema, on film, on alcoholism, on disruptions in America in the late 1980s and early 1990s. I felt that I had no license to talk about another person any longer.

Now, I'll just probably use up the rest of my time. It was when I discovered the performance framework. When I discovered, unbeknownst to me, that there was this group—many of them on this panel—in performance studies, who were creating poetic performative texts based on their own autoethnographic experiences. I began to feel some kind of liberation. So, then, what I was struggling with was what am I going to write about now if I want to go to this performative space? And that's what led me to my current project, which has been a series of interventions in what I call "Searching for Yellowstone,"[2] a reconstitution of history and nature and our rereading of Native Americans in popular culture. I locate myself at the intersection where those events cross. These texts I'm writing now are meant to be interventions into the history, the popular, popular memory. I'm using myself as a focus for moving the critique into the popular, into the current historical moment. And that's how I moved then from the second epiphany to where I am now. Thank you.

Yvonna: [from her seat] I'm passing.

Janice: [from her seat] I'm passing.

Laurel: [as she walks to the podium] What are we talking about?

Carolyn: Ethics.

Laurel: When I stopped talking before—the thing about the community—it's good to have the community, but you need to have something beyond that. And I want to make sure we give Norm credit not just for this congress, but in giving us places to publish. Without those publications, none of us gets promoted, tenured, and so on. So, not only did the space open where we could think about things differently and meet differently, but Norm really, and Yvonna, they really did provide places for us to publish. Norm, how many journals do you run? And how many handbooks do you edit? So, I think that's an important part. The publication absolutely matters. I wanted to make sure that was clear. I also wanted to thank these two people [Art and Carolyn] and Mitch Allen of AltaMira Press [now publisher of Left Coast Press] and the series of qualitative books so that people can write books and have them published. It's not just enough to love each other. There is a real world out there we have to deal with.

Ethics is always an important question for me, and I've had some minor experiences with them. I wrote a book called *New Other Woman: Contemporary Single Women in Affairs with Married Men* (Richardson, 1987), and one of the questions that become more interesting was men thinking they were in my book when they weren't. Some men thinking their woman came and talked to me when they hadn't. Now, those women are at risk, even though I never interviewed them. Whenever you do anything, you don't quite know what the consequences might be. In a later book of mine, *Fields of Play* (Richardson, 1997), I obliquely intimated that my cousin possibly had sex with her father and the baby was born very not okay and died shortly thereafter. The same day her father died. ... My cousins haven't read my book, but my sister and my brother-in-law are just horrified that I used that nonsecret.

In *Travels with Ernest* (Richardson & Lockridge, 2004), a recent book coauthored with my husband, I chose to accept the ethical decision he had made to tell the story of his father having been sexually abused and its role in his subsequent suicide, despite the grief we would both receive from his siblings for having revealed this family secret.

And I'll tell you about an ethical thing going on right now. I won't call it a crisis; I'll call it a challenge. A dear friend of mine is dying and I'm keeping a journal, I'm writing a book. The working title is *Death of a Friend*. I talk to her on the phone and I keep my journal. Have I told her I'm studying her? Should I tell her I'm studying her? No, I've not told her. And no, I'm not going to tell her. What if I told her? She has said to me, "I've lost everything and now I am losing my stories." And I have said back, "Would you like me to tell your stories?" "Would you?" she has said. That to me is a greater and more ethically grounded permission than me saying, "Hey, I'm writing about our phone conversations." There are other ethical challenges in this book, one being the telling/not telling of her secrets. So, I am thinking and writing now about these ethical challenges. But my ethics always have to be situated ethics. I'm telling her stories, which is what she wants to happen.

Thank you.

Art: The question, "What gives us the right to tell their stories?" raises a second question: "Are there stories that come to our attention that need to be told but have not been inquired into or requested?"

I have one example I want to give you briefly. It revolves around this project I did about five years ago on geriatric care managers, which was inspired by my experiences during the last four years of my mother's life when she was declining into dementia and Alzheimer's disease. I had received consent from a geriatric care manager I had interviewed three or four times previously to interview her in the nursing home. I was sitting and doing the interview and I had my tape recorder going, and she had signed all the consent forms, and we had done all the IRB stuff. Along came a nurse, my mother's nurse practitioner, and the tape recorder was running when she came over and greeted me at the table. She knew I had been looking for her that morning. We began to engage in a very spontaneous, unplanned conversation in which a number of stories were revealed about her and her industry's orientation toward death and dying. I've since written a story about this, but have not published it, though I think it's one of the best stories I've ever written. It's called "Paperwork," a title I chose to reflect how bureaucracy and paperwork are given priority over the impulse toward caring and empathy at the end of life.

I have about ninety minutes of tape of this conversation. Should I publish it? I never asked her consent. The story puts her in a very bad light. The people who read the story tell me how much they dislike her, though that really was not my intention. How do you answer a question like this? On the one hand, we need some guidelines about what rights we do have to publish stories that we hear. On the other hand, there's another argument that goes: if they hadn't behaved so badly, we wouldn't have the stories to tell.

Carolyn: I can't help myself. Though I am the moderator, I have to tell an ethical story. I hadn't planned to but I would really like to join in the conversation, because I did experience a real ethical dilemma.

I was educated as a qualitative methodologist, and I went

out into the field and studied isolated fishing communities for my first project. In one community that I studied, most of the people were illiterate. At that time to get IRB permission meant you just filled out and signed a short form, saying, "I have permission to study them, and I use pseudonyms," or in some way disguise who they are. My training then led me to think that you go out and interview people, and you participate with them, and you try to get all the information you can, hoping they forget you are a researcher. The more information you get, the better fieldworker you are, especially if you come back with information about their hidden lives.

So I wrote *Fisher Folk* (Ellis, 1986), and, to be honest with you, I didn't think that much about how the people would respond, though I thought, "They're illiterate; they'll never read this work." So, the work was published. And unfortunately—well, right now I think that it was fortunate—a professor of mine when I was an undergraduate, who had wanted to publish a book on this community and never had, copied parts of my book, highlighted sections, took them into the community, and read them to the fisher folk.

The fisher folk had known I was doing research. But I had been there for nine years, and they forgot. At this point, to them I was pretty much just Carolyn coming to the community to visit. They were extremely hurt by what they heard. I had described them as smelling like fish, and other things equally devastating. These people had become really good friends of mine. I loved them and cared for them, and what I said was very painful for them and for me. I went back to the community and talked with them. Some people forgave me. Some people never did forgive me.

This event led to a paper I wrote about this experience called "Returning to the Field" (Ellis, 1995a). The experience did not lead me to do autoethnography—which some think happened—because I was already doing autoethnography when all this happened. But it did lead me to start thinking about the ethics of research in a whole different way. That there are all kinds of ethical issues that the IRB doesn't concern itself with. These are issues that I talked about in another panel here, issues that occur in particular when you become friends with the people you study. IRBs are concerned only with procedural ethics; they assume that you go into a setting, that you don't know the people who are there, that you study them, and get out. That's the end of the relationship. When you develop friendships, as all of you know you do, the ethical issues are deeper and more complex. This experience has led me to be really concerned with doing ethical research from a relational standpoint and to think deeply about what we owe the people whose lives we want to put in our studies. Thank you for indulging me.

Round 4

Carolyn: The next question is: Do you have a favorite qualitative study and why? Some of you have addressed that already, too, so pass if you don't want to say more about it.

Ron: I think Carolyn's question is an impossible question to narrow down to one. So, I'm going to name several really quickly. I have to start with Carolyn's *Final Negotiations* (Ellis, 1995b) for the absolute power of that tale. I also think of Carolyn's *The Ethnographic I* (Ellis, 2004) for its wonderful ambition. I think of Lisa Tillman-Healy's *Between Gay and Straight* (Tilmann-Healy, 2001) because of the compelling stance of the researcher. I think of Dwight Conquergood's (1991) article, "Rethinking Ethnography," which powerfully situates performance in ethnographic work. I think of Lesa Lockford's *Performing Femininity* (2004) for the wealth of her insights and the eloquence of her style. And, of course, I think of Norman Denzin's *Interpretative Ethnography* (1996), which for me is one of the richest summaries of the contributing forces to a qualitative sensibility.

Norm: I just think that everything everybody at this panel has written is my favorite.

Yvonna: Leading an impoverished life as I do, I have two favorite books. I actually have a lot of favorite books and I've been recommending them to students. I'll mention two. One is Margaret

Wolf's *A Thrice Told Tale* (1992). I love that because she tells the story three different ways. It seems to me to be truly the first experimental text we ever had that experimented with different discourses and rhetorical forms. My other favorite book is something probably serious sociologists think is totally trivial, but I think John Van Maanen's *Tales of the Field* (1988) is the funniest doggone introduction to different genres and to some of the illusions that fieldworkers hand themselves. It's just a wonderful book and students come back when I assign it and they say, "You need more of these kinds of books."

Jan: I read the question to the letter so I have articles, not books. The first one that I give all my students is from archaeology and is called "The Golden Marshalltown: A Parable for the Archeology of the 1980s" by Kent Flannery (1982), and this is the funniest—but wisest—thing you can ever read! My favorite article that's ethnographic is "Some New Dying Trick: African American Youths 'Choosing' HIV/AIDS" by Silvy Tourigny (1998). It's about youth in Detroit who choose to become HIV positive so they can be eligible for the services provided for those with HIV. It's very powerful.

Laurel: I also like everything. There are so many things to read and the things I like are not so much by genre as the impact on me—when I'm surprised, when I'm delighted, when I didn't know it, when it moves me. And what I like best is whatever I last read that moved me.

Art: I echo all the choices of my colleagues on the panel. I'd like to mention a few other works that have had a huge impact on me. Laurel Richardson's *Fields of Play* (1997) and Jane Tompkins's *My Life in School* (1997) are two I'd choose because they tell very important stories about the life histories of teachers and the impact of how the institutional culture under which we labor influences our lives. I strongly believe that we should not only be focusing our critical lens on the sociopolitical culture of the countries in which we live, but also turning a critical eye to the institutions that have had so much influence over us.

I also mourn the death of my good friend Dwight Conquergood and virtually anything that you can find that Conquergood has written is worth the read and will change your life.

One other book that I think is very much, at least in my view, cutting edge is by Ross Gray and Christine Sindling (2002), which we published in our Ethnographic Alternative series with AltaMira. The authors studied breast cancer and prostate cancer survivors and based their book on some very traditional psychological research, including interviews with doctors, survivors, and friends of survivors, which was funded by a grant. They did a rather conventional orthodox empirical study and then turned it into a text and a performance script that was directed by a woman theatrical director in Canada. The survivors themselves took part in the performances, which were taken out into the community, including in hospitals throughout Canada during grand rounds. I think this has all the elements of basic research, performance, performative writing, and community activism in one, and I highly recommend it.

Carolyn muses about her favorite books and is glad she doesn't have to answer the question she has asked:

What would I say? *Presentation of Self* by Goffman (1959)—a classic. *Tally's Corner* (Liebow, 1967)—one of the first ethnographies that engaged me with its style. Norman's *Interpretive Ethnography* (Denzin, 1996)—extremely useful. Krieger's *The Mirror Dance* (1983)—that showed how writing could be different. Any and just about everything Laurel and Ron write—always evocative and provocative as they take the next step that needs to be taken. Plus whatever Art writes, especially the theories and stories piece (Bochner, 1994)—yes, I'm biased! Like the work of Norm and Yvonna, Art's work lays the ground and framework for all we do. And, of course, the books in our Ethnographic Alternative series, coedited with Art. Ruth Behar's *A Vulnerable Observer* (1996), Carol Rambo's articles, especially the one on being abused by her father (1995). ... Ah, yes, I'm glad I don't have to answer this question.

Rounds 5 and 6

Carolyn looks at her watch and notes that only a little time remains. First, no discussion among the participants; now, she wonders if there will be time for audience participation. She knows audience members would like to ask their own questions. How often does one get to ask questions of the leaders in the field? Still, the session is going well. The audience is quiet and attentive; no one leaves the packed room, in spite of how uncomfortable it must be to be jammed together in their seats and sitting on the hard floor. The room is so hot, she notes, glancing at the open windows along the side of the room and wiping the beads of perspiration off her face. She stands and says:

Carolyn: I'd like to combine questions five and six. Then, hopefully, we will have time for the audience to ask a few questions at the end. Question five concerns the current state of qualitative methods. How would you characterize the current state of qualitative research? For example, what are its strengths and tensions? How do you see the connection of qualitative work to humanities and to arts and sciences? To politics, culture, and social justice? And then I'm going to add challenges and goals. What are the major challenges qualitative researchers face in the next decade? What would you most like to happen in qualitative research politically, practically, and/or academically and intellectually? What goals do you have for yourself in your work? And yes, you have only two minutes to answer.

The audience laughs.

Ron: One of the things that stops me with Carolyn's question is that it is really hard to know what exactly we're saying when we say qualitative research. There's a journal in the speech field, *Qualitative Research Reports in Communication*. Not too long ago, I sent them a little essay. It was a simple phenomenology, boringly traditional in its approach. Probably the article was boring in and of itself, but that's another matter. What is interesting to me is that piece came back to me, without review, with the editor's note, saying, "I'm sorry, this isn't what we consider to be qualitative work." The question of what constitutes qualitative work and what we are pointing to when we say that becomes pretty tricky.

The other issue Carolyn's question evokes is the relationship among the sciences, the humanities, and the arts. I would like to suggest that all of these fields have been in the business of legislating how the "I" should appear. If we think about literary studies in the last century, we can begin with I. A. Richards (1926) and the distinction he wanted to make between science and pseudo-science. His distinction gave rise to the New Critics and the formalism that is still being taught in many of our undergraduate English departments today. This particular work takes as its primary task to discover, in part by removing the biographical and psychological dimensions of the reader, what is in the text. The idea is to get it right, to nail it down. This is a desire for objective truth, rather than for subjective truth.

An alternative logic situates the "I" quite differently; it invites the articulation of feeling and the enunciation of the possible. So, this privileging of the affective, the uncertain, and the possible seems to me a different way of thinking about qualitative work. There is a considerable amount of qualitative work that in many ways still mimics what's going in the sciences and certain branches of the humanities and certain branches of the arts. The work I like best—and I believe this is where the strength of qualitative methods resides—is when it articulates how claims matter on the level of the individual, when it shows how the material consequences of discursive systems, legislative policies, and interpersonal interactions happen on individual bodies.

Norm: When Yvonna and I put forth the notion of moments of inquiry, originally five moments I think, or seven moments, what we were attempting to capture is that in the last two decades there has been a profound revolution in the thinking about and the doing of qualitative inquiry. It's as if the field, in my mind, had sort of reached a certain steady stay for almost a half century and it just kind of stopped developing. Suddenly, it went into fast forward and went through so many iterations over the last two decades. Many of those iterations have been talked about in the editions of the *Handbook of Qualitative Research* (Denzin & Lincoln, 1994, 2000, 2005). So, there is so much to stay on top of and to understand in terms of these developments that weren't there when those of us on this panel came into the field and taught ourselves to do qualitative research. At the same time, to reflexively reflect on all of these transformations and to locate ourselves in the present in those spaces is a profound challenge because we really haven't had time to digest all of these changes and transformations.

As they've happened so quickly, I think there are centrifugal forces or contrary forces that are trying to move us back to what it was like before these transformations happened. As if we could go back to *Boys in White* (Becker et al., 1961) and stop time and say there's this group who don't count, they don't do numbers, but they contribute to the study of the world through their mixed methodologies and their interviews, and their narratives, and their life stories, and their case studies. And we like them, and we have one or two of them on our faculty, and they publish, and they do good work, and they're going to get tenure, and kind of leave it at that. But for this cohort that has come to this conference the last two years, the call is radically different. It is to transform and change the spaces in which we exist in the academy. And to take hold of the terms that define our existence in relationship to the other disciplines and the journals and the apparatuses and the departments, and tenure, and recruitment, and teaching, and instruction, and funding, and publishing, and journals. To take hold of our own existence, our own history, and make it into a dream that was there from the beginning when we were called into this space. To do something different than what we had been doing up until we got here.

The audience applauds loudly.

Laurel: [to Yvonna] How will you follow that "I Have a Dream" speech?

The panelists roar with laughter.

Yvonna: Oh man. ... I actually have two sets of questions from Carolyn and so I'm going to work off both of them. I had this long conversation with Lisa Shaw today. And she said, "What do you think about where qualitative research is?" I outlined a theory very different from what she'd been hearing. I think one of the strengths is the growing number of practitioners. And I think unless you're going to take those people out and shoot them, qualitative researchers are not going away. I'm sorry Grover Whitehurst [assistant secretary of education with the U.S. Department of Education]. I think that we have a compelling story to tell and I think there are more and more people interested in being a part of creating that narrative. So, I think one of the strengths is that we're onto something with qualitative research and it's not going to go away. And Bush can hope as much as he wants and we're not going anywhere.

I have a very hopeful look about the future even though I don't have a very hopeful look about funding for the future. I think that this is a field ripe and rife with tensions. Sometimes they get annoying, so I just go back to my room in the hotel. But sometimes the tensions are points where there are highly fruitful discussions, debate, and argumentation going on. One of those tensions currently going around is the influence of the right-wing methodological fundamentalists on qualitative research. I think one of the tensions has to do with the regulatory aspects of IRBs. One of the tensions has to do with how we describe ourselves, and this gets back to the story Ron was telling. Wait a minute, phenomenology is pretty fundamental, what do you mean you aren't interested in this kind of qualitative research? What exactly are you interested in if you aren't interested in this?

I think there are a lot of varieties, brands, subspecies, whatever, drifting around. Many of those different models have different criteria for judging them. But we knew that long before Norman and I got cognitively hooked up. Mary Lee Smith told us that in the late '70s. I think the tensions are very good. My notion is a metaphoric Gordian knot, and I'm always trying to keep the knot very loose. I rather resist having people wanting to tie down the knot and focus into one model, one paradigm, one set of this, one outline for that.

I like the fact that right now we're in ferment. That's where I see us. And I think that being in ferment is not one of the tensions, but one of the very real strengths. I think when we come out of the ferment it has to be not in relation to the National Research Council. It has to be in relation to this community. That we need to decide who we are. We don't need to decide who we are in light of who Grover Whitehurst and Dick Shavelson [School of Education, Stanford University] say that we are or are not. Those are decisions that we need to engage as a community. We are the scientific community in qualitative research. It's up to us to decide who we will be and when we will be that.

Jan: I want to talk about where we are now and where we are going. At the moment, I think we are in a good position, but we are not in such a fortunate position everywhere. We have pockets where qualitative research is striving to *be*, and pockets where qualitative inquiry is really struggling to stay alive. In his closing address of the Qualitative Health Research Conference in Edmonton a few months ago, Carl Mitcham, who is a philosopher of science and technology, made a very interesting argument that the sciences in quantitative inquiry have almost outdone themselves—quantitative inquiry is becoming increasingly expensive for smaller and smaller gains in knowledge and discovery. And that the time for qualitative inquiry is coming, for there is still much to discover qualitatively. I kept thinking of the $28 million project (S.U.P.P.O.R.T.) funded by Robert Wood Johnson on end-of-life care, which had no statistically significant findings. And at the end, they called in qualitative folk to try and save this project.

On the one hand, I'm very hopeful for qualitative inquiry. On the other hand, I believe the warnings that Julianne Cheek (Cheek, Garnham, & Quan, 2006) is giving us that we have to watch our back. There is game playing, and as a journal editor, I'm quite aware of the politics of impact factors and the perceived worthiness of information that is now regulating our universities, regulating what we do, and regulating who gets funded. So, one part of me is very hopeful and excited, but my other eye wary. We have to support each other. We have to cite each other, we have to cite qualitative journals, we have to fight or we are going to die.

Laurel: I started by telling you I was interested in knowing and telling. And I was talking about knowing, and now it's time to talk about telling. Simmel! Georg Simmel has been essential to my intellectual life. Simmel is interested in how form shapes content. How what you can say depends on the form you choose. You can't say everything in a particular kind of form. What you might say in a science article, what you might say in a poem, is different. The form is different and therefore the content is shaped differently. I know different things through different forms. What I'm so excited about for contemporary qualitative research is how the forms have burgeoned. How there are so many different ways in which people can tell their stories. Not just on the written page. On the Internet. Artistically. I'm doing altered books, as some of you know, which is another form. People do drama, they do performance, and they do music. The formats are just expanding. That means there are multiple ways, more and more different ways by which stories can be told and through which qualitative research can be reported and things can be known.

In most universities, you don't have to do that five chapter discipline thing. You can alter that. You can really expand and do different things. I'm really excited about the burgeoning of different kinds of formats because the content can just be amazing things you might know. What you might know, what I might know from you.

Along with that, I've been in Australia for almost two months and I had a fantastic experience doing qualitative research with communities I never thought even knew about qualitative research. The Sisters of Mercy are doing projects around the world with people with AIDS, and I got to work with them. I got to work with circus people; they wanted to know all about qualitative research methods. Three of them have e-mailed me subsequently that they want to get Ph.D.s in qualitative research—because they didn't realize that academia could be so much fun. So, we should take a broader view of the spaces where people do research. It's not just large research universities. It's all kinds of places in the world and sites in the world that we just didn't think about. Who would think that circus performers would want to do Ph.D.s in qualitative methods? That's fantastic. And how might they perform them? It's an emergent thing. And with the Internet, my university is going to forgo hard-copy dissertations. It's going to all be on the net. And once it's on the net, what difference does it make if someone is dancing on the net or writing a paper on it? So, there are all these new formats and therewith new content. I tend to be an optimist. I'm just always glad to be alive and I'm glad we have a world.

I like this last question. What goals do you have for you and your work? I have for me the same goals that I have for you. To do what you want to do. Enjoy it, love it, publish it, share it, and stay in my community, please.

Art: I'm just curious, how many of you out there hold tenured positions in universities? [About 15% of hands are raised.] Okay. That's quite a few of you. Some of what I have to say is especially addressed to you, because you are in a less vulnerable position then others in the room. It's interesting that we've called these last two meetings a Congress in Qualitative Inquiry. I think this project is about our own institutional activism and its political qualities. I think the question, "What will qualitative inquiry become?" is a political question. And it's in your hands. Most of the panelists here have a lot of gray hair. We've been around the block. We've done what little we can to initiate and advance this cause. The future is in your hands.

As I said in my opening remarks, I can remember a time in my own field, communication, when quantitative empiricists were just trying to get their foot in the door. There was just one per department. And that was only thirty years ago. Now, by and large, they are the gate keepers; they control the field. Thirty years might sound like a long time to some of you, but it's really not. Fifteen years ago, we didn't have *Qualitative Inquiry*. We didn't have the *Handbooks*. We didn't have the corpus of projects, or not many of them, that have been discussed or referenced at this congress.

It is up to you, the next generation of qualitative research-ers, to go back to your universities, or wherever you are working, and do what you can, in an activist way, to inspire some of the changes we've been talking about at this congress. I think this is a tremendously important part of our whole experience here. At this conference, I had conversations in the halls and in meetings with nurses, psychologists, social workers, educators, sociologists, performance artists, communication theorists, ethicists, political scientists, health and family practitioners, and counselors. All of them at this meeting. All of them coming because they feel a calling and a cause. Now we have to engage in some sort of political activism wherever we work. If you're called on or if you have any opportunity to serve on editorial boards, to serve in positions of any influence or power in whatever discipline you belong to or in whatever institution you are employed, you need to do this. And you need to nurture and mentor young students—I can't think of anything that is any more important that that. Giving them hope, encouragement, support, assistance, and the wisdom of your own experience. We all have a responsibility, an ethical and moral responsibility, if we believe in the work that is being done here, to do whatever we can individually and collectively to shape the future. Meet your colleagues in other departments who are doing similar work. Talk to each other. Have conversations. Form institutes. Form work groups. Get involved with each other. Don't isolate yourselves. The future belongs to you.

The audience claps loudly.

Carolyn feels she has been at a rally. "I'm ready to answer the call," she muses. "Take me," she wants to stand up and say. "Take me. I'll go." She feels the positive energy of the current state of qualitative methods right here circulating through this room. The excitement is with the interpretive/participatory/activist qualitative researchers who are called to follow their hearts, not model themselves after quantitative scientists. This panel puts an exclamation mark on the conference, reflecting the positive feelings that have been present among more than 900 delegates from fifty-five nations who have gathered to attend sixteen preconference workshops and present more than 800 papers and performances in more than 180 sessions. What energy! It's as though people have been let out of a locked closet or better they have unlocked the doors themselves. This is the future. We have moved from standing on the margins of mainstream orthodox research looking for acceptance and have formed our own centers, publication outlets, and conferences. Although there still is work to be done and barriers to move past, as these speakers note, the excitement of possibilities fills the air.

The hot room suddenly feels breezy as cold chills run up and down her arms, no doubt the effect of listening to the passion of her colleagues. The rest of the audience seems to feel the moment as well. They sit quietly, but lean forward, eyes wide open, taking it all in, wanting more: more speeches like these where panelists have fire in their bellies and emotion in their hearts; panels where people talk about what they feel and the mistakes they're made as well as their thoughts and accomplishments; panels where people want their work to matter; panels where audience members feel talked to or with rather than talked at.

Carolyn stands and speaks.

Carolyn: I've learned in my time in this profession that professors always fill up whatever time is available. We have managed to fill up the entire ninety minutes. We didn't get to have a discussion, but we at least got to talk informally and personally and hear some things about what scholars think and feel that you don't normally get to hear at formal conference presentations. My thanks to the panelists and to the audience for coming.

◊ ◊ ◊ ◊ ◊

The panel ends with Norman inviting everyone to the town hall meeting that follows, where a constitution for the organization and a policy on IRBs will be presented for ratification. He invites them to attend that evening an old fashioned cookout with a Cajun band.

For Carolyn and others, the music and the dancing that evening—the embodied engagement—will be
another highlight of the conference.

Carolyn thinks about how to design and implement panels where participants have a chance to
engage more with each other in conversations, building on what each other has to say, and where audience
members have a chance not just to listen but to speak
back and say what's on their minds and in their hearts
as well.

But for now, this is fine, real fine. She's ready to
dance.

Notes

1. This script comes from an edited transcript of a session entitled "Talking
and Thinking about Qualitative Research," which was part of the 2006
International Congress of Qualitative Inquiry, held at University of Illinois
at Urbana-Champaign on May 4–6, 2006. This special session featured
scholars informally responding to questions about their personal history
with qualitative methods, epiphanies that attracted them to qualitative work
or changed their perspectives within the qualitative tradition, ethical crises,
exemplary qualitative studies, the current state of qualitative methods,
and challenges and goals for the next decade. Panelists included: Arthur
Bochner (Communication), Norman Denzin (Sociology/Communication/
Critical Studies), Yvonna Lincoln (Education), Janice Morse (Nursing/
Anthropology), Ronald Pelias (Performance Studies/Communication),
and Laurel Richardson (Sociology/Gender Studies). Carolyn Ellis
(Communication/Sociology) served as organizer and moderator. Thanks to
Christopher McRae for recording and transcribing this session. After Cris
transcribed the original tape, each participant then had the opportunity to
read and edit her or his section of the transcript though I [Carolyn] asked
them to preserve the flow and informality of their speech. I then read the
transcript with the minor changes the participants suggested and listened
to the tape to get a sense of the emotion and tone of the speeches and the

occasion. I edited for consistency, omitting some of the redundancies and unnecessary words but attempting always to keep the meaning of the oral texts. And for consistency with other chapters in this book, I inserted relevant citations into the text. In the rewriting, I added my thoughts and feelings along with descriptions of the panel. Panelists then had an opportunity to respond to this version. This text is a co-production by all the panelists.

2. See, for example, Denzin (2001).

References

Bateson, G. (1972). Steps to an ecology of mind: Collected essays in anthropology, psychiatry, evolution, and epistemology. Chicago: University of Chicago Press.

Becker, H., Geer, B., Hughes, E, & Strauss, A. (1961). *Boys in white: Student culture in medical school.* Chicago: University of Chicago.

Behar, R. (1996). *The vulnerable observer: Anthropology that breaks your heart.* Boston: Beacon Press.

Blumer, H. (1969). *Symbolic interactionism: Perspective and method.* Englewood Cliffs, NJ: Prentice Hall.

Bochner, A. (1994). Perspectives on inquiry II: Theories and stories. In M. Knapp & G. R. Miller (Eds.), *Handbook of interpersonal communication*, 2nd ed. (pp. 21–41). Thousand Oaks, CA: Sage.

Bochner, A. (1997). It's about time: Narrative and the divided self. *Qualitative Inquiry, 3*(3), 418–438.

Campbell, D. T., & Stanley, J. C. (1966). *Experimental and quasi-experimental designs for research.* Chicago: Rand McNally.

Cheek, J., Garnham, B., & Quan, J. (2006). What's in a number? Issues in providing evidence of impact and quality of researcher(ers). *Qualitative Health Research, 16*(3), 423–435.

Conquergood, D. (1991). Rethinking ethnography: Towards a critical cultural politics. *Communication Monographs, 58*(2), 179–194.

Denzin, N. K. (1977). *Childhood socialization: Studies in the development of language, social behavior, and identity.* San Francisco: Jossey-Bass.

Denzin, N. K. (1987a). *The alcoholic self.* Newbury Park, CA: Sage.

Denzin, N. K. (1987b). *The recovering alcoholic.* Newbury Park, CA: Sage

Denzin, N. K. (1988). *The research act: A theoretical introduction to sociological methods.* New York: Prentice-Hall.

Denzin, N. K. (1989). *Interpretive interactionism.* Newbury Park, CA: Sage.

Denzin, N. K. (1996). *Interpretive ethnography.* Thousand Oaks, CA: Sage.

Denzin, N. K. (2001). Cowboys and Indians. *Symbolic Interaction, 25*(2), 251–261.

Denzin, N. K., and Lincoln, Y. S. (1994, 2000, 2005). *Handbook of qualitative research,* 1st, 2nd, and 3rd eds. Thousand Oaks, CA: Sage.

Ellis, C. (1986). *Fisher folk: Two communities on Chesapeake Bay.* Lexington: University Press of Kentucky.

Ellis, C. (1995a). Emotional and ethical quagmires in returning to the field. *Journal of Contemporary Ethnography, 24*(1), 68–98.

Ellis, C. (1995b). *Final negotiations: A story of love, loss, and chronic illness.* Philadelphia: Temple University Press.

Ellis, C. (2004). *The ethnographic I: A methodological novel about autoethnography.* Walnut Creek, CA: AltaMira.

Flannery, K. (1982). The golden marshalltown: A parable for the archeology of the 1980s. *American Anthropologist, 84*(2), 265–278.

Goffman, E. (1959). *The presentation of self in everyday life.* Garden City, NY: Doubleday Anchor.

Goodall, H. L. (1989). *Casing a promised land: The autobiography of an organizational detective as cultural ethnographer.* Carbondale: Southern Illinois University Press.

Gray R., & Sindling, C. (2002). *Standing ovation: Performing social science research about cancer.* Walnut Creek, CA: AltaMira.

Henry, J. (1965). *Pathways to madness.* New York: Vintage Books.

Krieger, S. (1983). *The mirror dance: Identity in a women's community.* Philadelphia: Temple University Press.

Liebow, E. (1967). *Tally's corner.* Boston: Little, Brown.

Lockford, L. (2004). *Performing femininity.* Walnut Creek, CA: AltaMira.

Milton, J. (2003 [orig. 1667]). *Paradise lost.* New York: Penguin Group.

Morse, J. M. (1984a). Breast- and bottle-feeding: The effect on infant weight gain in the Fiji-Indian neonate. *Ecology of Food and Nutrition, 14*(1), 109–114.

Morse, J. M. (1984b). The cultural context of infant feeding in Fiji. *Ecology of Food and Nutrition, 14*(1), 287–296.

Morse, J. M. (1989). Cultural responses to parturition: Childbirth in Fiji. *Medical Anthropology, 12*(1), 5–44.

Morse, J. M., & McHutchion, E. (1991). The behavioral effects of releasing restraints. *Research in Nursing and Health, 14*(1), 187–196.

McHutchion, E., & Morse, J. M. (1989). Releasing restraints: A nursing dilemma? *Journal of Gerontological Nursing, 15*(2), 16–21.

Rambo (Ronai), C. (1995). Multiple reflections of child sex abuse: An argument for a layered account. *Journal of Contemporary Ethnography, 23*(4), 395–426.

Richards, I. A. (1926). *Science and poetry.* New York: W.W. Norton.

Richardson, L. (1977). *The dynamics of sex and gender: A sociological perspective.* Chicago: Rand McNally.

Richardson, L. (1987). *The new other woman: Single women in relations with married men.* New York: The Free Press.

Richardson, L. (1993). Poetic representation, ethnographic presentation and transgressive validity: The case of the skipped line. *The Sociological Quarterly, 34*(4), 695–710.

Richardson, L. (1997). *Fields of play: Constructing an academic life.* New Brunswick, NJ: Rutgers University Press.

Richardson, L., & Lockridge, E. (2004) *Travels with Ernest: Crossing the literary/sociological divide.* Lanham, MD: AltaMira.

Tillmann-Healy, L. (2001). *Between gay and straight: Understanding friendship across sexual orientation.* Walnut Creek, CA: AltaMira.

Tompkins, J. (1997). *My life in school.* Boston: Addison-Wesley.

Tourigny, S. (1998). Some new dying trick: African American youths "choosing" HIV/AIDS. *Qualitative Health Research, 8*(2), 149–167.

Van Maanen, J. (1988). *Tales of the field: On writing ethnography.* Chicago: University of Chicago Press.

Webb, E. J., Campbell, D. T., Schwartz, R. C., & Sechrest, L. (1966). *Unobtrusive measures: Nonreactive research in the social sciences.* Chicago: University of Chicago Press.

Wolf, M. (1992). *A thrice-told tale: Feminism, postmodernism, and ethnographic responsibility.* Stanford, CA: Stanford University Press.

| Index

About the Authors

Editors

Norman K. Denzin is Distinguished Professor of Communications, College of Communications Scholar, and Research Professor of Communications, Sociology, and Humanities at the University of Illinois, Urbana-Champaign. One of the world's foremost authorities on qualitative research and cultural criticism, Denzin is the author or editor of more than two dozen books, including *Performance Ethnography*, *Reading Race*, *Interpretive Ethnography*, *The Cinematic Society*, *Images of Postmodern Society*, *The Recovering Alcoholic*, and *The Alcoholic Self*. He is past editor of *The Sociological Quarterly*, coeditor of the landmark *Handbook of Qualitative Research* (1st, 2nd, and 3rd editions, Sage Publications, with Yvonna S. Lincoln), editor of the *Handbook of Critical Indigenous Methodologies* (forthcoming, Sage, with Yvonna S. Lincoln and Linda Tuhiwai Smith), coeditor of *Contesting Empire/ Globalizing Dissent: Cultural Studies after 9/11* (Paradigm, 2006, with Michael D. Giardina), coeditor of *Qualitative Inquiry and the Conservative Challenge: Confronting Methodological Conservatism* (Left Coast Press, 2006, with Michael D. Giardina) coeditor of *Qualitative Inquiry*, founding editor of *Cultural Studies/Critical Methodologies*, series editor of *Studies in Symbolic Interaction*, and *Cultural Critique* series editor for Peter Lang Publishing.

Michael D. Giardina is a visiting assistant professor in Advertising & Cultural Studies at the University of Illinois, Urbana-Champaign. He is the author of *From Soccer Moms to NASCAR Dads: Sport, Culture, and Politics in a Nation Divided* (Paradigm, forthcoming) and *Sporting Pedagogies: Performing Culture &*

Identity in the Global Arena (Peter Lang, 2005), which received the 2006 "Most Outstanding Book" award from the North American Society for the Sociology of Sport. He is also the coeditor of *Globalizing Cultural Studies: Ethnographic Interventions in Theory, Method, and Policy* (Peter Lang, 2007, with Cameron McCarthy, Aisha Durham, Alice Filmer, and Miguel Malagreca), and *Youth Culture & Sport: Identity, Power, and Politics* (Routledge, forthcoming, with Michele K. Donnelly). His work on globalization, cultural studies, qualitative inquiry, and the racial logics of late capitalism has appeared in journals such as *Harvard Educational Review, Cultural Studies/Critical Methodologies, Journal of Sport & Social Issues*, and *Qualitative Inquiry*.

Contributors

Marie Battiste is a Mi'kmaq educator, professor of Educational Foundations, and academic director of the Aboriginal Education Research Centre at the University of Saskatchewan, Canada. Her research interests are in initiating institutional change in the decolonization of education, language and social justice policy and power, and postcolonial educational approaches that recognize and affirm the political and cultural diversity of Canada and the ethical protection and advancement of indigenous knowledge. A technical expert to the United Nations, recent books include *Protecting Indigenous Knowledge and Heritage: A Global Challenge* (Purich Press, 2000, with J. Youngblood Henderson), which received a Saskatchewan Book Award in 2006, *Reclaiming Indigenous Voice and Vision* (University of British Columbia Press, 2000), and *First Nations Education in Canada: The Circle Unfolds* (University of British Columbia Press, 1995, with Jean Barman).

Arthur P. Bochner is professor of communication and codirector of the Institute for Human Interpretive Studies at the University of South Florida. He has written extensively on ethnography, autoethnography, and narrative inquiry, and has published such books as *Ethnographically Speaking: Autoethnography, Literature, and Aesthetics* (AltaMira, 2002, with Carolyn Ellis), *Composing Ethnography: Alternative Forms of Qualitative Writing* (AltaMira, 1996, with Carolyn Ellis), and *Understanding Family Communication* (Gorsuch, 1990/1995, with Janet Yerby and Nancy Buerkele-Rothfuss). His work has also appeared in journals such as *Qualitative Inquiry, Journal of Contemporary Ethnography, Communication Theory,* and *Studies in Symbolic Interaction.* He is the current vice-president of the National Communications Association.

Gaile S. Cannella is professor of education at Arizona State University. She is the author of *Deconstructing Early Childhood Education: Social Justice and Revolution* (Peter Lang, 1997) and coauthor (with Radhika Viruru) of *Childhood and Post-colonization: Power, Education, and Contemporary Practice* (RoutledgeFalmer, 2004), and coeditor of *Kidworld: Childhood Studies, Global Perspectives, and Education* (Peter Lang, 2002). She is also the section editor for Childhood and Cultural Studies in the *Journal of Curriculum Theorizing.*

Julianne Cheek is a professor in the Division of Health Sciences and director of the Early Career Researcher Development program at the University of South Australia. She is the author of *Postmodern and Poststructural Approaches to Nursing Research* (Sage, 2000), and coauthor of *Finding Out: Information Literacy for the 21st Century* (Macmillan, 1995) and *Society and Health: Social Theory for Health Workers* (Longman Chesire, 1996), which won the prize for the best Tertiary Single Book (Wholly Australian) in the prestigious Australian Awards for Excellence in Educational Publishing for 1996.

Clifford G. Christians is the Charles H. Sandage Distinguished Professor of Advertising and Research Professor of Communications and Media Studies at the University of Illinois, Urbana-Champaign. One of the world's leading authorities on media and social ethics, Christians is the author or editor of numerous books, including *Good News: A Social Ethics of the*

Press (Oxford University Press, 2003, with John Ferre and Mark Fackler), *Media Ethics: Cases and Moral Reasoning* (1st–7th editions) (Longman, 2004, with Kim Rotzoll and Mark Fackler), and *Communication Ethics and Universal Values* (Sage, 1997, with Michael Traber) and the forthcoming *Normative Theories of the Media* (University of Illinois Press, with Theodore Glasser, Denis McQuail, Kaarle Nordenstreng, and Robert White). Professor Christians has also been a visiting scholar in philosophical ethics at Princeton University, in social ethics at the University of Chicago, and a PEW fellow in ethics at Oxford University. In 2004, he received the Paul J. Deutschmann Award for Excellence in Research from the Association for Education in Journalism and Mass Communication.

Carolyn Ellis is professor of communication and codirector of the Institute for Human Interpretive Studies at the University of South Florida. She is the author of many books, including *The Ethnographic I: A Methodological Novel about Autoethnography* (AltaMira, 2004), *Composing Ethnography: Alternative Forms of Qualitative Writing* (AltaMira, 1996, with Arthur P. Bochner), and *Final Negotiations: A Story of Love, Loss and Chronic Illness* (Temple University Press, 1995). Her current research projects investigate autoethnography, narrative writing, and issues of illness and loss.

Michelle Fine is Distinguished Professor of Psychology, Women's Studies, and Urban Education at the Graduate Center of the City University of New York. Committed to participatory action research in schools, prisons, and communities, her writings focus on theoretical questions of social injustice: how people think about unjust distributions of resources and social practices, when they resist, and how such inequities are legitimated. Recent books include *Silenced Voices and Extraordinary Conversations* (Teachers College Press, 2003, with Lois Weis), *Construction Sites: Excavating Race, Class, and Gender with Urban Youth* (Teachers College Press, 2001, with Lois Weis), *Unknown City* (Beacon Press, 1999, with Lois Weis), and *Off White* (Routledge, 2004, with Lois Weis, Linda Powell Pruitt, and April Burns).

Corrine Glesne is an independent scholar specializing in qualitative research methodologies and educational anthropology. She has conducted ethnographic research in Mexico, Costa Rica, and St. Vincent and the Grenadines, as well as qualitative research and evaluation in Surinam and Puerto Rico. She has also done archaeological work in Kenya and Israel. Her research interests focus on rural youth, women, and grassroots organizations, their nonformal means of education, and their adaptations to "development" and the forces of globalization. She is the author of *Becoming Qualitative Researchers: An Introduction* (1st–3rd editions) (Allyn & Bacon, 2005).

Sandy Grande is associate professor of education at Connecticut College, where she also serves as special adviser to the president for institutional equity and diversity. Her current research examines the intersections between critical theory and American Indian intellectualism. Her approach is profoundly inter- and cross-disciplinary, and has included the integration of critical, feminist, and Marxist theories of education with the concerns of American Indian and environmental education. She is the author of *Red Pedagogy: Native American Social and Political Thought* (Rowman & Littlefield, 2004), as well as numerous article that have appeared in such scholarly journals as *Harvard Educational Review, International Journal of Qualitative Studies in Education*, and *Journal of Environmental Ethics*. In 2004, she was named "Higher Education Multicultural Faculty of the Year" by the Connecticut chapter of the National Association of Multicultural Education.

Yvonna S. Lincoln is professor of higher education and human resource development at Texas A&M University, where she holds the Ruth Harrington Chair of Educational Leadership and University Distinguished Professor of Higher Education. She is the coauthor of *Effective Evaluation, Naturalistic Inquiry, and Fourth Generation Evaluation,* the editor of *Organizational Theory and Inquiry,* and coeditor (with Norman K. Denzin) of *The Handbook of Qualitative Research* (1st–3rd editions, Sage Publications) and the journal *Qualitative Inquiry.*

Janice M. Morse is professor of nursing at the University of Utah. She is the author or editor of eighteen books, including *Nursing Research: The Application of Qualitative Approaches* (Stanley Thorne, 2003), *The Nature of Qualitative Evidence* (Sage, 2001), and *Preventing Patient Falls* (Sage, 2001). She is also the editor of the journal *Qualitative Health Research* (Sage) and the Qual Institute Press.

Ronald J. Pelias is professor and director of graduate studies in the Department of Speech Communications at Southern Illinois University, Carbondale. He is the author of many books on performance studies and performance methodologies, including most recently *Performance Studies: The Interpretation of Aesthetic Texts* (St. Martin's Press, 1992), *Writing Performance: Poeticizing the Researcher's Body* (Southern Illinois University Press, 1999), and *A Methodology of the Heart: Evoking Academic and Daily Life* (AltaMira, 2004). In 2000, he received the Lilla A. Heston Award for Outstanding Scholarship in Interpretation and Performance Studies and the Distinguished Service Award, both from the National Communication Association.

Laurel Richardson is Professor Emeritus of Sociology at The Ohio State University. She is an international leader in qualitative research, gender, and the sociology of knowledge. She has written numerous groundbreaking books, including the landmark *Fields of Play: Constructing an Academic Life* (Rutgers University Press, 1997), which received the 1998 Charles Cooley award from the Society for the Study Symbolic Interaction. Other publications include *Travels with Ernest: Crossing the Literary/Sociology Divide* (AltiMira, 2004, with Ernest Lockridge), *Writing Strategies: Reaching Diverse Audiences* (Sage, 1990), *Feminist Frontiers* (1st–7th editions) (McGraw-Hill, 2003, with Verta Taylor and Nancy Whittier), and *The New Other Woman: Contemporary Single Women in Affairs with Married Men* (Macmillan, 1985).

Thomas Schwandt is professor of educational psychology at the University of Illinois, Urbana-Champaign. He is the author or editor of numerous books, including *Evaluation Practice Reconsidered* (Peter Lang, 2002), *Exploring Evaluator Role and Identity* (Information Age, 2002, with Katherine E. Ryan), *Linking Auditing and Metaevaluation: Enhancing Quality in Applied Research* (Sage, 1998, with Egon G. Guba and Edward S. Halpern), and three editions of the highly acclaimed *Dictionary of Qualitative Inquiry* (Sage, 1997, 2001, 2007). His research has also appeared in such scholarly journals as *Educational Theory, Pedagogy, Culture, and Society, American Journal of Evaluation,* and *Studies in Educational Evaluation.*

Eve Tuck (Aleut) is a doctoral candidate in urban education at the Graduate Center, City University of New York. Her interests are in indigenous and decolonizing theories, participatory action research, and education policies and practices, particularly those that unfairly exclude indigenous youth, poor youth, and youth of color. In 2006, she cofounded the Collective of Researchers on Educational Disappointment and Desire (CREDD), a New York City–based youth participatory action research collective that in its first endeavor, the *Gateways and Get-aways Project,* investigated the lived and perceived value of the GED, push-out practices in New York City public schools, educational options to testing-based curricula, and the myths of meritocracy and the American dream.